ENGLISH PERSPECTIVES:
ESSAYS ON LIBERTY AND GOVERNMENT

Also by C.H. Sisson from Carcanet

POETRY
Selected Poems
Collected Poems
God Bless Karl Marx!
Antidotes

PROSE
Christopher Homm (novel)
The Avoidance of Literature
English Poetry 1900-1950
On the Look-out (autobiography)
In Two Minds: guesses at other writers

TRANSLATIONS
Lucretius, *Poem on Nature*
Virgil, *The Aeneid*
The Song of Roland

EDITIONS
The English Sermon 1650-1750
Christina Rossetti, *Selected Poems*
Jonathan Swift, *Selected Poems*
Jeremy Taylor, *Selected Writings*

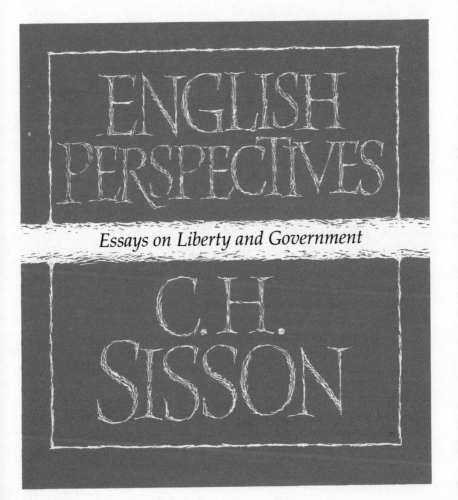

ENGLISH PERSPECTIVES

Essays on Liberty and Government

C. H. SISSON

CARCANET

First published in Great Britain in 1992 by
Carcanet Press Limited
208–212 Corn Exchange Buildings
Manchester M4 3BQ

British Library Cataloguing in Publication Data
Sisson, C.H. (Charles Hubert), *1914-*
  English perspectives: essays on liberty and government.
  I. Title
  323.44

  ISBN 0 85635 980 7

The publisher acknowledges financial assistance
from the Arts Council of Great Britain

Typeset in 10½pt Bembo by Bryan Williamson, Darwen
Printed and bound in England by SRP Ltd, Exeter

Contents

Preface   9

I   Orientations 1937-1940
   Charles Maurras and the Idea of a Patriot King   15
   Remarks on a Letter of Junius   17
   Prejudice as an Aid to Government   19
   English Liberalism   22
   A Study in Public Opinion   24
   The Argument for Federal Union   26
   Reflections on a Bureaucrats' War   28
   Order and Anarchy: an essay on intellectual liberty   32

II   Post-war Reflections
   Charles Péguy   51
   Epitaph on Nuremburg   55
   T.S. Eliot on Culture   57
   Lord Beveridge Explains Himself   63
   The Crisis in the University   68
   Charles Maurras   71
   Looking back on Maurras   87
   Philip Mairet   96

III   The Practice of Government
   The Nature of Public Administration   111
   Administrator and Law in France   118
   The Judge and the Administrator   127
   The Administrator as Governor   137
   The Politician as Intruder   146
   The Mind of the Administrator   155
   A Note on the Monarchy   167

IV   A Touch of Whiggery
An Enlightened View of Government   179
The Art of Money   199
The End of Walter Bagehot   217
Epilogue on a Founding Father   236

V   Native Ruminations
Introduction   247
A possible Anglicanism   249
An Essay on Identity   255
'Call no man happy until he is dead'   259
On the Eros of Poetry   263
A Note on Morality   266
On poetic Architecture   268
Le Roi Soleil   270
By Way of Explanation   272

Sources   279
Index of Names   281

Preface

Some apology is needed for a book of political essays of which the first was written when the author was twenty-three and the latest nearly half a century later. Could there be any excuse? A volume published in 1990 under the title of *In Two Minds* brought together a number of literary essays written over a span of thirty years, ending more or less at the moment when the book went to press. There are many changes in the literary scene in the course of a generation, but literature at least pretends to a more permanent interest, while in politics – it is alleged – even a week is a long time.

There is, however, more to politics than the weeks and days of politicians and the surprises they attempt to spring on one another, or which uncontrollable events spring on them all. It is the way of the media to represent the public world as in daily mutation. So, in a manner, it is, if hardly in the manner shown by newspersons and commentators whose principal expertise is in a plausibility which serves the great commerce of ratings. But even in our age there remain other ways of looking at politics. There have always been those who have felt impelled to question the assumptions on which the public affairs of their times have been conducted. Such reflections are part of the natural curiosity of mankind about itself. The great names of philosophical and religious enquiry have their place here and, less obtrusively, the host of unimportant people who are habitually sceptical about the ruling preconceptions of their times – a class certainly not limited to those who make it their business to go on record about such matters.

It is to the casual and occasional productions of this unnoticeable class that the pieces collected in this volume belong. The title, *English Perspectives*, is far from being an exhortation to any particular line of political action. It is intended rather to be merely historical and factual, in recognition of the limitations imposed on the author's viewpoint by birth, interests and occupations. The book is divided into five parts. The first consists of a series of brief articles by someone just settled in his first employments, already long captivated by literature but highly uncertain as to what, if anything, he would ever be able to do in this field himself. The articles reflect the obsession with politics which was common in the 1930s and a groping after some scraps of lucidity amidst the confusions of the immediate pre-war period. Most of them were contributed to *The New English Weekly*, an uncommercial outlet of a type unthinkable in the conditions of the 1990s. It was acceptable in that journal to comment on authors long dead as on books hot from the press. There was no question of payment. Philip Mairet, who had succeeded to the editorial chair on the death of A.R. Orage in 1934, was sympathetic and open-minded to an extraordinary degree, the perfect editor for a newcomer. The last piece in Part I was published as war broke out, in what was to be the last number of a small – likewise non-paying – quarterly called *Purpose*, which had several contributors in common with Mairet's journal.

The New English Weekly survived the war, and Part II opens with an article I wrote for it in 1946 on Charles Péguy, who had had a new lease of life at the hands of the Free French in war-time London. Before the journal died of inflation in 1949, I had contributed a number of other pieces, represented here by – among others – one on T.S. Eliot's social writings which, I had reason to believe, did not please the great man, and by one on Beveridge, who was then in full flower. Part II ends with longer articles on the very un-English figure of Charles Maurras – who had had a place in my first contribution to *The New English Weekly* in 1937 – and on Philip Mairet himself.

Part III reflects more directly than any of the others my practical experience as an administrator, as well as the first-hand knowledge I acquired in 1956-7 of the operations of my European counterparts. The essays are largely derived from *The Spirit of British Administration, and some European comparisons* (1959, 2nd edition 1966) which, whether or not it is, as one reviewer alleged, characterised by 'agnosticism and empiricism' and 'a brilliant attack against the theoreticians', at least certifies that *English Perspectives* is not the work of a writer who has merely dreamed about government. One chapter of the 1959 volume was originally contributed to Michael Oakeshott's *Cambridge Journal*, and another to the *Church Quarterly Review*, and for the purposes of the present book it seemed best to give them in the form in which they appeared in 1953.

Part IV is pillaged from *The Case of Walter Bagehot* (1972). Bagehot was so profoundly influential that he may be said to represent the ethos of British government from his day to ours, and echoes of him are still not infrequently to be detected. Part V veers back to more remote English roots which, it is the main import of *English Perspectives* to suggest, are by no means irrelevant to the future as to the present of this country.

The time-scale of the volume as a whole precludes the possibility of anything programmatic. It does not propose solutions, but raises questions which need to be asked. The experience of any septuagenarian must be largely irrelevant to the detailed plans which current political business requires: it might even be suggested that the franchise should be withdrawn from everybody at seventy, as having at that age only a limited interest in the future disposition of things. On the other hand, the present and the future, in politics as in literature, are intelligible only in the light of the past. Troubles go on, and most decades, once past, appear to have been largely misguided in their conduct of public affairs. If the public opinion of the 1930s now seems to have been for the most part a tissue of illusions, is there any reason to suppose that what is peddled to us now is any different? The present book touches only lightly and occasionally on political events; where it does so – as on the German-Soviet Pact of 1939 – it is not to congratulate the perspicacity of contemporaries. There was about the same time a movement in favour of Federal Union which is by no means irrelevant to some of the European hopes being declared now. And what could be more relevant to the recent proposals to resume the trials of war criminals than Montgomery Belgion's pamphlet, virtually unnoticed when it appeared in 1947, on the great show-business of Nuremburg? Much has changed in France and Germany, as in this country, since my explorations of the working of their government machinery in 1956-7, but if what was done in pre-revolutionary France, to say nothing of Napoleonic times, was perceived then to affect profoundly administrative habits and structures, can there be any reason for supposing that the lapse of thirty years or so has so changed the scene that what was observed in the mid-1950s has no significance for the current fantasies of European integration?

The final 'Native Ruminations' may appear unbearably idiosyncratic, as the conclusion of a book of political essays. Their idiosyncrasy turns, however, on the thesis of the opening sentence, that 'the conduct of government rests on the same foundations and encounters the same difficulties as the conduct of private persons.' The ultimate questions as to the meaning and scope of political liberty depend on the finally unanswerable question of the nature of the freedom of the individual, and on how far what we think about the latter is determined by the manner in which the history of several millennia bears down upon our local situation. Our notions of individual liberty cannot be otherwise than individual: their lesser or greater sophistication, and greater or lesser haziness, depend on who we are and on what we have done. Mine are the notions of an Englishman born in 1914 who early preferred literature to propaganda and turned out to be a poet – and who chanced to earn his living by serving what in many places is called the State but with us is, constitutionally, the Crown.

I

ORIENTATIONS 1937-1940

Charles Maurras and the Idea of a Patriot King

We have several political poets and too many publicists, yet scarcely any writer since Hulme has formulated a precise political idea. Inevitably, both poetry and political analyses are the worse for the lack of political doctrine. I believe that Charles Maurras is almost the only writer capable of re-directing our political enquiries. He is not, by Englishmen, to be swallowed whole, but to be used. What is needed is a transposition of his ideas to fit our own place and prejudices. That difficult transposition is not attempted in this essay, which is a simple experiment. I have taken a single idea of Maurras (an idea not peculiar to him no doubt) and placed it beside an idea of Bolingbroke; the two are allowed to react in such a way as to expose a common contemporary English error.

Maurras finds in the identification of a king's interest with the public interest a chief guarantee of the efficacy of monarchy. While not without a good word for personal qualities which his taste disposes him to admire, he aims at showing the value of the monarchy independently of the value of the monarch.

Bolingbroke is concerned with a 'rare phenomenon', a patriot king, but there are fortunately passages in his essay which are susceptible of commoner application. He claims at the start that his method is sceptical, yet he is soon engaged in discussing 'duties' in a manner which is not sceptical. His intention, however, is coherent. '"Salus reip. suprema lex esto", is a fundamental law: and sure I am, the safety of a commonwealth is ill provided for, if the liberty be given up.' Liberty is justified because it contributes to the safety of the state. Similarly, we read:

> I speak not here of people, is any such there are, who have been savage or stupid enough to submit to tyranny by original contract; nor of those nations on whom tyranny has stolen as it were imperceptibly, or had been imposed by violence, and settled by prescription. But I speak of people who have been wise and happy enough to establish, and to preserve, free constitutions of government, as the people of this island

15

have done. To these, therefore, I say, that their kings are under the most sacred obligations...

The king must be moral because the people has a mind to be free. The constitution is such, Bolingbroke says elsewhere, that 'no king who is not a patriot can govern with sufficient strength'. The need for morals arises from the nature of the constitution. The famous English talent for humbug is not all stupidity; it corresponds to the facts of our situation.

Maurras, despite his comparative unconcern for rights and wrongs, does not represent a contrary point of view. The government he wishes to realize is decentralized; the monarchy is therefore not unlimited. In national affairs, however, the king exercises a power which he may delegate but which he shares with no one. The English constitution provides for a division of power in national as well as in local affairs; the business of the king is merely to prevent the disintegration of the central authority. The difference between the theories of Bolingbroke and Maurras, therefore, arises out of the difference of function of the English and French monarchies; it is accidental. In essence, Bolingbroke and Maurras aim at the same thing – the utilization of the king to secure the unity and coherence of the nation.

The morals of Bolingbroke are forced into their place in an empirical system. They are in no sense the starting point of his political theory. In this, Bolingbroke is at one with Maurras, who, at every point more consistent, declares himself an atheist.

If we are content to identify, as for this purpose we may, the 'justice' and 'injustice' of the Pinks with the 'absolute standards' of the Oxford Group and the 'development of consciousness' of the Artists' International Congress, it will be clear that this relegation of morals, or sentiments, to a position of dependence in politics, is in conflict with the assumptions of a wide section of political writers in this country. While Bolingbroke, attempting to justify the position of the king deductively, was taking notice of the habits of his countrymen to such an extent that his method was in fact empirical groping, most contemporary writers, while claiming to adhere more or less to scientific schools of political thought, deduce their politics from their ethical and sentimental prejudices. An English interpretation of the ideas of Maurras would make their fault evident, and might rid us of those humane philosophies which provoke violence by demanding excessive change.

Remarks on a Letter of Junius

Un jour arriva promptement que Charles-Augustin Sainte-Beuve sut préférer la vérite à son cœur.

Those who are pink in politics or religion will have wondered at, or will not have noticed, the letter in which Junius attacks Lord Mansfield for preferring justice to law. We are acquainted with the distinction between law and justice, but we have forgotten the reasons for preferring the former. Those reasons are, none the less, the principles of exact observation in politics.

The fashion of believing men perfectible is, for the moment or century, out. The present error is to think the State perfectible. To take power from persons and hand it to the State is a common aspiration. It is not thought that at present any State is good, but the myth of the State's perfectibility is abroad. An abstraction is more to be trusted than men are.

Our difficulty in understanding foreign countries, and in seeing ourselves, arises from an inability to translate. We look too simply for similar social machinery abroad and at home. The significant likenesses, however, are not structural; they are in motive. The same motives may result, in different countries, in different forms of words and government. Englishmen are often astonished at German *Freiheit* – the freedom of the nation to do as it pleases – and assert their own freedom is of another kind. Yet most would think of the liberty of the individual as one of the things the good State would secure for them (like drains). It is not considered that government is in itself a corrupt practice, or that the effort should be to keep clear of governors rather than to get the State to make one free. One might consider whether asking the State to provide liberty is not a way of inviting it to take what liberties it pleases.

The view that the State should provide liberty (and other moral goods) arises from inattention to the individual, where he should be attended to, and from asking his views on questions on which he should have none. Incapable of action in modern society, the

17

citizen projects a fantasy on the State, which thus acquires the appearance of a person. The State has to appear to be the voice and conscience of the individual. The statesman is regarded less as a man skilled in tricky negotiations than as a voice for popular sentiment. When the State becomes a personal fantasy statesmen become impersonal and responsibility is not properly attributed.

Junius objected to justice and conscience as legal criteria because when the judge becomes 'human' and swayed by prejudice his power is unlimited and there is no freedom. In place of justice, therefore, Junius wished, in the English fashion, to put precedent. One might say that he opposed to the state of fantasy the state of fact. He wished to limit the public exhibition of virtue, in order that people might escape from the tyrannical consciences and appetites of others. His task remains to be done again. Without a clear conception of the State liberty is not attainable.

Prejudice as an Aid to Government

> *permitting the innocent to be possessed with laziness and sleep in the most visible article of danger.*

In the fourth and fifth books of *De l'Esprit des Lois*, Montesquieu defines three springs of government and describes the education which favours each. Honour is the spring of monarchical government, fear of despotism and virtue of democracy. The 'principle' of a government is what makes it work. The government does not, however, entirely stand on its own legs; an appropriate education is required for the production of suitable citizens and subjects.

No European state now belongs wholly to one or other of Montesquieu's three types of government. England, for example, is a democracy pervaded by snobbery which is in part a decadent left-over from a monarchical caste system and by a little tyranny more lately introduced. Democracy is, of Montesquieu's three, apparently the chief ingredient of England as it is of all modern European states. (All are at least governments in which the people appears to have some voice.) We should therefore examine more closely the virtue which makes democracy work.

This virtue is, Montesquieu insists, a 'vertu politique' and has nothing to do with morals. In a later book, he illustrates this by telling us that the avarice of the Chinese is a 'vertu', whereas the honesty of the Spaniard is bad for the prosperity of the state. These examples, however, prove nothing about the nature of 'vertu politique'; they merely show that a moral virtue may cause the state to disintegrate, and a vice may hold it together. 'Vertu politique' is more closely defined in the fourth book, and there it is not successfully distinguished from moral virtue. As one might expect, if many are to govern they must be possessed of honest manners, uprightness and forbearance. Otherwise the government will disintegrate or be transformed either into a monarchy or a despotism by the vice of one man or of a group.

The 'sentiment de l'éducation' which, according to Montesquieu, is appropriate to democracy, is the honesty learned from the manners of one's parents. Englishmen, with their long democratic tradition, should obviously be instinct with this honesty. As everyone knows, however, the young do not imitate their parents; rather, perhaps, the old prefer to be like their children rather than to be models for them; the family, except as a breeding-ground, is disappearing. There are few opportunities of exercising virtue in public life. The citizen drops his paper in the ballot-box with a cross against the name of one of two or three distasteful candidates. This action may help the state to cohere; the mere repetition of it produces a sense of easiness; it is not, however, 'virtuous', or in itself even 'politically virtuous' and it has little to do with democracy. There is virtue in the air, however, in England, of the sort that the League of Nations was built on. We may examine it more closely.

The first thing to notice is that the citizen does not do anything with it politically. He carries it about with him and he can produce it like a driving licence. It does, however, enable him to react in a certain way, or rather, it is a label which tells one how he will react. If it is useless to him, therefore, it may still be of use to someone else and it is in fact useful to the man who makes him react – the advertiser with something to sell, or the politician. The passive sense of what is right does therefore help to hold the state together. It is, however, a mechanical sentiment and by no means an active quality.

The political thoughts which drift in most minds in England are 'Is it right?' and 'It's not fair'. That these should be the most popular thoughts is due partly to our tradition of democracy and partly to our liking for religion of a certain brand. It is clear, however, that the function in the state of passive virtue is precisely the same as that of the passive sense of national honour which is exploited by the leaders of Germany. Hitler has said that the German soul has two or three strings, and one can count on getting a certain response by plucking them. An English statesman might say the same of the English soul. The notes would be different, that is all.

The modern governor uses in an unprecedented fashion the sentiments of his subjects as an instrument of government. The typical modern state is in fact run by propaganda. Wherever the nominal government is, the power will lie with whoever controls opinion and a government which offends public opinion will go under. Most governements, of course, once established, take care that they shall more than anyone else control opinion.

The sentiments appealed to usually are of some nobility. In England they are moral and sporting canons; everywhere they are meant to dispose people to be disinterested. Hitler has written in *Mein Kampf* an interesting chapter on propaganda. He says: 'All propaganda must appeal to the people and must be put at the intellectual level of the most limited of the minds it is directed to... The capacity of the mass of men is very limited, their understanding small, but their forgetfulness great.' The second sentence at once recalls Machiavelli – 'It is to be asserted in general of men, that they are ungrateful, fickle, false, cowards, covetous...' Hitler is speaking of peaceful persuasion; the fact that he is an unpleasant Nazi should not blind us to that. His words might be used by any politician or man with muffins to sell. Machiavelli recommended the utmost violence. If he were our contemporary he would change nothing in his view of man; he would, however, no doubt see that a subject who can be clubbed into obedience by propaganda is not in need of rougher treatment. One may, by friendly words, give a despotically-governed people the illusion that it is free. The nobility of the sentiments the new despot governs by, makes it hard for people to understand his tyranny. Blows have this advantage, that even the stupidest do not think them signs of good intentions.

English Liberalism

Anthony Ludovici's thesis in his new pamphlet, *English Liberalism*, is that the Anglo-Saxons, a race of particularists, were civilized against their will by wise rulers from Henry I to Charles I and forced to admit the authority of the state to order certain matters for the common good. Then the Puritans got the upper hand, defeated the king and made property absolutely private, at the same time re-admitting to the country the Jews, an 'uncivilized' race (in the proper sense) little better than the Anglo-Saxons. Despite the Tories of the king's party England declined from that day. Englishmen grew both sentimental and scraggy and the stock declined so far that some are now born liberals.

I am not competent to discuss Mr Ludovici's account of the history of our decline, but on his methods I will offer a few observations. It is undeniable that races, or at any rate nations, have peculiar characters, but these characters are difficult to define. Wherever it is possible, therefore, to explain a change in a society without reference to them, one should, I think, in the interests of clarity do so. There is a further reason. Whoever talks of the national character comes near to encouraging it, and I do not think that the national character should be encouraged. It is the fund of vitality from which the conscious life of a nation springs, and if one exploits it one debauches the source of life. To develop a personal life it is perhaps best to fix one's eyes on impersonal values and it may be better to criticize past changes in constitutions in the light of the values one at present entertains than to consider them in relation to 'national character'. 'National character' can only be a name for one's ideals and if one judges by it one is still judging by present values, only more blindly because less explicitly. Mr Ludovici would have made a more convincing case if he had not dragged in the Saxon character, as everyone must feel on reading 'The Study of Celtic Literature' that Arnold would have made a more serious attack on his contemporaries had he not used the clownish abstractions of Celt and Saxon. The changes Mr Ludovici deplores are not peculiar to England, and his case has much in common with the case which for many years M. Maurras has been making out in France.

Mr Ludovici's belief that our history is a struggle between the particularist natives and the rulers who cared for the common interests causes him to observe our present conditions erroneously. He desires for the worker a status which only the possession of property can give, but he none the less overlooks the fact that people are now forced to do more for the state than before and the life of the ordinary worker is regulated by the state as never before. 'Particularism' is a vice few can now afford to practise.

I have written chiefly about what I consider to be the faults of Mr Ludovici's pamphlet, but the reader would do well to expend sixpence to discover the virtues for himself. In the course of the pamphlet Mr Ludovici raises many of the questions which must be considered by anyone concerned about the future of England, and he raises them with the right intentions.

A Study in Public Opinion

The pact between Russia and Germany, and the events which followed, have a little thrown off their balance the many enlightened people who habitually thought well of Russia. A short time ago any profound doubts of the virtues of Russia were regarded as being in bad taste; they were even taken as signs that the doubter was at least a potential Fascist. It was not considered proper to mention, for example, the views of the *Action Française* or of Mr Wyndham Lewis on Russia's part in the Spanish war. The enlightened public was sure that the Fascist states were the only instigators of iniquity. At present, the situation is different. Russia is somewhat in disgrace, and it is considered not improper to impute to her manoeuvres of which only Fascist powers were formerly thought to be capable. It is not that we know very much more than before about Russia's intentions, which indeed remain obscure, but as a result of her unpopular acts it has become licit to think ill of her.

Popular opinion, therefore, which before on insufficient evidence, and chiefly on the assurances of the domesticated communists of Western Europe, concluded that Russia was for the democratic states, or at least in some manner for the common people in the democracies, is now engaged in reconstructing the history of the last few years. The people who have been most misguided adjust themselves to the new situation not by developing their earlier views and by tracing the consequences of those views in the present, but by altering the past.

The evidence on which popular judgements of events are formed is almost always insufficient, and in fact the judgement is usually made first and then goes in search of facts to support it. Consistency in opinion is commonly persistence in a prejudice without regard to facts, not the patient extraction of a principle from that part of political events which is intelligible.

The method of popular discussion of politics is to attribute moral praise or censure according to the prejudice's of one's education and temperament, and having, at an age of outward

maturity, taken one's stand, to continue as long as possible, whatever the facts may be, to deduce the import of events from the
virtues or vices attributed to the actors. As it is often difficult to
explain events on the system of dividing powers into the virtuous
and the vicious, and as the disputants commonly enter the discussion with the intention of ending where they began, discussions
conducted by this method are usually heated and futile. As they
are heated, they are often wearisome, and as they end where they
started, the participants get nothing by them. The discussions
are, in fact, irrelevant to the conduct of life. If one relies on what
one really knows about political events, one finds that although
the matter for speculation is large, the matter for partisanship is
small. The taste for politics exhibited by so many people in the
last few years is merely a taste for a vicarious and printed existence, in which attention to the things which may be directly
apprehended by the wits and senses is replaced by attention to a
fantastic battle which owes what reality it possesses as much to
the emotions within the skull as to the evidence outside it.

The Argument for Federal Union

I – As Westminster knows what is best for Dorset, New York will know what is best for England.

II – As we are adequately represented by our Parliament, and as the French are adequately represented by their Chamber, we shall both be perfectly represented by the Federal State.

III – As every elector understands the government of his country he will still better understand the government of the Federation.

IV – As no one is at present distracted from the affairs of his own town by the voices of politicians in London, no one will be distracted from the affairs of his country by the voices of politicians in Moscow.

V – As we have perfected the art of governing a small territory we are proper persons to undertake the government of a larger one.

VI – As the countryside flourishes under the care of the Lords and Commons, it will blossom as never before under the care of the Senate of New York.

VII – As the voter is better able to judge the conduct of his Prime Minister than he is that of his local dustman, he will be better able to judge the conduct of the Federal President than he will that of the Prime Minister.

VIII – As there is no possibility of intrigue in the French Chamber, the example of France may be followed by the whole Federation.

IX – As men care most about ethical ideals, less for their country and least of all for money, there will be no conflict between inclination and duty in the minds of the senators.

X – As there is one philosophy to which all men give assent the senators will easily agree on what principles their policy is to be decided.

XI – As language is merely a vehicle for conveying abstractions, representatives ignorant of one another's tongues will easily understand one another's ideals.

XII – As the nations of Europe have always been wonderful examples of docility, history will have left on their characters no trace of mutual suspicion.

XIII – As the most powerful nations have always been the freest, the largest state of all will be the freest of all.

XIV – As strong nations habitually respect the rights of weak ones, even when it is not in their interest to do so, a strong federation will inevitably be a just one.

XV – As the rights of the federated nations will be guaranteed by the word of the central government, it is convenient that the central government should control the army.

XVI – As the tenure of office usually improves men in proportion to the greatness of the power they exercise, the central government will be a school of virtue.

XVII – As great office produces magnanimous governors, there is no possibility that the power of the Federation will be abused.

XVIII – As the federated nations will always retain the power of the vote, they need not fear the central executive which disposes of the power of the sword.

XIX – As great nations are less often at war than small ones, the great federations will scarcely ever be at war at all.

XX – As the wars of great nations are less disastrous than the wars of small nations, the wars of the great federations will do good.

XXI – As a foreign army is less ready to oppress a country than a native army, it will be less dangerous for the people of England to support an army of Prussians than to support an army of Englishmen.

XXII – As there is little inconvenience in fleeing to another country there can be none at all in fleeing to another continent.

Reflections on a Bureaucrats' War

We may felicitate ourselves that the present war is, as compared with the last, rather well organized. We have been spared certain inconveniences, such as ladies with white feathers, and the exhortations of politicians, considering the gravity of events, been subdued if not inaudible. We are not urged to be up and doing, or rather, we are urged to be doing but not up: each man is to wait and in time a benevolent and omniscient government will tell him where he is wanted. No man is to presume to judge for himself; his capacities will be justly measured by the central government and his function accordingly determined.

There are great benefits. The War Office is not shaken by young men demanding arms, and the young men are not accosted by harpies who want to see blood spilt. The government is not affronted by the moral determination of the people, and the people, for their part, have not to make any personal decision. Our personalities are not of course annihilated; it is even recognized that some of us – I believe about two per cent – have consciences, and the colour of these consciences is recorded and their proper activity determined. But the responsibility of personal decision is taken from us. The state does not assert that it has any right over free spirits; indeed it asserts that it has none, and this absurdity of doctrine – absurd in view of the practice – forces it to oppress with a soft and gentle pressure which will provoke no vivacious reaction. It does not oppose the individual will, or it does so as little as possible, but it limits the will's field of action always more and more, so that the latter slowly reduces its force to a measure appropriate to the condition it lives in. The vitality ebbed from the parts goes to feed the gross power of the central authority. But as spirits do not migrate lightly from one body to another, and as they are particularly little apt to congregate from many bodies in a few, energy passes from restless and undisciplined individuals not to others who become radiant with the addition, but to an organization. The force passes from persons to things, and to men only as acting for them.

'We do not wish,' assert the democratic governors with impeccable correctness, 'to become more radiant at your expense. This little organization we have constructed is for your benefit. We are also diminished by it.' Diminished statesmen and people alike, in difficulties to discover the personal advantages of the régime, assert that they support it for the common good. This may well be the answer, but it is puzzling. These gentlemen our governors are not philosophers, and no one would demand that they should be. But the matter is worse. They are not even unconscious carriers of any coherent philosophy. And being neither one nor the other, it is difficult to see how the common good should concern them or how they should be able to apprehend it at all. Perhaps indeed it does not and they cannot. When one listens to their discourses one discovers that they are protecting us against evil rather than governing us in accordance with good. In peace they preserve us from illiteracy, vice and destitution: in war they can produce with triumph as their *raison d'être* an unpleasant and ferocious enemy.

In an age of philosopher kings, each engaged in tearing up a society in order to rebuild it according to his own theories, this negative view of government has its attractions. One observes abroad martial and unpleasant philosophers forcing their peoples to become the instruments and symbols of their philosophy, and one might suppose that the negative rulers at least gave their subjects freedom. This is of course the negative ruler's invariable plea, and in England it is given plausibility by relics of liberty still left to us from the days when other policies than theirs prevailed. 'They have their system of politics; our ancestors grew great by another.' But the appearance of freedom and even the appearance of negativity is false. The negative ruler says either: 'I have not an idea in my head, therefore I am a person well qualified to give you freedom'; or 'I have my own ideas and you yours. We need not quarrel about them and, better still, you need not investigate mine.' Neither of these propositions promises to be a firm foundation for liberty. At the kindest interpretation both promise liberty to the ruler: it is he, rather than we, who is to be free. A free and irresponsible governor is the definition of a tyrant, and the ideal negative politician is in fact that. He represents pure government, freed from its connections with moral tastes and prejudices. He should never consult the people about his activity, which he is able correctly to describe as a purely technical matter. He is in principle the same as most of the philosopher kings now current abroad, but he has the advantage of not having to produce his philosophy on the public stage. He has achieved the final success of making that too a technical matter; for the people he has some stuff about liberty which they can imagine they understand because their ancestors once understood it. It is this contradiction between the philosophy the negative politican talks and the philosophy he appears to act by which deprives the one and the other of their force and makes the politician himself appear incoherent.

A country going to war must act so far as possible as an entity. It aims at ceasing to be a collection of people and at becoming a thing. The chaotic people becomes, in the mind of the governor, a machine at his direction; the governor aims in fact at the annihilation of the people and at their replacement by something else. When his work is complete he should, ideally, find the fifty million units responsive to his smallest vocable. Complete government would so transform the people that they would be useless to everyone but the governor, and would, in fact, become meaningless except in so far as he could pose for them an external problem which, as an entity, they could resolve. Although peoples are complex and the tender animals who constitute them are anarchic, the organized state is simple and the number of things a people can do organized in a state is limited. It can only move against something; only thus can it be given the appearance of having a will.

The typical action of the state is an act of war; it is only in war that the people can act with the unity of method which makes them cohere in a mechanical entity. The method of their unity is force, and their proper act is conquest. As government, as such, always aims internally at the elimination of the individual will, so externally it aims at the destruction of boundaries. Government is a concentration of force, and to maintain itself it seeks to destroy the free person under it and the free state outside it.

Government as such has its private ends, and the tendencies evident in principle will appear in each particular government no matter who is in charge of it. They will appear less or more in accordance with laws which we cannot here enquire into, but no particular government, however virtuous, is without the seed of the principle in it. In governments one has to consider less the kind than the quantity; the further a government extends its powers the less freedom there can be in a state, and a complete government is a tyranny. A country in which government is being extended is one which is approaching the state of tyranny. And as the internal function of a complete government is the exercise of force on its subjects, its external function is the exercise of force on its neighbours. The highly organized state is good for nothing but war, and as it is evoked by war it is itself a provoker of war. For it seeks to make its organization ever more complete, and the organization reaches completeness only at the point where the people is ready to be hurled in a mass at its neighbour. And at that point there is nothing to be done with the people but to hurl it, for it has become unfitted for any complicated function. It has ceased to be capable of its active and chaotic functions as a people and has become passive in the mould of the state.

As ideally the aims of government are servitude within and conquest without, it is obvious that the ideal governor could not confess himself in England. It is impossible for government, as government, in England, to have any war aims, because the principle of government is contrary to the prejudices of the nation. An English government cannot easily announce conquest as its aim, yet as government it can have no other. If there are to be war aims; if the war is to be for anything at all, it must be for something proposed by persons other than the governors and by the governors only as repeating the voice of the people. If therefore the extension of government (so that it approaches the frontiers of tyranny) is a technical necessity of war, its limitation is a condition of peace. If the people is to be preserved as a people, and not to be compressed into a mechanical state, certain imperfections must remain in our organization. There must be a certain amount of disorder: a number of important actions must be placed beyond the government's control. It is not a question of the tolerated semi-official voice being permitted to censure or abuse a government department or of 'initiative' being permitted within an officially laid plan. It is not a question of permission at all; some boys must remain out of their places however hard the master scowls, and some who remain in their places must silently recognize what principle their master represents.

Order and Anarchy:
an essay on intellectual liberty

Introduction

The relation of the free mind and person to the state is at present a chief concern not only of writers of every kind, from the low and high journalists to our half-a-dozen men of genius, but more obscurely, of everyone whom an extraordinary fortune has not politically neutralized. The subject has often been treated explicitly; more often it is an implicit part of some subject itself of more or less importance. It has acquired the quality of an obsession as the problem of morals did in Arnold's day. And it is, for moralists, itself a problem of morals.

This essay is concerned with the relation of the individual and politics, but the subject is limited in several ways. It contains no recipe for preventing any political or unpolitical person or group from starving or maltreating the reader or depriving him of his goods. It is concerned with the relation of the independent mind with society. Certainly I do not pretend that there are not practical conditions which must be satisfied before any complicated thinking can be effected. On the other hand, those conditions granted, whether the thinking is fruitful or sterile depends to a considerable extent on the methods of thought employed. This essay is a study in method.

The subject is further limited by the fact that, in writing, my eyes have been on British democracy. Other forms of government have not been forgotten; it would have been an act of genius to forget them and to think for a moment of England alone. For my present purposes the difference between British democracy and the fascist and communist régimes is insignificant. I shall not treat of morals, but that does not mean that the difference between the several kinds of states is necessarily insignificant for morals. My subject is the method of thought which best solves the question of the relationship of the free intellect with politics to the advantage of the intellect. Politics too may, I believe, derive some advantages. Naturally I do not suppose that I have added much to what better writers have said.

The future of Europe is to wars and military governments, but this essay is written with the gaiety which is obligatory in an intellectual.

I   *Motives and subject of the essay*

There have been of late many books on political matters, but few among them in which the principles of politics are enquired into. Enquiry into principles is not perhaps publicly discouraged, but anyone who turns his attention from certain popular questions is likely to be accused, in one manner or another, of inhumanity, as tomorrow he may be accused of lack of patriotism. This essay does not deserve to be called an enquiry into political principles, but it may be regarded as a demonstration made in favour of such an enquiry. In it certain questions are asked which, if they were truly answered, would make ease of mind more attainable, and all its inhumanity is there. I am aware that there are persons of good sense who believe that one should immerse oneself as fully as possible in the torments of the age, and who will therefore be out of sympathy with the motives of the essay. The motive of the essay is not, however, its subject, and the humane reader will not be shocked by an account of the virtues of the serene life. He may, I hope, be induced to consider by what gentle roads one may come upon fanaticism.

The essay concerns the state of the free person. Most of the words in our English vocabulary have become debauched and depraved, and it is difficult to speak unironically of 'liberty' or to use the word with much conviction that one knows its meaning. It will be necessary to define at the outset the manner in which the word is used here if the whole of what follows is not to be hopelessly misunderstood.

II   *An account of freedom*

We are to consider intellectual liberty. I am not concerned with the liberty of lives or properties or with the freedom of the body from hurt. The reason for my unconcern is certainly not that

I think these matters unimportant, but that in order to say one thing one must keep silent about others. And my reason for keeping silent on the matter of civil freedom is that I think one can have nothing of interest to say about it until one has proposed a solution to the more obscure question of the freedom of the mind, for if the civil freedom one devises is to be freedom at all, it must first allow the mind to be independent.

Freedom, whether of body or mind, is independence, and it assumes the existence of something on which one might, but does not wholly, depend. The freedom of man in a state is independence of the state. It is evident that one cannot be completely free; it is even evident that complete freedom would be meaningless, but, supposing the reader to agree that some measure of independence is possible, we may examine the principle of independence, leaving the question of the degree in which the principle might or should be realized to politicians and their theorists.

III The definition of freedom is negative

It may be objected that the definition of freedom we have adopted, having no positive content, is meaningless or in some manner valueless. To that we must reply that a positive definition of freedom would contain something besides the idea of mere freedom; the question of what liberty is is not the same as the question what liberty is for. The definition of freedom as independence has, it is true, no meaning until one has defined the thing of which one may be independent. It implies a definition of the state, which is not the same thing as a political theory.

IV The principle of government

There are several kinds of state, but we are not in this essay interested in distinguishing them. We have not to describe the mechanism of particular states but to identify the principle of government.

Statesmen talk so much of liberty that it is forgotten that the state is a machine that governs us independently of our wills. If it governed us according to our wills – supposing such a thing to be possible – it would become invisible and die because there was nothing for it to do.

It may be argued that the state need not govern independently of our wills and that in a democracy the government merely organizes the wills of the people and may in fact be in accordance with them. The answer to this argument is that the work of organization is the work of suppressing those whose wills appear not to coincide with that of the state. Further, the state should for our present purposes be looked at not from the point of view of the 'people' – an abstraction so nebulous as to be meaningless – but from the point of view of the free person, an abstraction less difficult to apprehend because it is realized less or more in every reader. And it is clear that in a democracy it is impossible that the will of the free person should become the will of the state, for if it did the state would cease to be a democracy and would become a tyranny. In a tyranny the wills of the members, other than the tyrant, are by the definition of that state incapable of realization.

It may still be objected to our account of the state that the members of at least democratic states may pay their taxes and perform their civil duties of free will. One performs these duties, however, in the knowledge that the state may force one to comply with its polite requests, and when therefore one acts in accordance with the will of the state it is hard to be certain that one is not acting because of the state's threat of force.

V *The relationships between person and state*

If the state is to be regarded as independent of our wills and capable of constraining them it will not be improper, from the point of view of the free person, to identify the principle of government with force. And if government is the exercise of force, the person will not be free so far as he is subject to it. The delimitation of the frontiers of government is a matter of some difficulty which will be attempted in succeeding sections of this essay, and it may at present be sufficient to say that, as the means of compulsion are many and people commonly succumb to them, we shall assume the relationships between state and person are affairs of force wherever it is not evident beyond doubt that they are free.

VI   The impossibility of the citizen being free

One consequence of the accounts we have given of government
and of freedom is that it becomes necessary to regard the citizen
as in a condition of servitude. There can be no such thing as
a free citizen in the sense in which we are using the term free,
and a person is free in so far as he is something other than a
citizen.

It should be understood that in this section the term citizen is
used in its most limited sense, and the duties of citizenship are
taken to be not those which a private taste or conscience imposes
but solely those which the government exacts for the reason that
it is a government.

VII   The notions of civil liberty compatible with intellectual liberty

We have said in an earlier section that it is not possible to devise
a satisfactory theory of civil liberty until one has solved the question of intellectual liberty. It may, however, be of assistance in
understanding the limits of government if we now say what kind
of theory of civil liberty will be in accordance with the account
of intellectual liberty we are giving in this essay.

It follows from our account of the state as the embodiment of
the principle of force that civil liberty will be the freedom of life,
person, property and action from the control of the state. And
it follows that this freedom will exist only so far as the state
tolerates it, or so far as the principle of government is inoperative
in the state.

In what manner may the state tolerate the existence of civil
liberty? In so far as it embodies the principle of government, it
will do so by allowing apparent disorder which it has force to
reduce to order. Persons will appear to be outside its system of
force when in fact they are not so.

This idea is implied in the definition of liberty given by Montesquieu and others as liberty to live according to the laws. The
state may change the laws, and in any case one did not choose
the laws which have already been made, but one has liberty in
the sense that one will suffer no violence so long as one acts in
accordance with the pronounced will of the state.

The extent of one's freedom, according to this definition, may
be small, and one may be much at the state's mercy. The content

of certain of the laws may, however, be such as to give an appearance of more liberty under certain conditions.

The chief method of giving an appearance of greater liberty than the naked person could have in the face of the laws is to legislate for the security of property. This is the matter of interest in Locke's otherwise dull book. The position of the owner of property may in practice be more secure than that of the man without property, but his position before the state is fundamentally the same. The law may be changed and the privileges his property gives him may be suspended or destroyed.

The idea that civil liberty may depend on property is of interest in this essay for another reason. Property means force and a man with property may be more free than a man without because he is temporarily able to resist the state's force with force and to obtain civil liberty by making a local disorder.

VIII   The mind as a force in public affairs

Unlike the body, the mind does not secure its liberty by force, although the body may, of course, obtain certain of the conditions of liberty for it. The conditions the body obtains for it will, however, be the conditions in which the mind *may* be free, and it is to succumb to a delusion of the most dangerous kind to suppose that there are physical conditions (and in particular, political conditions) in which the mind will inevitably enjoy independence. Its freedom is a result of its own act or attitude.

In speaking of the mind, I have attempted to give no definition of it. I am aware that this may lead to difficulties. It would have been possible to give a definition, but I am not sure that it would have been possible to give a satisfactory one, and I have preferred to take the word with all the looseness with which it is commonly employed and to allow the sense in which it is here used to appear gradually as the context exhibits it. The reader is asked to remember this in reading the present and following sections.

Although people often speak as if the mind was, or could be, a power in the conduct of public affairs, they often do with a notion even vaguer than the one we entertain of what the mind is. It is obvious that they cannot mean that reason, as the mere power of observing contradictions, in any way governs. They may often be thinking of the part of morals in politics. It is not necessary to understand the philosophical notions of the state which their view of morals may imply to discuss the part of morals in politics, so long as one discusses it from the point of view of politics and not from the point of view of morals. From the point of view of politics, morals are sentiments whose political function depends on the fact that they are common to a number of people, and usually more nearly identical in people grouped together in one state than in people in different states. The function of morals, as well as the distinction between different kinds of morals, will be the subject of later sections of this essay. What is important here is that these sentiments may be used, as physical objects are used, as the weapons of a directing mind, and that it is not the mind as director, but the weapons which constitute the force. The question whether the force can exist without the directing mind is a separate question which we need not discuss.

The mind as governor must on our account of government be the utilizer of force. Its function is, in the simplest terms, the employment of violence, and fraud, ruse and treachery are methods proper to it.

IX Propaganda

We are little concerned, in this essay, with the effects of physical violence on the free person, but much with the manipulation of sentiments. The latter method of exercising force supplements the method of physical violence and government is complete only when both methods are used. As literacy has spread, the manipulation of sentiments has taken a larger part in government, and it may be said to have replaced some physical violence.

All propaganda has this characteristic, that it tends to make of one opinion those to whom it is directed. The opinion is not necessarily that of the person who is responsible for the propaganda, but it may be assumed to be an opinion which he desires for good reason that people should hold. Propaganda unites the people in such a manner that they are more useful to the propagandist.

It is only the people influenced by the propaganda who are united by it, and propaganda diffused by people of opposed interests is likely to form hostile groups. Propaganda in favour of a race and propaganda in favour of a class have the same effect in this: they unite some people only to divide them more sharply from others. It may be said, I think, that, *ceteris paribus*, the more propaganda there is in any group the less physical violence there is, but propaganda tends to intensify the feeling of difference of one group from another and therefore causes more hostility and probably more violence between them.

It follows from what has been said of the unifying effect of propaganda that liberal propaganda, which none the less claims to exist, is a contradiction in terms. The propaganda invites one to abandon one's individuality, and propaganda pretending to be in favour of individualism really serves some other cause. It forms a compact mass of minds which tends, when it moves, to move as a whole. Even if the propaganda which united the mass was not consciously directed, its effect is to form a mass which may with ease be directed. The mass may, moreover, be directed by persons whose sympathies are not at all with those (supposing, what is not difficult, a case in which they exist) who originated the propaganda because they believed in it. The great efficacy of liberal and individualist propaganda lies in the fact that it denies that it is propaganda. The innocent individualist, by helping a work of propaganda, produces a result which is the opposite of his intentions. With great enthusiasm and good will he plays into the enemy's hands.

The battle of the individualist in politics must in the nature of the case always be lost, and in the nature of our case the battle must today be more than ever completely lost. That may of course not be a reason for declining to fight it, but the matter of this section should provide reasons for not fighting it with the enemy's weapons.

X   Public displays of sentiment

The efficacy of propaganda depends on the persons to whom it is directed sharing certain sentiments. The common sentiments will before the intrusion of the propagandist be among the things that hold the group together, but the propagandist will make them more efficacious for that end in several ways. He will upset the organization of sentiments which before his intrusion was related to the people's factual environment, and he will over-develop certain of them so that, finding no satisfaction in their immediate environment, people project a fantasy on the state and live vicariously. The sentiments are no longer directly related to the people's activity.

It is impossible to distinguish neatly between these detached sentiments and those directly related to private life, and it is with some reluctance that I attempt it. It is necessary, however, to remark that the increase in public displays of sentiment marks some change in the function of sentiment. The change is not, however, a complete change of kind, nor is it entirely recent. It is merely that we have the privilege of observing detached sentiments in a more than commonly inflated condition, and we have that privilege because our public life is more than commonly disgusting.

XI   Democratic morals

The moral sentiments which are prominent in British democracy are detached sentiments of the kind we have been describing, and the amoral spectator may think that they are part of a moral method different from that of La Rochefoucauld and Pascal. One of the differences may appear to be that Pascal and La Rochefoucauld observe, whereas the morals commonly displayed in British politics appear to be the work of a prophet rather than of an observer. It must not be thought that I am accusing my country in particular; I am describing, in local terms, a political mechanism which is also to be seen elsewhere. The mechanism happens to work particularly well in England because we are politically so mature.

On closer enquiry the public morals of England may appear to be after all the work not of a prophet but of a statesman. It is notorious that to continental observers it appears that our moral indignation subserves some end of imperial policy. They imagine our public men hatching plots with an entertaining duplicity of which certainly not all of them are capable. That duplicity is sometimes conscious I would of course not deny, but more often it is the effect of political tradition. The successful policies of the past have left behind them a sediment of feelings which indicate the way statesmen should behave in certain circumstances.

That the phenomenon is not a new one may be understood by a reading of *The Idea of a Patriot King*. Bolingbroke invites the king to be moral because, in a country where the people have a mind to be free, it is for his safety.

XII   The modern popular governor and the people

In modern popular states, whether they are called democratic or fascist, the governors appear to be at one with the will of the governed. They appear not only to be part of the same system of force as the governed, but to be the same kind of part. They share, or appear to share, popular feeling, and act as they do because of, or apparently because of, those feelings. They do not stand above the people and direct it: they usually like it to be thought that any other man (of the same race or nation) would have done what they did, had he been in office and had he had the wits to think of it. The directing will be supposed to be the people's. I am aware that this description may appear to be inapplicable to Germany and Italy, but it must be remembered that I am talking of the matter as the leaders intended it to be viewed by the common person and not as it may appear to the wary reader of the more conscious and acute pages of *Mein Kampf*. The description I have given is, however, in some ways more obviously relevant to the democratic states.

The local democratic statesman is one who is merely a part of the sentimental system of the whole people. It has already been demonstrated that a democracy cannot express the will of the people composing the state, and a corollary of this proposition is that the ideal democratic statesman cannot exist.

XIII   The common man of action

The common politician is half governor and half one of the governed. He does not exercise force in such a manner that his will embodies completely the principle of government; he is partly sentimental and acts partly at the orders of sentiments which he shares with the governed. I am not speaking now of the governor who takes account of and makes use of the sentiments of the governed; that procedure, as we have shown, is perfectly in accordance with the principle of government. I am speaking of the politician who is partly deceived by his own propaganda.

The unconscious politician is the type of the common man of action. The ordinary man at his work takes the floating propaganda about him and makes it his own. He uses it, unconsciously, and he is deceived by it. Within a system of force, he brings himself to believe that the floating ideals are the reasons for his action. And in a manner that are, for he is sustained by the illusions created by the propaganda.

It is more often vanity than avarice or the desire for any tangible good which is the motive for action. The common man of action cannot bring himself to believe that he is merely part of a system of force, as he most often is, or that the motives of his actions do not deserve to be called by exalted names, as they most often do not. He cannot think any action he engages in unimportant, and appears to reason at the back of his skull that *he* engages in it and *therefore* it is important.

It will be seen that the error arises because he believes himself to be free where he in fact is not so.

XIV   The Machiavellian and popular sentiments

The Machiavellian prince is the opposite of the democratic states-man. He stands apart from the people and he does so not only because he is the source of physical power in the state but because he is highly conscious of the moral forces at work in it and is therefore able to manipulate them. He is not sentimental, and observes popular prejudices only so that he may use them to bring the people more entirely within his system of force.

The Machiavellian dissimulates because the objects of the persons composing the state are not the same as his own, and he has to appear to share their prejudices in order to render them patient. Dissimulation is necessary in manipulating both the sensible and the moral interests of the people. It is necessary for the people to think that the prince's ambitions will not make impossible the realization of their own, and it is necessary for them to find the prince a man tolerable to their consciences so that they will feel no moral discomfort in living under him, and so that they will be able to trust him not to lay hands unjustly on their goods.

XV   The special position of the Machiavellian in the state

The position of the Machiavellian governor in the state is unique. He is as it were the point of intelligence in the system of force: the people, so far as they are deceived by him, are the blind parts. They pursue, as they think, their several ends, and he in every act perceives the mechanism of the state.

It is evident that the Machiavellian statesman comes nearer than any other to embodying consciously the principle of government. He is the utilizer of force, physical and moral. For what purposes he may utilize it does not in this essay concern us.

XVI *All government is Machiavellian*

The Machiavellian differs from other governors only in the degree of consciousness with which he exercises his function. All politicians, so far as they really govern, are utilizers of physical force and manipulators of sentiment. None is entirely in sympathy with the people and the distinction of the Machiavellian is merely that he understands that he is not in sympathy.

XVII *The freedom of the governor*

Having defined the position of the governor in the state, we may enquire whether the privileges of his special position include freedom. Freedom we have defined as independence, and it is clear that the governor cannot be independent of the state for the reason that he is the state. We have seen that the subject's civil liberty is made by the creation of a condition of disorder and this disorder is only apparent so far as the state really governs. The 'freedom to live according to the laws' is conditional on the will of the governor. We saw also that real disorder may be creeated by a man who has sufficient force to resist the demands of the state, and this, so far as it is maintained, is real civil liberty. The liberty of the governor is of the same type as the real civil liberty of the subject: it is obtained by the exercise of force against whatever threatens it. Only it is not the state, but other forces which are potential governors, which threaten the liberty of the ruler.

The liberty of the governor and that of the disorderly subject are both liberties of action, and it is by action that they are maintained. It is therefore useless for us to look here for intellectual liberty, although a political theorist might look here for certain of the physical conditions of some of the free activities of the mind. It may be added that in any system of force few can take part in government, and few can be disorderly subjects. If liberty of practice were the only kind of liberty we could enjoy, we should enjoy very little of it: and only few would enjoy even a little.

XVIII   The free activities of the subject

The free activities of most persons in the state are made possible
by apparent or conditional liberty. By free activity we mean here
any activity which is irrelevant to the state's system of force. It
may be expected that people will not in all cases be in agreement
as to what activities come within the system of force, and about
one kind of activity people are particularly likely to disagree.
That activity is the reading and writing of literature.

XIX   Literature and intellectual liberty

It is not my intention to attempt, in a section of a brief essay, to
propound a new theory of art, nor have I one to propound. But
because any conception of intellectual liberty which is of any
interest must allow for the free production of works of literature,
and because I was stimulated to write this essay partly by a feeling
of dissatisfaction with the verse of certain of my immediate
seniors, it may be well to make a few observations on the relations
of literature and government. I should perhaps add that these
remarks are not made in the belief that political criticism can
replace literary criticism, but in the belief that the two are complementary. The uneasiness one feels in reading faulty political
verse is due to literary faults, but political criticism may be able
to account, in part, for the manner in which the faults arise. And
this may be of use to the common cause which literary and political criticism serve.

The political critic would have nothing to say about the verse
of Mr Herbert Read (although he would no doubt have something to say about Mr Read's recent theorizings). The faults of
the verse, which give most of it, interesting though it is, too
low a degree of tension for poetry and make it fall without impact
on the mind, are faults which can be explained satisfactorily without going beyond the limits of literary criticism. Mr Auden's
work is different: its method, no less than its subject matter,
invites one to examine its author's political position.

The position of Mr Auden is well known. Expensively taught,
and then an expensive teacher, he professes socialism. I am not
sure that a purely proletarian communist movement could exist,
and I am aware that there are theories which justify the position
of the bourgeois instigator of revolution, but I do not understand

the virtue of a socialism whose vital parts are bourgeois. It looks extremely like the usual politician's game of liberating the people for the politician's advantage.

In this essay it is not the virtues and vices of Mr Auden's socialism as such which concern us, but the effect which the contradictory position he stands in has on his writing. Because he is Communist, Mr Auden must appear to oppose the bourgeoisie, and because he is a bourgeois he cannot do so by having the sentiments of a proletarian. Every writer in a manner opposes his class when he sets his original perceptions beside the popular and sentimental productions which embody the prejudices of the class. This opposition would not, however, suffice for Mr Auden and his friends, because it would not be a political opposition. For a political opposition it is necessary to pit one body of prejudices against another, and because the prejudices of the working class are not his to use, Mr Auden had to make an artificial opposition. This is the function of the group of friends whose names appear often on the poems and dedications. They form a band which fights a harmless and often imaginary battle against our rulers. The prejudices of the group are a variety of the prejudices of the bourgeois proper, and they are in fact part of the sentimental means by which we are governed. It will scarcely be denied that Mr Auden's best work is that in which these prejudices have least part, and in which he merely records his perceptions. The bad part of his work is the sentimental and political part.

This distinction between public sentiments and private perceptions appears to me to be fundamentally the same as the distinction between good writing and bad. If this in fact is so, it may be said that bad writing is writing which expresses the politically manoeuvrable sentiments and is therefore part of the system of force which is government. Good writing alone may be described as independent of government, and one has intellectual liberty just so far as one has the capacity to distinguish between valid work and invalid.

XX *Methods of political thought*

If popular sentiments are to be regarded as part of the instruments of government, and if one is to be regarded as free only so far as one is not at their mercy, it follows that thought which takes them as its premises will not be independent of the state. The position of abstract thought is not radically different from that of art. Its starting point is the perception of the thinker, and if the thinker sees nothing for himself his work will be valueless.

It follows from what has been said in the preceding sections that free judgement on political events is not common. It is rarely that people are able to judge without becoming part of the instruments of government, for it is only when they abandon the usual categories of thought and protest as an act of art that their judgement is free.

It is not, however, my intention to recommend that we should replace political thought by intuition; the example of the surrealist politicians effectively warns us against that. Attempts to think about politics in a manner appropriate to artists ends in the same manner as attempts to think about it in moral terms. One must persuade, and one finds that one has therefore abandoned one's personal perceptions and is speaking in terms of the popular sentiments exploited by propaganda. One becomes a fanatic.

It is evident that in our account of literature and of government political thinking must be anarchical if it is to be valid as thinking, but that is not to say that it must be such as will tend to reduce existing governments to a condition of anarchy. There are two kinds of political thought compatible with our idea of intellectual integrity. One is that of the person who criticizes the state in terms of his private tastes (as distinct from the popular prejudices he entertains). This will be a kind of protest against the conduct of politicians, but the anarchical thinker will hardly hope to have a notable effect on them. He will understand (what M. Benda has pointed out) that ideas have political effect only when the popularization has denatured them. The other kind of political thought compatible with intellectual liberty will consist not in protesting against government but in understanding it. It will consist in considering every political situation in terms of force, and it will seek to discover in any situation how far the influence of force extends. In some cases it will at that point come near to the frontiers of literary criticism.

XXI   *The method appropriate to intellectual liberty*

Art, and protest of the kind that is akin to it, are uses made of freedom, and a definition of them is not a definition of the method by which freedom may be attained. It is not now difficult for us, however, to give an account of the fundamental condition of free intellectual activity. The method of thinking which makes free intellectual activity possible is to look in the state, as in all organization, for the principle of order, which is force, and to detect the action of that force on actions and opinions. The present essay is a modest illustration of this method.

XXII

It may be well to state, in conclusion, several implications which this essay has not, and to give an opinion on another resolution of the difficulties which are the subject of it. In doing so certain of my own preferences, which I have so far tried to suspend as the writing of a critical essay demands, may become evident to the reader. The preferences do not, however, affect the validity of the method described in the essay, and the reader who has understood, and who has no taste for the tastes of others, need read no further.

It is not my intention to conclude in favour of political anarchism, nor of any form of government. As for political anarchism, I do not know whether the conditions which would make it possible could anywhere or anywhen obtain, so the question whether it is desirable is of no importance and perhaps of no meaning. As for the various forms of government, none for itself commands my loyalty, but I think that one may be justified in having a strong preference for one or another in a particular time and place. I admit the practical necessity of government, and my interest is to see that the form of it I live under is as little as possible offensive to my taste. But I should not expect to find my taste satisfied by any state.

Because the method of thought we have described includes a method of political thought which comes near to that of the Machiavellian, it is in a manner a resolution of the opposition between the practical and the speculative intellects. The politician will almost certainly not be a complete Machiavellian, and in any case he will be concerned to act, but the anarchic thinker will understand his function and we have shown that he will not be a fundamental political agitator. There is no reason why a man should not both enjoy a certain intellectual liberty and be a political actor, but if he does so he will be concious of his duality. The mind will not go waving its arms with the body.

I am aware that this solution will not be satisfactory to those who entertain belief, and for them this duality will not exist. It exists for the unbeliever because action is inevitable and in any case for the pleasure of life proper, and because the tastes are not satisfied in action, and so long as they are only tastes and not beliefs there will be no motive for unsuccessfully trying to satisfy them. It is to my liking to recall in my final sentence that several of the most profound minds of England in the last hundred years have been believers: but to recognize them is not to be converted.

II

POST-WAR REFLECTIONS

Charles Péguy

He never wanted for anything. They say he was poor, but it's not true. All that he wanted, he had; a book, a box of paints.

A pride that is almost savagery must have dictated those words, spoken by Péguy's mother to M. de Poncheville and preserved for us by Barrès. Pride for her generation, savagery perhaps for most of ours, whose greatest social effort has been to make dependence respectable. Madame Péguy's claim to her own son is established by her words. For if she was a peasant, of a family that for generations had cut wood and tended vines, his merit is to have introduced into letters an individuality tempered as it could only have been by peasant virtues. Laborious and frugal, – and these are adjectives that sound harsh in the England of today – the years served merely to expose the stamp of his beginnings: is not every sincere life, in a sense, a journey to the first years? 'There is nothing more mysterious', and it is with these words of Péguy that Halévy opens his story, 'than those dim periods of preparation which every man encounters on the threshold of life.'*

Charles Péguy was born and brought up in the shadow of Orleans, in the faubourg Bourgogne. His father had died before Charles was born, and the boy was brought up by his mother, who earned a living by mending rush seats, and by his grandmother, through whom he had contact with the (dare one say it?) vivid and irreplaceable world of illiteracy. 'We didn't even know what school was', his grandmother would say, 'I can't even read the names of the streets. I can't read the papers.' This deprivation, like others, brings its rewards.

'A child brought up in a town like Orleans between 1873 and 1880 has literally touched the old France', wrote Péguy, 'the people in the old sense, the people in fact, he has literally had his

* Daniel Halévy, *Péguy et les Cahiers de la Quinzaine*, translated by Ruth Bethell (Dennis Dobson, 1946).

part in the old France, in the people... The break-down came, if I may say so, all in a rush and covered a very short space of time.' The break-down came, though it was so much less complete when Péguy died than it is now, and it is Péguy's distinction to have carried certain virtues of the old France into the new; not in an actual, social form (no one man could do that), but in letters, in such a manner that they can nourish and inform those living in a world where human dignity is less respected.

Péguy started his education, as was to be anticipated, at the primary school, and it was a piece of good fortune that he encountered, among the early directors of his studies, M. Naudy, who determined that he must learn Latin. He learned Latin; he learned Greek; and became a master of both languages, and although he was too hard-worked ever to become what is called widely read one cannot doubt that, in what he did know, he had read deeply. His studies took him to the Lycée Lakanal, then to Sainte-Barbe and to the Mont Ste-Geneviève which was to be, in a sense, the central stage on which his industrious and provocative life was played. At Sainte-Barbe (which Jaurès had recently left) he encountered the brothers Tharaud, and a number of others who became his friends, including Marcel Beaudouin whose sister he later married. He went then to the Ecole Normale, where his studies were broken and never brought to their anticipated conclusion because, before the end, he had married (in order to know at once all the responsibilities of life) and turned printer, publisher and bookseller (in order, mainly, to print, publish and sell his own works). His life after that date was outwardly little varied; two weeks each year with the army by way of training and for all his holiday; a pilgrimage in time of need to Our Lady of Chartres; the war which was for him a conclusion. Péguy's life was not gaudy with honours or events; it was the negation indeed of such a life and a proof that renunciation is also a form of fulfilment.

At the outset of his work as a writer we find Péguy associated with unlike and unlikely figures – Jaurès, Léon Blum: men who were, in Péguy's phrase, *capitalistes d'hommes*. A motion of the Socialist Congress of December, 1899, is quoted by Halévy:

There is entire freedom of discussion on all matters regarding doctrine and method; but as regards action to be taken, the [Socialist] papers must conform strictly to the decisions of the Congress as interpreted by the General Council.

Furthermore, newspapers are asked to refrain from all statements of a polemical nature likely to incur the displeasure of one of the organizations.

Now after nearly fifty years, we know more about this 'displeasure of one of the organizations'; but Péguy's attitude to this sort of thing involved something deeper than mere dissociation from a party line. His portrait of Jaurès, lightly drawn, is yet damning; not merely for Jaurès but for all his kind. Between that which is genuine and contracted, and what is false and inflated the difference is absolute. Péguy divides men (in *Jean Coste*) into two classes, in the one men 'whose care is work, and whom we should call classical', in the other men 'preoccupied with representation' and whom he called romantic. The terms may be changed at pleasure, but nothing can change the division. There are those who work, and there are those who fuss after something more impressive.

It is impossible to give here any adequate idea of Péguy's work. That work is bulky; none but a specialist or a man of leisure would read it all. It has been called diffuse and repetitive, and in a manner it is. But it is integrated as only the work of a man who has found himself can be. And it is a certain spareness that strikes us in Péguy's sentences, which are all bone and muscle. Suarès has said: 'For him there are no synonyms. There are none for the artist, but the artist decides. Péguy could not. He wants to contain in his thought all the twists and inflections of conscience. He does not choose. So he gives us all the variants. And scruple completes the system of digression.' The characteristic of his style (or styles) could hardly be better defined. There is no question of perfection. Much, it must be admitted, is unsatisfactory. Only the rhyme, often, reminds one of the order of the lines of some of Péguy's quatrains. Of the most famous Gide has said that they are '(to speak moderately) very mediocre'. Maybe, though no technical fault could rob them, as they stand against the background of the whole *oeuvre*, of their significance. But Péguy's circuitous method, his tact in approaching a subject, giving an indication, receding, then trying again by a slightly different approach, is perhaps found at its best in such prose as that of *Notre Patrie*.

That book is a marvel. For that precious writing which is also discovery Péguy's style is a perfect instrument and here, under the German menace of 1905, Péguy discovers the *patrie*. To that discovery he added another – had he ever really forgotten it? – that of Catholicism. That brings us to the completed man in whom, but without any of the trappings of antiquarianism, the old France was resuscitated. The voice he had carried with him from the cradle spoke; the word was made flesh. His death on the Marne in 1915 was so much a fulfilment as to seem almost an indulgence. Those most famous verses which, Gide warns us, are imperfect, cannot be trite from such a man nor, one may add, from France.

> Heureux ceux qui sont morts pour la terre charnelle,
> Mais pourvu que ce fût dans une juste guerre.
> Heureux ceux qui sont morts pour quatre coins de terre,
> Heureux ce qui sont morts d'une mort solennelle...
>
> Heureux ceux qui sont morts pour des cités charnelles.
> Car elles sont le corps de la cité de Dieu.
> Heureux ceux qui sont morts pour leur âtre et leur feu,
> Et les pauvres honneurs des maisons paternelles...
>
> Car ce vœu de la terre est le commencement
> Et le premier essai d'une fidelité.
> Heureux ceux qui sont morts dans ce couronnement
> Et cette obéissance et cette humilité.

He was found face-down among the beetroots.

Epitaph on Nuremburg

'Je me demande', said Henri de Montherlant after listening to the French official broadcasts of 1940, 'pourquoi il est si rare que les hommes parlent à leurs semblables un langage humain.' And it is alarming indeed how seldom any real voice is heard in discussion of public affairs. The reasons are easy to find. For it is, after all, a somewhat rare talent to be able to speak one's mind at all; it is perhaps a still rarer one to be able to speak it on subjects distorted by the stress of rival interests which include one's own. But Montgomery Belgion's voice, it goes without saying, is a real one; he writes a prose which follows the conformation of a subtle and sensitive mind. The subject of the Nuremburg trials was treated with ugly relish by the popular press, and by many of us it is regarded with nothing but weary repugnance. Neither of these two attitudes is likely to produce observations of any value. Mr Belgion, however, has somehow preserved through the corruption of the last eight years a sensitive conscience, and it is this uncommon faculty which, in his little book *Epitaph on Nuremburg*, is to be observed agitating among the lies and prevarications of the Inhuman Voice.

Mr Belgion starts from the observation that there has been no convincing explanation of the Nuremburg trials, and that 'the absence of one is significant. An explanation fails to convince', he goes on,

> when it is not true. If the public of the world has not been given the true explanation of the Trial, it is not to be supposed that the lack of this explanation was accidental or aimless. The true explanation was kept back for a reason. I suggest the reason to have been that it was of the very heart of the real object of the Trial, and essential to its attainment, that it should not be disclosed.

Evidently, the author of this pamphlet is a man who has smelt a rat and is determined to go after it. Mr Belgion proceeds to a critique of the thesis that the trial was the outcome of a 'demand'

55

for 'justice'. He concedes that the 'demand' was made, but demonstrates with a wealth of detail the equivocation in the use of the word 'justice'. There would be no point in recapitulating here all the stages of the argument; it is to be hoped that the reader will get hold of the book and follow them for himself. It may be mentioned, however, that Mr Belgion thinks that there was a deliberate desire on the part of the authors of the Charter '*to pretend* that no persons except Germans could commit, or be suspected of deeds defined as "war crimes" or as "crimes against humanity"'. He goes on to show (what is obviously not difficult to show) that the Allies, and one ally in particular, did commit such crimes. 'There was not one kind of deed specified in the Nuremburg Indictment as a "war crime" which one or more of the chief victorious Powers, who arrogated to themselves the task of punishing the so-called "war criminals" among the defeated, was not open to being accused of.' From this it is an easy step to the statement that the trials and condemnations, which ignored 'the principle of equality before the law', were 'in accordance with the official morality of the defunct National Socialist Government of Germany'. The object of the trials was to establish the guilt of Germany 'in the eyes of the whole world, and also in the eyes of the German people themselves'.

This conclusion is a commonplace and would, I believe, have been readily accepted by nine out of every ten English people at the time when the trial was first mooted. It is the merit of Mr Belgion's little book that he shows, with a brilliance of exposition that holds the attention from the first page to the last, what dangers lurk behind this simple and commonly accepted belief. The ordinary man would be very astonished to hear that the object Mr Belgion discovers behind the trials is an improper one for any proceedings that aim at justice. Yet of course Mr Belgion is right.

He is right but... In the present state of public morality, it is doubtful whether politicians in states ruled by the popular will could in fact have acted much otherwise than as the allied leaders in fact did act. The 'demand for justice' was there, however equivocal the justice it asked for. The error goes back to the root of our troubles, of which the Nuremburg trials were perhaps no uglier a fruit than were the false ideological 'line-ups' of the 1930s, without which... But it is useless to speculate.

T.S. Eliot on Culture

When Mr Eliot first presented himself as a writer of prose, it was in the character of a literary critic. The essays collected in *The Sacred Wood* changed the course of literary criticism in this country, so far as it had a course; and so far as it did have a course, it was time it was changed. The stream started by this whang of the magician's rod is still flowing – if the analogy of a stream can properly be used at all for anything that has become dessicated. For Mr Eliot, however, *The Sacred Wood* was only a partial statement; he quickly became uneasy, like a man who has made a remark that has been overheard out of its context and so feels obliged, not to take back what he has said, but to qualify and expand it. The first major public demonstration of Mr Eliot's reservations was made in *For Lancelot Andrewes*. In the preface to that volume Mr Eliot spoke of a wish to dissociate himself 'from certain conclusions which had been drawn' from *The Sacred Wood*: he also spoke of a wish 'to indicate certain lines of development', and from this one may gather that there had been a widening or at any rate a deepening of certain interests since the publication of the earlier volume. It was in the preface to *For Lancelot Andrewes* that Mr Eliot introduced the ghosts of three unborn books which haunted his readers for some years. *The Principles of Modern Heresy* was the happiest of these ghosts, for it found embodiment, perhaps in slighter form than was originally intended, in *After Strange Gods*. *The School of Donne* had, in a sense, been written already. No doubt, had Mr Eliot carried out the work as he intended in 1928, he would have made a number of distinctions, and we should have found that the school of Donne was not quite what we thought he had meant, in his earlier essays, to indicate to us what it was. But that ghost was less haunting because we thought, with whatever imprudent assurance, that we knew the sort of form she would take. *The Outline of Royalism* was as near to being a figure of fun as ghost could be; at that time, and for some years afterwards, it was generally known that Marxist socialism was the only manifestation of government that one need take seriously and that monarchy was merely part of the monstrous opposite – called fascism, capitalism, imperialism – by which socialism then, even more than now, defined itself. Those who had ventured beyond the permitted fields, or asphalt pavements, of Marxist socialism, and read some pages of Charles Maurras, could generally only regret that Mr Eliot was plotting to resuscitate an outworn political philosophy; outworn, for to them it was evident that people who enjoyed a free and pacific life under the stable protection of the Third Republic could have nothing to learn from the *ancien régime*. The point about the announcement of the three books in the preface to *For Lancelot Andrewes* was that it involved a declaration of unpopular loyalties. There was widespread regret that Mr Eliot had gone wrong. When I became aware of these things in 1931 people told me that I might read the poetry and *The Sacred Wood* but that I was to consult *The Left Review* before believing a word that was said in Mr Eliot's later writings in prose.

After Strange Gods appeared in 1934, and bore witness to Mr Eliot's theological preoccupations and, more important and more characteristic, to his determination to take these preoccupations into studies to which they were, at that time, more often than not thought not to be relevant. To apply the word heresy at all to the writings of ordinary irreligious people, who had put forward fallacious propositions without considering their relationship to Christianity, was by way of being an innovation. The introduction of the term 'heresy' in this context is an example of that confrontation of ancient and modern, or rather of the modern and the permanent, which every sound critic of letters or manners must make, and which Mr Eliot himself has on numerous occasions made so singularly well. Mr Eliot was driving back further into the roots of our culture without losing – and indeed while gaining – in awareness of the contemporary scene.

A more significant book, from the point of view of our approach to Mr Eliot's new study, was *The Idea of a Christian Society*, which appeared in 1939. By contrast with what was adumbrated in the preface to *For Lancelot Andrewes*, the book savoured less than one might have anticipated of practical politics, or of a close application of principles to the particular needs of this country. Perhaps it may seem a little absurd to talk of practical politics – which are, among other things, more long-winded – in connection with the somewhat rarified little books I have been speaking of. But one certainly got the impression, from *Lancelot*

Andrewes, that Mr Eliot was taking a stand in something other than, or in addition to, a theoretical sense, and there are few of his writings in prose after the date of that book that do not show, as the Commentaries in the *Criterion* showed, a growing sense of the urgency of public affairs, and of the relevance of the permanent values which Mr Eliot was concerned to uphold to the day-to-day goings-on of politicians and other public men. The extent to which *The Idea of a Christian Society* falls within the world of theory or the world of practical politics, however, hardly matters. What does matter is that during the last ten years Mr Eliot's pronouncements have had a simultaneous force and relevance in both worlds. The development that has brought Mr Eliot to his present position looks like an organic growth.

The *Notes Towards the Definition of Culture* are, in a sense, a synthesis of various interests which have been exhibited in Mr Eliot's earlier writings in prose. Characteristically, he tells us, in the first lines of his Introduction, of some purposes he had *not* in mind in writing the book. He did not, he tells us, intend to outline a social or political philosophy, nor to make the book merely a vehicle for his observations on a number of topics. His aim was 'to help to define a word, the word *culture*'. In short, he is concerned to make the thing look as little like a synthesis, and as much like an analysis, as possible. In the course of the book he does the things he disclaims the intention of doing, and several other things as well. But the words of the Introduction serve to warn us that Mr Eliot is here airing only such of his views on social and political philosophy as are relevant to the definition of culture, and no one, therefore, should suppose after reading this book that he has more than partial indications of Mr Eliot's views on these matters. The book goes beyond its nominal subject-matter only in the sense that it is impossible to talk sociology without talking several other things at the same time.

In the first chapter of *Notes Towards the Definition of Culture*, Mr Eliot endeavours 'to distinguish and relate' the uses of the word which differ according to whether one has in mind 'the development of an *individual*, or a *group* or *class*, or of a *whole society*'. 'It is part of my thesis', he says, 'that the culture of the individual is dependent upon the culture of a group or class, and that the culture of the group or class is dependent upon the culture of the whole society to which that group or that class belongs. Therefore it is the culture of the society that is fundamental.' Mr Eliot then goes on to 'try to expose the essential relation of culture to religion', and here he comes to a point which is original in more senses than one, and somewhat abstruse. He wishes to 'make clear the limitation of the word *relation* as an expression of this "relation"'. Mr Eliot conceives 'culture and religion as being, when each term is taken in the right context, different aspects of the same thing'. Therefore neither can culture be preserved or developed in the absence of religion, nor religion preserved and maintained without reckoning with culture. But, if there is question here of the unity of religion and culture, there is no question of their identity. Hence 'aesthetic sensibility must be extended into spiritual perception, and spiritual perception must be extended into aesthetic sensibility and disciplined taste'. It is true that Mr Eliot speaks as if religious standards and aesthetic standards were really identical; or, to report him more accurately, as if to judge by either of these standards 'should come in the end to the same thing', but he is careful to add that that 'end' is one 'at which no individual can arrive'. The whole of the passage from which this is taken must be studied in Mr Eliot's own words – in all his own words and not merely in summary, comment or even quotation. It is, I think, the central point of the book and, incidentally, it is the point at which Mr Eliot's prose exhibits the maximum of suppleness, passion and refinement. In these pages Mr Eliot seems to be struggling to express the perception which is the basis of all his subsequent ratiocination, and the writing shows at moments almost an excess of its own essential quality, just as a paragraph of Sir Thomas Browne may seem, even when the intensity of the writing is at its greatest, pleasurably over-burdened with its own very different self.

After explaining his theory of religion and culture, Mr Eliot goes on to discuss three of the conditions for culture. 'The first of these', he says,

> is organic (not merely planned but growing) structure, such as will foster the hereditary transmission of culture within a culture: and this requires the persistence of social classes. The second is the necessity that a culture should be analysable, geographically, into local cultures: this raises the problem of 'regionalism'. The third is the balance of unity and diversity in religion – that is, universality of doctrine and particularity of cult and devotion.

The first two are conditions that were evidently likely to strike a man whose political philosophy was of the kind to which Mr

Eliot's was supposed to belong, but it would be unfortunate if readers who do not share the views that they imagine to be his were thereby distracted from a careful study of the relevance of the persistence of social classes and regional differentiation to the persistence of culture. The reception Mr Eliot gets as a sociologist is bound to suffer from the fact that he has long ago declared certain loyalties, contrary to the practice of the typical modern intellectual, who looks up from his books or his test-tubes and announces that his long sojourn in the world of thought has taught him that he should join the ———— party, and that he advises other chaps who want to be thought thoughtful to jolly well hurry up and do likewise.

It is the later chapters of this book, I think, and particularly the notes on education, which are likely to receive most immediate attention from the public at large. There would be no great harm in this, if people were thereafter and thereby coaxed into a consideration of the more fundamental matters with which the book starts. That may not always happen, however, for Mr Eliot's remarks on education are not only of great intrinsic interest but of great emotive force. There are several wholesome but unpopular truths in this final chapter, and it is unfortunate that Mr Eliot's presentation of them has in it an element which is bound to alienate certain readers more than the truths themselves would do. Mr Eliot's long residence in this country has not, one might guess, enabled him to see the country's social structure otherwise than as an outsider. The result is, one suspects, that he has an unduly simplified notion of what constitutes the governing classes, and perhaps attributes undue weight and value to the upper and upper middle classes. It may not be altogether extravagant to suggest that the fact that he tolerated – even from a collaborator – the sort of 'working class' dialogue that appears in *The Rock*, shows that his perception of what goes on in the working classes is or was somewhat blunted. In a note to the *Idea of a Christian Society* which is of special interest to the reader of the present book, Mr Eliot says: 'Britain will presumably continue to be governed by the same mercantile and financial class which, with a continual change of personnel, has been increasingly important from the fifteenth century.' That was hardly perspicacious, even for 1939, and a man of much less remarkable gifts, born and brought up in this country, would have avoided such a presumption. A similar defect of social perception marks some of the comments on education in this chapter. It is difficult, in the context of present society in England, to attach much meaning to being 'educated above the level of those whose social habits and tastes one has inherited', at any rate in the cases where the education has had any appreciable effect on the subject. And it is a pity that, in discussing the case against equality of opportunity in education, Mr Eliot has, as it were, looked at the problem from the top side only and spoken of the educated being unpleasant, or merely too numerous, and not concerned himself with the lot of the underdog, who would be deprived of his natural protagonist in the person of the man of lively wits who remains in the subordinate classes. One wonders, too, what Mr Eliot considers constitute advantages of birth in present-day England. The idea is not a simple one at any time; one might always ask whether a high degree of literacy in several consecutive generations may not deprive the heir of those generations of more than it gives him.

Without any major questions of principle being settled, or even more widely agreed upon, much that is done in this country might be better done if certain assumptions were less lightly made. Mr Eliot's approach to a definition of culture might be recommended to politicians, but for the fact that politicians are rarely of an age or temper to be persuaded to abandon their assumptions. To Mr Eliot's ordinary public, recommendation of any of his books is superfluous, but one may say that this one has a special interest for those who follow the elusive line of the *New English Weekly*. It is, by the way, inscribed to Philip Mairet.

Lord Beveridge Explains Himself

The title of Lord Beveridge's new book is *Voluntary Action*. That is, one might remark, an exceptionally vague title, but we have heard something of the author that enables us to place it in the appropriate field of discourse. Lord Beveridge helps us further by adding a sub-title: 'A Report on Methods of Social Advance'. The word 'report' is helpful, for it tells us what literary *genre* we have to do with. When we hear that word we do not expect, generally speaking, to find an individual expression of opinion, or the organic work of one man's thought or imagination. The characteristic report is the work of a number of people and its multiple origins are commonly betrayed by a vagueness of language hard to avoid when many are trying to speak as one. Lord Beveridge takes sole responsibility for this report, but he had, he tells us, a number of people working with him in his inquiry 'as Assessors' and these ladies and gentlemen – some of them, unless I am much mistaken, themselves famous committee-men and committee-women – 'acted as a committee in interviewing representatives of organizations and individuals. . . and in discussion'. It is is not to be wondered at, therefore, if this report has some of the faults, as well as the merits, of the report of a committee. The author of a committee's report does not keep both his eyes on his subject and use words in an attempt to give precision to his thoughts about it. He keeps one eye on his subject and one on the committee-men and on the organizations that are milling around behind him, each trying to make his or its own point of view felt by pricking the author with it. The result is that the report-writer's words are not the words of an individual man; they are what manages to get itself most clearly heard of a babel of voices. The trained committee-man learns to speak, as the trained report-maker to write, as if he were himself a babel, and I believe that some of the best of these people are quite unaware of their proficiency in this trick. It is not, of course, in the recording of a statistical fact – 'The total number of societies for 1910 is shown as 26,773' – that this trick of speech or writing shows itself. The common agreement about the facts of arithmetic is fairly genuine. The trick shows itself when the writer or speaker has to refer to the assumptions about values which underlie every discussion about action 'for a public purpose'.

It is important to inquire at the outset what Lord Beveridge means in the report by 'social action'. The explanation of the theme of the study that is given in the preface does not take us very far: 'Voluntary Action outside each citizen's home for improving the conditions of life for him and for his fellows.' The fact is, of course, that Lord Beveridge is what is called a 'representative figure' and he does not feel the need to be precise as an individual enquirer would have to be about the matter. His name has become a household word, and it has become so very quickly precisely because he is not an innovator but someone who, with an outlook shared by millions and methods shared by thousands, happened to find himself sitting in the right chair at the right time. He is a good sample of the serious-minded Englishmen of his generation who do not think that such terms as 'social advance' and 'improving the conditions of life' call for any explanation beyond themselves. This insensitivity to the problem of value that lurks behind such phrases is well illustrated by a quotation Lord Beveridge gives, apparently with approval: 'without the background of a sense of vocation, social service will have no basic principles'. That may be good enough for a lady who has to work herself up to do some task not intrinsically agreeable, and who feels the need for some such verbal stimulant; it should not be good enough for someone conducting an inquiry into 'methods of social advance', who should have a somewhat more precise notion of the way the advance is heading. It is true that the lady went on, as Lord Beveridge tells us, to name her basic principles. The first was 'a real belief in brotherhood and in the equality of man'; and I know not what suspicion that the belief might be bogus led to the addition of the adjective. The second was a 'reasoned and intelligent understanding of those for whom we work'; again the superfluity of adjectives. The third, 'a passionate sense of justice'; ditto. The fourth, 'a wider outlook beyond the palliative as to the constructive'; one can only add, *sic*, and note that this principle begs all questions of principle. The fifth, 'a determination to do everything possible to fit us for the work in hand'; that may have been all right for the particular task the lady had in mind, but if it is meant to be a 'principle' of social service in general one is still left wondering: 'What is the task in hand?'

I am not suggesting, of course, that Lord Beveridge would be capable of writing such clap-trap as this which he thinks worth the trouble of quoting, but I would not have dwelt on this particular quotation if I had not found difficulty, in reading the report, in formulating the principle on which it is based. I imagine that if one were able to corner the noble lord and to question him about first principles, his answer would be something like this: 'Of course, one can raise a lot of theoretical questions about ends, but all reasonable people are agreed' on whatever Lord Beveridge proposes. And I think it only fair to say that Lord Beveridge appears to hold, pretty consistently, much the same body of prejudices and opinions as the vast mass of those in England who would be generally recognized as 'social workers'. I do not think it possible, however, to make a satisfactory study of any 'social question' at the present time without examining the validity of those prejudices and opinions. Lord Beveridge is wisely economical of expressions of principle, but his report is rich in statements which can only be called tendentious and which cannot be examined without raising questions of principle. 'That there are more divorces and more broken families now than before the World Wars is undeniable. But the conditions are also different and more trying.' The trying conditions are put forward as the explanation of the phenomena noted. Yet there have been times of war and public disorder when there were no divorces at all, simply because divorce was not permitted. 'Ah, but the *facts* were the same; people drifted apart', the apologist for Beveridge might say, betraying a queer notion of what a fact is, and of what marriage and divorce are. '. . . to recognize housewives as . . . members of a team rather than as dependents on their husbands' – That is part of a plea for the atomic fission of the family. '. . . the day nursery to give the housewife freedom to do paid work, where this is necessary in the public interest or her own' – That sentence recognizes the demands of the 'public' (the state) and *certain* demands of the individual which are compatible with the former. 'The state has undertaken to see that irrespective of the means of his parents, every child shall have education fitted to his abilities.' – The problems raised by that sentence are innumerable: it may be sufficient to say that, even supposing that a child has identifiable abilities to which a particular education could be known *a priori* to be fitted, the state can carry out its undertaking only by being omniscient as well as all-powerful. Lord Beveridge, it may fairly be said, reveals himself as an apologist of the state. The glimmerings we get of his philosophy show him as one who, perhaps unconsciously, makes it his business to persuade people, in disarmingly gentle tones, to a subservience, not to the policies of the Government, but to the policy of government which is working itself out now in all the industrial countries of the world. He is one of those who are set on destroying whatever stands between the individual and the power of the state. 'In giving to each one social security according to his needs', he says ingenuously, 'Britain is nearer to the communist formula than Soviet Russia.' But Lord Beveridge means no harm. He believes that the ugliest possibilities of government cannot realize themselves in this country. One need only note with what equanimity he talks of certain recent developments in the financing of universities.

> The end of the First World War saw the beginning of Exchequer grants to universities; the end of the Second World War has seen a large increase in the scale of grants made. The total disbursed through the University Grants Committee in 1946-47 was more than £6 million and represents about half the total income of the Universities. Yet the public grants are given without destroying self-government.

It is small wonder, after this, to find Lord Beveridge proposing that there should be a 'Minister-Guardian of Voluntary Action'. 'If voluntary action for social advance is to be part of public policy, it is important that the voluntary agencies should have a voice and protector in the Government itself.' At this point the reader can only stick pins in himself. Either this is a particularly nasty dream, or Lord Beveridge has conducted us into a ghastly world of totalitarianism. The reviewer can only say that, as the pins didn't work, the latter must be the case. It is true, of course, that for some time 'voluntary bodies' have been becoming less voluntary. Lord Beveridge quotes in his preface from a publication produced in connection with the Nuffield College Reconstruction Survey: 'A generation ago "voluntary" was normally used to denote "unpaid". A "voluntary" worker was someone who gave unpaid service in a good cause... Nowadays many of the most active voluntary agencies are staffed entirely by highly trained and fairly well-paid professional workers.' While this process has been going on something has been happening to the trade unions. 'They remain voluntary associations in the sense given to that term here', says Lord Beveridge, 'but in many if not most occupations they are no longer voluntary in the sense of its being free to an individual who wishes to pursue that occupation to decide whether he will or will not join them.' And meanwhile, a new type of association has been invented. The W.V.S. is voluntary in the sense that a woman can join it or not as she likes, but it 'has taken as its aim assistance of statutory authorities in the discharge of their obligations'. Neither the organization a man serves in order to keep his job, nor the organization that 'assists the statutory authorities' can be one in which the individual as innovator counts for much: such organizations may be regarded as extensions of government. Less and less, in all the countries called 'more advanced', remains out of the clutches of whoever can, by popular favour or by force or fraud, make himself the boss. One can share Lord Beveridge's serenity only if one believes that the perfect machine will always find a benign master.

The Crisis in the University

It has been the conviction of others besides ourselves, in ages other than our own, that they lived in a time exceptionally given over to error. The constant renewal of such convictions is no doubt due in part to the fact that the world is filled with people of all ages, and when one man dies, or reaches a faith so settled that it puts him beyond trouble, another is sure to be just reaching an age of sufficient reason to reflect that unregenerate human life is a thing of unspeakable squalor while a third, yet younger, entertains aspirations that are due for disappointment before his next birthday. We may fairly suppose that any embracing crisis in which our age is involved has in it a large part of the general human trouble. It is the blight we were born for. It is legitimate to try to describe the peculiar forms the sickness may take in our own time and place, but any diagnosis that does not go back to incurable causes is bound to be wrong. The fundamental sickness is always the same, but the complications are various and may be worth study.

One of the complications, in our time, is that there are so many complications. Our malady is difficult to chase precisely because it seems to pop up everywhere at once. Someone sees a crisis in science, and everyone looks that way. While backs are turned, up pops a crisis in religion. Everyone looks round, but before they have time to collect their thoughts, someone has found the crisis in sex. Then someone else comes along carrying a horrid picture: he has found the crisis in art! Small wonder, with all this going on, that Sir Walter Moberly, who is in a position to know, has found the crisis in the university. That it is the same crisis that disturbs society at large is a main point in Sir Walter's thesis. 'La lutte qui ébranle la Cité, c'est d'abord en nous-mêmes qu'elle fait rage'.

Sir Walter Moberly accepts the description of what he calls 'our present communal condition of mind' given in *The Idea of a Christian Society*: 'We have a culture which is mainly negative', he quotes Mr Eliot as saying, 'but which, so far as it is positive,

68

is still Christian.' The problem he is concerned to answer is how, if this description answers to the fact of the matter, universities in this country should be organized, or rather, what principles should govern their organization. The nature of the answer he gives derives, not only from the author's own religious beliefs, and from his integrity of mind which cannot do otherwise than pursue the consequences of these beliefs into every cranny of practical life, but – if a guess may be forgiven – from a character of naturally liberal temper to which a varied administrative experience has given a further docility. The ordinary administrator, with no dearly-held beliefs – or none of general importance – or who is unable to see how he can relate his beliefs to his administrative acts, tends to become a tool of whatever masters will use him. He bends, but it is to the will of another, to the *vox populi* of the moment. There are virtually no limits to his tolerance. Sir Walter Moberly's mind is of a different kind. Contact with many men has made it flexible, but with the flexibility of an instrument teleologically designed and directed. Its tolerance is limited by the purpose for which it was made, and you would be rash to try to use it for a purpose other than that. The author's answer to the question he sets himself is that of a Christian, and of a Christian not of the schizophenic variety (with half his life shut off from his beliefs); and it is the answer of a wary man, too much experienced to suppose that he can go directly to an end simply because he holds it to be desirable, or even because it *is* desirable.

It is part of the answer proposed, in *The Crisis in the University*, to the question of what principles should govern the organization of universities, that their teachers should abandon an 'impartiality' which is bound to be deceptive, and bring to light their beliefs and preconceptions. If cards were laid on the table, the Christian who understood his own theology would be seen to have the strongest hand. The end of making the university Christian cannot be gained in any immediate future, but Christians should not 'decline responsibility for a machine' which they 'cannot hope to control'. They should 'aim at exercising influence in the university as a whole'. For (following Mr Eliot once more) our culture cannot 'remain in its present state; it must become wholly secular, unless it becomes more Christian than it is'. The Christian university teacher will have his part to play in making our 'culture' more Christian, if that is what it is to be; meanwhile, while we are in a condition in which Christianity commands no wide allegiance, the university must have 'a common basis' which cannot be 'specific Christianity'. 'Admittedly', says the author, 'such a basis will prove in the long run to be a precarious and unsatisfactory compromise'. It is likely to do so indeed, for it is merely 'a common moral outlook . . . which sees the challenge of our time in personalist rather than technical terms'; beyond that, there is no more common ground that 'intellectual honesty' which perhaps is meaningless in default of some agreement on fundamental points of belief. That the residuum is so small, when points of possible disagreement have been allowed for, must be, for a Christian, a sad consideration; that the author holds it none the less to be worth something perhaps reflects an intuition, renewed in innumerable encounters with university teachers, that the common agreement, if not extensive, may be profound. Sir Walter Moberly might say, with Jeremy Taylor, that 'it concerns all persons to see that they do their best to find out truth, and if they do, it is certain that, let the error be never so damnable, they shall escape the error or the misery of being damned for it'. Universities, however, do not comprise solely persons who 'see that they do their best to find out truth', and many who are taught by men who are themselves seekers of truth go down carrying nothing more than an opinion. It is not to be taken as axiomatic that at all times all opinions can be allowed; nor that it is always prudent, even if it is philosophic, to hear an argument out. But those doubts are not for the university teacher, and Sir Walter is right not to entertain them. That is someone else's job. In Jeremy Taylor's words: 'let the prince and the secular power have a care the commonwealth be safe'.

Charles Maurras

Charles Marie Photius Maurras was born in 1868, two years before that Third Republic whose enemy he was to become. The place of his birth was chemin de Paradis, Martigues (Bouches-du-Rhône) and it was there that he was domiciled when, seventy-seven years later, he stood on trial for his life on a charge of treason.

Scattered here and there in the writings of Maurras are indications enough to satisfy the imagination, if not the more popular faculty of curiosity, as to the conditions and circumstances of his childhood. His parents had three sons, of whom he was the second, but the eldest died before Charles was born. For several years Charles enjoyed the privileges of an only child, and soon after his younger brother came into the world his father left it. The father was a minor official, punctilious in the performance of his duties but with energies and interests left over for ideas and a mind on which Racine, La Fontaine and Voltaire had left their traces. Above all the father was, in the recollection of his sons, the source and embodiment of songs and dances. 'Sacred, profane, whatever is sung in church or at the opera, French, Latin or Provençal, or a mixture of the three, he knew everything and forgot nothing and . . . he conveyed the movement of his resonant soul to the ear of his wonderstruck child.' That was not without significance for the journalist whose passion for letters was second only to his passion for the doctrine he taught and who was to say, in the course of a superb apology for his supple and lucid prose, that 'reason may convince, but it is rhythm that persuades'. Madame Maurras was of a different temperament from her gay and ingenious husband, and Maurras claims to have inherited from her whatever he has of will and seriousness. The two parents differed in political outlook as in temperament. Madame Maurras never had the slightest faith in the republic: 'but your father', she would dutifully tell the young Charles, 'took the opposite view.' She would recall how, when she was a small girl, the Prince de Joinville had visited her parents' house; she had expected a prince out of a fairy tale and met a young man whose naval uniform associated him with the forces that govern the world. If there was this reminder in the recollections of Madame Maurras, that royalty has a modern dress and function, there was in the popular aspirations that centred round the comte de Chambord an imagination that lifted contemporary politics into the timeless and pastoral world: *'S'Enri V deman venié!'* An old servant, Louise Espérandieu, had seen the King and Queen pass over the bridge at Avignon on their way to Paris. Maurras carved on his school-desk again and again V.H.V. *(Vive Henri V)*. Then, at the age of twelve or thirteen, these loyalties were swept away by that philosophy of liberty which, in one form or another, has had to be encountered by every youth since at any rate the eighteenth century, and which indeed represents a persistent illusion to which local philosophies and aspirations have perhaps at all times given shape. The form the illusion took in the mind of the young Maurras was determined by Lamennais, a reading of whose *Paroles d'un Croyant* was the occasion of its inception. Maurras became a theocratic republican. Absolute justice demanded community of goods, equality of parents and children, masters and pupils. Maurras had swallowed all the claptrap. He was, however, unlike those who go mumbling mouthfuls of it all their lives, able to digest it. The period of rumination was one of that lofty and sceptical indifference which is a common feature of adolescence. It lasted roughly from Maurras's sixteenth until his twentieth year. Meanwhile, objective studies supervened, and he was drawn to consider the relationship between laws and institutions and the strength and weakness of states. He discarded the idea, essential to the romantic insurrectionism of Lamennais, that there is an irresolvable opposition between the interests of governors and governed. He began to reflect on the function of élites, which serve the multitude whether they will or not. His scorn for the 'many and absurd opinions' of the multitude grew at the same time as his passion for 'a small number of coherent and reasonable propositions'. This development marked out the shape of the finished man.

Maurras had taken his baccalaureate at the Catholic college of Aix-en-Provence, and in 1885 he had taken up residence in Paris. It was in the capital that he pursued those studies of history, philosophy and the social sciences which first enabled him to define his position. He was not, at first, much interested in practical politics, but the ideas that were ripening within him were bound to bring him, sooner or later, to take his stand in public discussion of matters affecting the government of France. Inseparable from the Provençal revival with which he had contact through the Ecole Parisienne du Félibrige was an aspiration towards decentralization and the revival of the provinces. The stories which Maurras wrote in the early years and collected in his first book, *Le Chemin de Paradis*, were dominated by a concern, somewhat general and theoretical in character, for the public good as well as for the purity and clarity of the abstract idea. The book, under the influence of a contemporary fashion and, perhaps more intimately, of Dante, was allegorically or analogically constructed so that, when one meaning was stripped off you were left, like the reader of a palimpsest, with others. These ingenuities have faded, and it is unlikely that anyone now, unless it be some student burrowing for a doctorate, will disengage from these stories more than is to be got at a normally attentive reading. But that much attention will show with what sort of man we have to do, and the author, as if already, in May 1894, doubting the efficacy of his allegorical method, made the main outlines of his mind clearer in the preface he addresses to Frédéric Amouretti. He laments that in his generation even those young men who seem to love ideas love them 'as dead beauties'. There is a touch of romantic and melodramatic gesture about this, but in retrospect there seems to be still more of the impatience of one for whom ideas are heavy with personal experience. 'The doctrine of the *Chemin de Paradis*', he says, 'is that the good life consists in misprizing nothing... and then... creating interior harmonies.' Knowledge and self-discipline are enjoined, and the two points at which it is possible to achieve a little discipline and agreement are said to be science and the love of one's country. Those who try to weaken those two supports of a public and objective reason are treated with the same contempt or disdain as those who waste their energies in an absurd pity for themselves or others, and those who seek to awaken concupiscence in the brains or bowels of merely instinctive people who might blessedly have died without having lived. The preface contains also the germs of those ideas about the Roman church which were to cause such scandal. Maurras describes his chain of ideas as 'sufficiently pagan and Christian to deserve the fine title of Catholic which is that of the religion in which we were born'. He speaks of 'the odd Saint-Simonian Jesus of eighteen-forty' to whom he opposes the Jesus 'of our Catholic tradition, who was on earth crucified for us'. 'Divinity is a number; everything is numbered and limited.' He has in mind particularly, in this part of his plea for harmony and measure, the Germans with their passion for the infinite. 'I am horrified above all by these Germans.' At this point his most abstract studies are touched and enlivened by his deepest passions. For he belonged, as he had occasion to recall at Lyons in 1945, to that generation which the socialist Jules Ferry reproached for being 'hypnotized by the blue line of the Vosges'. The defeat of 1870–1 had made 'revenge the Queen of France', and Maurras was not the man to fail to pay her a proper tribute.

The seedling ideas springing in the work of Maurras at this time showed that the moment was about to come when he could take his full and active part as a political controversialist. The year in which, in the little essays of *Trois Idées Politiques*, he extracted and defined the political sense of Chateaubriand, Michelet and Sainte-Beuve with a dexterity and firmness which showed him to be the complete master of his method, was the year when the Dreyfus case broke upon France. It is difficult, in the battered and bludgeoned Europe of today, with its inattention to ideas and its hebetude under repeated crises, to make present to oneself anything of the impact which the allegedly false condemnation of a single army officer had on the France of 1898. It was, however, not the fate of the mere individual officer that interested and impassioned the public. The case was something which, dipped into the politics of the day, caused the ideas therein held in solution suddenly to take shape and cluster about it. Dreyfus was a Jew, and it was alleged that he had been condemned on account of his race. The Minister of War affirmed that Dreyfus had been properly and regularly convicted. Those who put the safety of France before the rights of an individual were content to leave the matter there. Those who thought that justice must be done though the sky fell sought a revision of the case. No doubt it was possible for a patriotic Frenchman to take either view of the matter, and ranged with the Dreyfusards were such men as Péguy. It was not patriotism merely, but his understanding of certain principles of state, which put Maurras on the anti-Dreyfusard side of the discussion. Justice as well as patriotism, he contended, were on that side. There was much fevered discussion as to whether Dreyfus was innocent or guilty. Maurras did not concern himself much with this question. His view first and last was that 'if it happened that Dreyfus was after all innocent, by all means make a field-marshal of him, but a dozen of his principal defenders should be shot for the triple wrong they were doing to France, to Peace and to Reason'. Maurras, already himself convinced of the necessity of the monarchy, drew a moral from the *affaire* in an article entitled 'What good would a king be?' In the disquiet of the fully developed *affaire*, Barrès had said: 'There is no possibility of a restoration of the commonwealth without a doctrine.' His words must have reflected a need of which many patriotic and thoughtful Frenchmen were beginning to be aware. Maurras was, among the young nationalists of his day, the man equipped to indicate a doctrine and to give it precision. The original members of the *Action Française* group, which came into being under the shadow of the *affaire*, were not royalists. But they held like Maurras that the *patrie* was above everything, and it was inevitable that their views should give way to the more precisely formulated views of the latter. The *Action Française* was the movement of 'nationalisme intégral'. It was Maurras who showed them that that doctrine required objective embodiment in a king. The *Enquête sur la Monarchie* began to appear in 1900.

And so, at the beginning of the century, the stage was completely set for singularly coherent action which Maurras was to lead for fifty years. The paper, which became a daily in 1908, already existed in 1899. Names which long appeared in its pages were already associated with the movement. There was Vaugeois, the founder, Maurice Pujo who was at Maurras's side at the trial in 1945 and who was condemned with him, and Jacques Bainville whose lucid analytical mind commanded respect in quarters which viewed with suspicion or dislike the more polemically-minded members of the group.

The Ligue d'Action Française was founded in 1905. The declaration which had to be signed by its adherents contained, as was proper, a sufficient abstract of the doctrine Maurras was teaching. 'A Frenchman by birth and spirit...' it began. The doctrine was not one for all comers. It was not designed to correspond with an emasculated, Kantian reason. It was of France, and for the French: '...in mind and in will, I undertake to conduct myself as a patriot conscious of his duties'. The *ligueur* was expected both to understand and to act. Then came the declaration of enmity to the republic.

I promise to fight against republican rule. The Republic in

France is the rule of the foreigner. The republican spirit dis-organizes national defence and favours religious influences directly inimical to the traditional Catholicism. France must once more be given a system of government that is French.

Our future therefore lies in the Monarchy as personified by His Grace the Duke of Orleans, heir of the forty kings who, in a thousand years, made France. The Monarchy alone ensures public safety, and making itself answerable for order, prevents the public ills which are denounced by anti-semitism and by nationalism. The Monarchy is the indispensable organ of the common interest, and enhances authority, liberties, property and honour.

I associate myself with the task of restoring the Monarchy.

I promise to serve it by every means in my power.

One hears there echoes of the Dreyfus affair and of the current controversies which centred around the Christian democrats of the time. The monarchy was the means whereby alone could be secured the safety of those things to which the 'Frenchman by birth and in spirit' would be devoted.

Maurras had three main subjects of study and polemic in the years preceding World War I. They were: the weakness of the republic and the correlated strengths and benefits of monarchy; the religious question; and the German question. All three left their traces in the declaration. The references to the German ques-tion were, it is true, not explicit, for the declaration naturally kept to generalities, but it was that question which gave urgency to the other two. The *Action Française* grew up under the shadow of the German menace.

The doctrine of monarchy which Maurras conceived was determined, like every branch of his doctrine, by an acute sense that his beloved France was without adequate protection either from external enemies or from the enemies who weakened and denatured her from within. 'Yes or no, is the institution of a traditional, hereditary, anti-paliamentary and decentralized monarchy a matter of public safety?' Yes, ran the answer, put in a thousand forms as opportunity and occasion arose. France must have a central power which is strong, independent and essentially national. A traditional monarchy can provide this because by definition it gives perfect continuity, and independence of the popular storms and prejudices of the day. It is something to be accepted without dispute, an institution beyond the control of subjects, something handed down, *given*, like an indestructible monument or the original proposition of a geometry. It must be hereditary, because inheritance obviates those struggles about succession which are the weakness and distress of states under the hand of a mere Caesar or lifelong dictator. Moreover, the continuity of heredity binds the ruling family to the fortunes of the country for an immeasurable future. The hereditary monarch cannot conceive any future either for himself or for his family which is not dependent on the future of the country. The monarchy must be decentralized, so that people can go about their business and their business can be something that they know about. It must be anti-parliamentary, for the king must be a king who governs, and the meddling of a parliament could only weaken the unity and continuity of royal power and hamper the identification of the king's interest with the national interest which is the guarantee of the efficacy of monarchy. The king has the whole cake, and is likely to guard it jealously. The members of an elected assembly, no less egotistical, will quarrel over the size of their slices. The king's egotism will serve the common good; that of the members of an assembly will be hostile to it. Moreover, an elected assembly is driven hither and thither by the claims and complaints of those who put it in power, but 'a cry, even a loud one, is worth just as much as its cause is worth', and the independent government of the king will judge of things as they are and not as the people or their tribunes make them out to be. Maurras respects the people, vehicles of ancient traditions and the arms and legs of France, but he might say with our Charles I 'as for government, it is nothing pertaining to them'. He was fully aware of the difficulty of 'any reform that is a little noble', and did not expect to rally the mass of the populace to his side. The scheme of revolution he favoured was the revolution from above. Monck and Talleyrand were the models he admired. He conceived an action discreed, economical and effective, carried out by a handful of determined men. The means of communication in the hands of a government of the twentieth century make it possible for a competent government to resist insurrection, but also make it possible for insurgents who have seized a few key points to exercise an instantaneous and powerful influence over a wide area.

The treatment Maurras accorded to the religious question, no less than his treatment of monarchy, was determined by his concern for the safety of France. His writings on this matter had, he said, no other object than 'to unite the separated members of the French nation'. He declared himself an atheist. Differing from Catholics as to what is true, he sought reconciliation and agreement on what is useful. The useful was sufficiently defined for him by the idea he had formed of the needs of France. He had no concern for the truth of the revelations the Church teaches; he was concerned to support her merely as a vehicle of a Latin tradition. '*I am a Roman* because Rome, from the time of the consul Marius and the divine Julius... sketched the first outline of my France. *I am a Roman* because Rome, the Rome of the priests and the popes, has given the eternal solidity of feeling, manners, language and worship to the political achievement of the Roman generals, administrators and judges.' You could not have a more complete Erastianism of principle. Maurras maintained that 'societies of higher type exclude all forms of religious difference. The city-states of antiquity did so, and with very good reason. With very good reason too, the Roman Empire did so.' Maurras would have been on the side of Julian the Apostate. He would have shared the horror of those Roman men of letters for whom Christianity appeared as the substitution of a barbarous and formless semitic literature for the measure and order of the classical texts. In the twentieth century, he defended the institution of the papacy because he thought that, but for the Pope, 'the written monuments of the Catholic faith would necessarily acquire whatever religious influence was taken from Rome. The texts themselves would be read, and read literally. The literal text is Jewish and if Rome does not explain it, it will exert a Jewish influence.' Maurras was giving a new, anti-Semitic twist to the Counter-Reformation. It was the influence of the Jewish spirit, not merely the undisciplined voice of the individual conscience, that he wanted to suppress. He regarded the language and the poetry even of this country as 'infected, for the last three centuries, by dishonouring hebraisms'. At this point his treatment of the religious question touches his criticism of literary romanticism. He stood, as in the days of the *École romane*, for 'the restoration of classical taste and of feeling for tradition in letters'. The safety of France, for him, was the safety of these traditions: armed defence and literary criticism were complementary.

One might say that Maurras, with a habit of mind so unlike that most commonly and complacently admired among Anglo-Saxons, believed in the effect and force of ideas. If a man holds ideas that directly or by long implication, threaten the state, beware of him! It is not merely Maurras's taste as one for whom Paris is the unique surviving and the third in historical order of the capitals of the civilized world, that is offended by the Protestant and Judaising elements in the French thought of the time. Whatever weakens a man's loyalty and subordination to Latin traditions makes him a less reliable Frenchman. The criticism of ideas is at one with the hostility of those foreigners, often Jews, who drift in and out of the country at the call of interests and conveniences which have nothing to do with the welfare of France; who enjoy civic rights, but exercise them with regard to sectional interests. For them Maurras employed the designation 'métèques'; we might say, after Blackstone, 'denizens'.

Maurras, the devoted servant of his Latin heritage, execrated the Germans. He attributed to them, and to the Jews who had worked like a leaven in their country, everything that is formless and crude in the thought of the time. The northern barbarians who from time to time came, in Montesquieu's phrase, 'to break the chains forged in the south', according to Maurras came to destroy an order and harmony to which they were insensible. The marks in their behaviour of an immature civilization – so acutely noted by Barrès in *Claudette Baudoche* – their passion for gazing inwards, where there is no measure, instead of outwards into the world of shapes and colours, the tactless elaboration of their metaphysical systems, all evoked his contempt. He feared the 'servitudes...threatening to weigh upon Gaul', and feared that France would let herself be overwhelmed by the barbarians. Later, when the barbarians had in fact come, as he had foreseen, and had been turned back at the Marne, he addressed them thus:

> O toi, plus basse que les terres
> D'où sont vomis tes combattants,
> O dans ta paix et dans ta guerre
> Singe inutile des Titans,
> Race allemande qu'enfle et grise
> L'impunité de la traîtrise
> Et l'ignorance de l'honneur,
> Aucun reproche ne te presse
> Comme du manque de sagesse
> Qui de tout temps souilla ton coeur.

But if Maurras held Germany and Germanism in abhorrence, he did not fail to make that dissociation, failure to make which has, in this century, led to such wide aberrations, on the part of statesmen and public, from political courses obvious to plain reason. Loathing Germany, he could yet admire the mechanism whereby unity of power at the centre gave strength to the periphery. Why should the civilization of France, so much better worth preserving than that of Germany, be denied a similar source of strength? The principle of absolute rule was, anyhow, a Latin principle. The Germanies had been distinguished until the ideas of the Revolution had awakened them, by a fissiparousness which found expression in the innumerable principalities of the old Empire.

It was in the light of national struggles which they to some extent concealed that Maurras understood the progressive movements of the century. He did not particularly admire nationalism, preferring in principle the international orders of the Roman Empire and the Middle Ages. But no such order exists in our century, and meanwhile it is nonsense to talk about the brotherhood of workers. The socialism of France weakened and divided her; the socialism of Germany was made to serve the cause of national unity on which its survival depended. There were only two ways of bringing about the political unity of the world. The first was by a universal and simultaneous outburst of goodwill, which an educated man, or any man with his head properly screwed on, could see to be an impossibility. The second had the advantage of having been tried already. 'The people of Rome seized the world and imposed on it by force or by ruse its language, its laws, its manners. Catholicism repeated the same fortunate and spiritual effort.' The fearful question that recurred in the writings of Maurras was: what if the same success should come 'to the power of Germany? to German thought? to both at once?'

If Germany was the primary menace, it was not only against her that the interests of France had to be defended. England was in those days also something of a power. A sentence Maurras wrote in 1921, in elucidation of his views of 1905-14 on the foreign policy of France, carries its echoes to a date much nearer us. 'A country like ours, placed physically between Germany and England, does not have to choose one or the other; it should first of all love itself.' The alliance with England was *necessary*. Maurras had no doubt about that, because the interests of France and England, so different in certain respects, were in other respects identical.

When the war broke out in 1914, Maurras who, while Jaurès had been dreaming of brotherhood with German workers, had been announcing 'une épreuve que tout prépare', made a truce in his hostility to the Republic and supported the successive governments which undertook to lead France to victory. No one seems to have doubted Maurras's patriotism during those years – no one, that is, except Paul Claudel, who took the trouble to testify to the court in 1945 his impression that the enemy had during World War I found Maurras's articles useful in compiling his own propaganda. A moving dedication dating from 1915 shows in what spirit Maurras addressed himself to the tasks of that time: 'With you, if my body had had the worth of my mind, I should have armed myself and fought...' One need not envy those who, having read anything of Maurras's work, can doubt the sincerity of that dedication.

The judgement of Maurras on the treaty of Versailles is summed up in the title of the volume of his contemporary writings on the subject: *Le mauvais traité*. The treaty was bad because it failed to encourage German particularism and left the country more united than ever. It was bad because it failed to resuscitate the Austrian Empire and so facilitated the course of Pan-Germanism. The basic error, which Maurras attributed in particular to President Wilson, was to regard the struggle in Europe not as one between Germanism and civilization but as one between the lily-white principle of democracy and the evil demons of autocracy. This false antinomy has persisted ever since in the minds of the statesmen and publics of the western powers. If it were possible for all the international disasters of the last thirty years to be due to a single intellectual error, this would be it. For Maurras, it was a matter of indifference whether or not Germans were allowed to drop little bits of paper into ballot boxes. Nor was the complexion of the alleged principles of the government resulting from this or some other procedure of primary importance in his eyes. What mattered was whether a German government was put in a position from which it could control a unified national machine. If it could do this then it would, sooner rather than later, give expression to the historical Pan-Germanism. The Second World War was implicit in the treaty which had ended the first. This was not, as was the identical, though differently motivated contention of practical Germans and of the more unpractical Anglo-Saxons, because the treaty was too harsh. It was because it was mechanically wrong. It did not arrange the forces in play in such a way that the balance could remain stable. Behind this error was Wilson's false antinomy. There was the ingenuous faith that nothing much could go wrong with a Europe where every person had a vote and every nation a House of Commons.

The recovery of Germany between 1918 and 1933 was what Maurras had anticipated. He supported every move which, like Poincaré's initiative of 1923, tended to improve the relative position of France at the expense of Germany. Such moves were rare and inadequate enough. Moreover, the treaty which had sanctioned the Weimar Republic had completed Bismarck's work of unifying Germany. It had provided the machinery for a national action. The republican form lasted as long as it served any national purpose. Under its tutelage the German army survived and was re-formed. At the same time, the conduct of German democratic politicans under various pressures from their electors and from the western powers inevitably provided matter for criticism which was exploitable and was in fact exploited by the nationalists. Maurras did not see 1933 as another stage in the imaginary battle between democracy and autocracy. He saw it as an act of resolve by the barbarians, who now once more felt sure enough of themselves, and of the weakness of their prey, not to trouble themselves any longer to hide their intentions.

It was a sign of weakening national consciousness and growing befuddlement in the west that this obvious interpretation of events commanded little interest. Indeed, in the 1930s the old false antinomy of principle, in a slightly modified form, became a popular obsession. The term 'Fascism', which should properly have been reserved to denote a certain Italian nationalist movement, enjoyed the success of the century in a widely extended sense. Such coherence of meaning as it possessed derived from Marxist theory, and its popularity served no one but the Communists. Meanwhile, there was increasing confusion as to the meaning of 'democracy', the other half of this precious pair. There was an increasing tendency to suppose that the more left-wing a party was, the more democratic it was. This delusion likewise served the interests of Communism.

Maurras disdained the false antinomy in the new form as in the old. It was indeed beneath the attention of a literate man. He continued to see the conflicts in Europe as national conflicts. Italy and Germany in turn had had national revolutions. One did not have to suppose that they must necessarily be permanently in league because both had disposed of the anti-national, including pro-Russian elements within their borders. The old national differences would remain and perhaps become more marked. It would be one of the objects of a prudent foreign policy to distinguish the differences and to profit by them. Moreover, if one were able to allow oneself the luxury of a preference, there was no question but that the preference would go to the country whose civilization was the sister of that of France. It was these considerations which led Maurras to oppose action against Italy at the time of the Abyssinian war. No action must be taken which would jeopardize Italy's participation in the Stresa front and perhaps throw her into the arms of Germany.

When civil war broke out in Spain, Maurras at once recognized the independent and national character of Franco's movement. An independent Spain was to be preferred, in the interests of France, to one under the influence or direction of Moscow, Maurras supported Franco and did what he could to discredit the Reds.

In 1938, Maurras counselled against a war which he knew France was not ready to fight. He thought the declaration of war in the following year ill-advised. A rational foreign policy, in his view, must be based on force: the foreign policy of France must be based on force in the service of France. No doubt war with Germany, some time or other, was inevitable; no one had watched its approach with more open eyes than Maurras. But France should not, in Maurras's view, do anything to provoke war while she was weak and Germany was strong. That was to invite a disaster which might be mitigated if it were deferred. To those who said: But if you let Germany go on unchecked, she will consolidate her position in central and eastern Europe and be stronger than ever, Maurras replied: Even if you declare war, you can do nothing for Poland; do not threaten what you cannot perform. If France herself is attacked, then there will be no help for it. Then you must fight.

The pact between Russia and Germany which was the curtain-raiser to the war can have caused Maurras little astonishment. For years he had been saying: In certain matters the interests of Russia and Germany go hand in hand. Russia aims at provoking a war in the west. It is odd to recall that in the thirties there were respectable, even eminent, people in England and France who imagined that Russia was burning to defend the rights and interests of the common people of the west. Surely Stalin had read all the Marxist pamphleteers, and knew about the menace of fascism?

Hitler and Stalin were, of course, looking after the interests of their respective countries as they conceived them. That was what one expected of a head of state who had real power. The laws that govern the strength and weakness of states are the same for Roman and barbarian. Meanwhile, who was looking after the interests of France? The answer, Maurras was convinced, was: Nobody. A congeries of politicians at the centre of things was no substitute for a king.

Once war had been declared, there was no further room for debate on the merits of the declaration. France must be defended. Maurras did not support those who called for displays of non-existent strength against Germany. The trial of strength would come. Meanwhile, France must try belatedly to make herself strong. When the trial of strength came it was settled according to the immutable laws that govern such matters. The government was handed to Pétain by the President of the Republic which had had its day.

Maurras left Paris when it was known that the city was not to be defended. The *Action Française* re-appeared on 1 July 1940 at Limoges and then, in October of the same year, the office was moved to Lyons, where it stayed until the Allies arrived in 1944. In those four years Maurras was the brilliant apologist of the Pétain régime. He did not think it necessary to approve or disapprove the Marshal's acts. Obviously, Pétain would be subjected to various pressures from the enemy; obviously he would not be able to speak his whole mind in public. But he could be trusted to serve the interests of France with honour and discrimination. Maurras had long admired Pétain, and had perhaps considered him as a possible General Monk. However that may be, 'the worst of our defeats has had the good result of ridding us of democracy'. The assumption of power by Pétain gave Maurras the hope that some possibility of future greatness for France might still be saved.

From the days of Limoges onwards, the *Action Française* daily carried the *manchette* 'France, and France alone'. The words were a summary of the policy of the paper, indeed of Maurras's whole thought. France should love herself first, Maurras had said years before. What made people in England assume that, if Frenchmen showed signs of unwillingness to serve England, it must be because they wanted to serve Germany? It was probably that the question was put in a form which excluded the third possibility. In spite of the Russo–German pact, which should have enlightened the dullest, thought was still conducted in the obfuscating categories of Democracy and Fascism. Maurras was not a democrat, *ergo*, he was a Fascist; he would flock with birds of a feather, *ergo*, with the Nazis. Yet 'France, and France alone' was a reasonable policy for (to employ an antiquated phrase) a man of honour.

France had suffered military defeat, which is inexorable. In these hard circumstances, Maurras no doubt recalled that France had rejected an armistice in 1870 only to be forced to accept harder terms in 1871. No doubt, in 1940, France was at the mercy of Germany. But even such a disaster as 1940 was not to be treated as if it were the end of the world. France must go on. And for this there must be a French government on French soil. This government would do what it could for the people of France. In the face of the powerful barbarians this might not, physically, amount to very much. None the less, a French administration would do what it could to mitigate hardships which could not be avoided. The people would not be abandoned. The head of the state, watching over the fate and interests of France, would be able to seize opportunities of improving her position. The war would not go on for ever. Had not the very enemy who had overrun France herself been a defeated power in 1918?

It is not to be supposed that Maurras approved the actions of all those about the Marshal. He did not. Some, including Laval, he considered to be traitors. Only those who, with complete loyalty, served the French interest, were to be tolerated. No doubt it was not, in the conditions of 1940-44, easy or indeed always possible to distinguish those people, but the principle was clear. When the Militia was formed to defend the will of Vichy, it was 'Oh what happiness'. But when Maurras discovered later that organizers of the Militia were in contact with the Germans, he took them for traitors. He opposed the *maquis*. If the government which he thought essential to the future of France were to survive, it must govern. It must not permit dissident elements to take the law into their own hands. If it did permit disorder, the Germans would inevitably intervene and French government in France would be at an end.

'France, and France alone.' To a German officer who repeatedly saluted him in the hope that the salutation would be returned, Maurras at last said: 'It is useless, Monsieur, I do not even see you.'

Maurras was arrested on 8 September 1944. On 27 January

1945 he was condemned to imprisonment for life for intelligence with the enemy.

The *Action Française* has failed. What Maurras did during the war was no doubt, as he said, 'a form of resistance like any other, less romantic, perhaps', but it would have served its purpose fully only if the democratic régime in France had been permanently overthrown. On the desirability of that we, who are not French, have not to pass judgement. Our British interest is merely that France shall be strong. Pétain is in prison, and de Gaulle is at large in France, a restless critic of the Fourth Republic. We have not to suppose that, in the eyes of history, the two will be held to have served different causes. And history will record that among the *maquis* were many Communists, who were only temporarily and provisionally the friends of France.

But although Maurras and his movement have failed, for his lifetime at least, to bring back the monarchy to France, it would be rash to say that even that practical objective has been brought no nearer by their action. At the trial, when Maurras confronted the representatives of the Republic in what was almost certainly the last of his many encounters, the moral victory was his. The reader of the trial, now or a hundred years hence, is unlikely to envy the role of *'Monsieur l'avocat de la femme sans tête'*. The record remains, and crowns the work of a lifetime. It may yet operate as the record of the trial of 1649 operated in 1660. At least it will work as the trial of our Charles I has done to form and direct minds applied to the issues, rarely enough considered, on which the health and fate of states finally depend.

The work of Maurras has its point of departure in the Revolution of 1789. The work of Hooker perhaps contributed something to our being spared a disaster similar to that of the French, but the rebellion of 1642-60 has left upon our history and in our minds scars that go deep, and 1789 and 1917 were salt in these old wounds. No doubt Maurras is not the man to set all to rights for us. He is a Frenchman, speaking for France. But he can help us, inasmuch as a preliminary to any satisfactory synthesis of our political ideas must be a re-statement of that side of the case whose apologists have so miserably defaulted.

Fervet opus.

Looking back on Maurras

The influence of Charles Maurras is something I should like to shake off. Its work on me was done long ago, so far as I can judge, and I am puzzled that he has not fallen into place, with Eliot, say, or Yeats, as a figure to whom I acknowledge a debt from a distance: an historical debt which, unpaid as such things always are, no longer concerns one very much. With Maurras it is different. The seduction remains, even though I cannot read through any of his books with approval. And if I am asked to summarize his achievements, I find myself usually talking about his limitations, even his vices. If I am asked what books of his one should read, to get some idea of his importance, I do not know what to point to. Did he in fact write a satisfactory book? Each of the books is nothing, in itself, and the compendia he himself produced – such as the *Essais politiques* in the volumes of *Oeuvres capitales* he prepared during his final imprisonment – seem jejune and inadequate when one turns to them after a long acquaintance with his performance. They must be a poor starting-point to the reader who comes fresh to his work, and give nothing at all to the inquirer who does not come with a measure of sympathy and understanding, from the rumours he has heard of them. And it has to be admitted that an intelligent inquirer, interested in the political questions which obsessed Maurras, is as likely to have gathered from rumours matter for a lack of sympathy, or for plain hostility.

Perhaps a parallel case, so far as the nature of influence is concerned, would be that of Voltaire. What did Voltaire write? Everything and nothing. If there are masterpieces, such as *Candide*, they are much as one might expect from a smaller man. All the life of Voltaire is in them, in a sense, yet none of them gives one anything which could possibly account for his influence. So it is with Maurras. If you turn to the *Enquête sur la monarchie*, which from its title one might suppose to be a magisterial demonstration of the case for the monarchy advanced by the most famous monarchist of the twentieth century, you find nothing but a number of beginnings. And so elsewhere. Everything is provisional, linked to the quarrels and events of the moment, or rather of a series of moments which have already passed, as moments do, leaving the need for a different approach to the apologia. The book most to be recommended to anyone seeking an initiation is the autobiographical *Au signe de Flore*, which deals with the foundation of the *Action française* between 1898 and 1900. But again, it is in the excitements of the moment – the Dreyfus affair in particular – that the author discovers his principles. The reader who finds other principles more vividly illustrated by those events, or who feels an understandable reluctance, at this time of day, to turn over that particular dunghill again, will not find this book a very good starting-point for an inquiry into the modern case for the monarchy, which might be supposed to be Maurras's central subject though, truth to tell, it is not, and the question of what does lie at the centre of his work is not easily answered.

The most sympathetic matter in the book, for the reader without passionate political bias, is likely to be the idyll the author there makes out of his early years in Provence. Avoiding the circumstantial except when it embellishes the romance he is building, Maurras sets out his early recollections of his childhood in Martigues, Bouches-du-Rhône. The whole aroma of old Provence rises from a few pages. Nothing of the more squalid predicaments of the family of a minor official, living in a little fishing town presumably already in steep decline. Not a word of the industrial menace of Marseilles, almost on the doorstep, and containing more Provençals than the whole of Provence, as the England of the villages and shires is outnumbered and overwhelmed by the inhabitants of Liverpool, Manchester, Birmingham and London. How narrow Maurras's basic sympathies were, how narrow, really, the world of his imagination is curiously indicated by his reference to Nîmes (in a letter of 9 June 1894, to Barrès) as 'un ramassis de protestants, de juifs, et d'anciens mercantis beaucairois'. Or to Marseilles itself (letter of January 1903) as 'une ville *ignoble*. J'y respire l'ignomonie', he goes on. 'Aix est pur. Martigues est chaste. Arles a la goût de tous les mystères de mort, Marseille est d'une vie obscène, et vous le pouvez constater.'

It is a Provence of the imagination, of which one cannot deny the seductions. And so, in Athens, where he went to report on the Olympic Games in 1896, at the age of twenty-eight, the splendours of the Acropolis leave him no eyes for anything else; as when he went to London two years later, it was to see the Elgin Marbles without being distracted for a moment by the living city which, after all, has and must have had a certain human interest. In Greece it was only the peak of the classical period which interested him; before and after that, there was only ugliness. It was the aesthetic of a man who had already found all he wanted to know, 'la science du sentiment', as he accurately defined it. 'Une ANTHINÉA, fleur du monde, printemps des pensées et des arts, s'élargit nécessairement.' It includes the country, 'douce et nerveuse' of Racine, Voltaire and La Fontaine. Maurras feels its intimate bonds with his own Provence. He has travelled, one may say, in order to find his roots. Yet it is not exactly that. For in *Anthinéa* itself he explains that beginnings are not beautiful. 'La beauté véritable est au terme des choses.' Dangerous to contemplate, one would think; and perhaps Maurras thought so. It is difficult to fix a point in the ultimate thoughts of this man who, for all his dogmatisms, was so full of reactions and qualifications. Looking at the instability of his own Martigues, built among the sand-dunes of the Étang de Berre, he reflects that it is a place of death, where 'le néant et la mort ont soulevé... leur voile' and 'Celui qui ne meurt point de cette vue en tire une nourriture très forte.' The whole of Maurras's career is, in a sense, a revulsion from this vision of death, on which he none the less feeds all the time. The aesthetic of an unattainable finality broods over it all, yet Maurras knows better than to try to embody this finality in any work of his own.

All this may seem far from the Maurras known to those who see him only as a political figure, bitterly involved in the Dreyfus affair, in antagonism with Léon Blum and the *Front populaire*, standing behind Pétain during the occupation in 1940-44 or in the dock at Lyons in 1945. But it was never far away – not far enough, it might be said, for Maurras tried to impose his vision on that singularly inharmonious background, the technological Europe of the late nineteenth and the first half of the twentieth century.

II

Although I had some glimmerings of Maurras, while still an undergraduate in 1931-4, from the *Speculations* of T.E. Hulme and the pages of *The Criterion*, and indeed had read *L'avenir de l'intelligence* without those glimmerings becoming a light, it was in the two following years, under the full impact of my first visits to the Continent and prolonged stays in Germany and in Paris at a time of tempestuous international politics, that I really had my apprenticeship. Everything in my approach to him was coloured by the dangers and controversies of those pre-war years. A residence of eight months in Hitler's Germany, with all the intimidations that offered to a very young Englishman whose heart did not readily beat in time, as invited, with the then thumping hearts of his German cousins, determined my direction. As an undergraduate, though at a provincial university, I had already undergone the full onslaught of left-wing politics. It was the time of unemployment and hunger marches, as well as of the early poems of W.H. Auden and Stephen Spender. The few fashionable intellectuals my university boasted were, as was proper, members of the Communist Party. My sympathies had been with the hunger marchers. I had gone to hear Saklatvala speak and had assumed that he was talking the language of the future. Through the good offices of T.E. Hulme, my scanty political reading had extended beyond *The Communist Manifesto* to take notice of Georges Sorel. The brilliant representatives of the Communist Party had not, however, talked me round. Auden and Spender were impressive in their language but their social attitudes were unconvincing to someone brought up in a working-class area and a complete stranger to the social facilities of the upper and even the middle classes. I belonged I supposed to one of the lower middle classes, those barely distinguishable people who – perhaps because I have belonged to them – I believe had their roots deeper than anyone, in what England used to be. At any rate I was, in the end, stubborn as a mule to the political dogmatisms of student politics, and when I set off for Germany, in October 1934, it was as a more or less complete political agnostic.

As I tried to arrive at an orientation of my own, living in the Hamburg and Berlin and Munich of the Storm Troopers and a Prague already threatened by the Sudeten Germans, it was not as an adherent of Right or Left – those great, vague, pan-European conceptions – but as an Englishman whose country was threatened by attack. The Nazi party at that time was putting itself out quite noticeably to be pleasant to the British. While a dogmatic anti-Fascist passion raged among the British Liberals and Left, fanned by those who were particularly moved by the threat to the Jews, what one might call the ordinary stupid British tourist was not infrequently won over by the partly assumed, partly real, admiration of the Germans for the race which was supposed to be enjoying stable government, to be running a great empire, and anyhow to be given to manly sports in a manner which made them worthy companions of a movement in which young men were for ever flexing their muscles and admiring their physique. I was not a candidate for this ingenuous flattery and had no difficulty in seeing the Nazis for the menace they were. I was, moreover, of a reflective nature and thought of 1870 and 1914 as well as of 1933. My sympathy for France grew *pari passu* with my alarm for England. It never occurred to me to doubt that the French cause was also ours. When I finally got to the Rhine it was to hope that the poplars of Alsace concealed plenty of guns pointing east. It was at this time, while a student in Freiburg, that I sought out my first book by Léon Daudet and so came a step nearer to becoming an addict, as happened in Paris later in 1935, of the *Action Française*.

The political events of those years were confusing enough, and did in fact confuse many better qualified observers than I. There was the Abyssinian war, to which the liberal reply was supposed to be in the operation of the League of Nations in Geneva, where H.M. Government, represented by Anthony Eden in his best-tailored period, still cut quite a figure. At home there was a Peace Ballot, a much-canvassed expression of the will to peace which was supposed to be an answer to rising militarism. Briefly, the politics of opinion, against the politics of action as represented by Hitler's Germany and Mussolini's Italy. All good courses were supported by the Soviet Union; all bad courses were supported by Hitler, Mussolini, and in due course, Franco. There was a high degree of plausibility in all this. The merit of the commentaries which, as I found when I got to Paris, appeared day by day over the signature of Charles Maurras, was not that they took a sympathetic view of Mussolini and, when he appeared, of Franco, or the vain dream – not without connection with Maurras's Provençal obsessions – of creating a Latin block against the Germans. It was in the nature of the analysis which – this little Latin deviation apart – ignored the clamour of sentiment, however popular, and operated wholly on a calculation of interests and forces. The rights and wrongs of, say, the Abyssinian war, as they appeared to most of the public in France as in England, the widespread sentiment which supported the League of Nations for the good it was supposed to be capable of, were brushed aside. England still had a reputation for morality in those days, and all the manifestations of that virtue were treated with a fine irony. Churchill, at this stage still a relative outsider, was pointed to as a statesman with the wit to support the League solely for the advantages of interest which could be extracted from it. 'Cependant il n'est pas des nôtres', I remember Maurras writing in one of his daily articles. The interests Churchill sought to preserve were, of course, British imperial interests. France must look to herself.

And so, day by day, I ingested these radical commentaries, in cafés on the Boulevard St-Michel or in my little room in rue du cardinal Lemoine. I was living in a pension where the opinion was, predominantly, liberal and leftish; and day by day I talked over Maurras's analysis with people who did not agree with it. What came out of all this, so far as I was concerned, was a complete disenchantment with the popular categories of 'democratic' and 'fascist', at a time when it was usual to see all political events, wherever in the world they took place, as a conflict between these ill-defined antagonists.

I became so far a convert to the *Action Française* as to try to see these events from the point of view of the bleakest national interest – but I retained wit enough to try to effect my calculations from the point of view, not of France, but of my own native country, which involved sometimes a certain effort of transposition. It was one of the enlightening features of the Maurrasien analysis that the idea that Russia was on the side of European socialist movements had no part in it. The Russian moves were seen as manifestations of a government as conscious of its national interests as was Hitler's or Mussolini's; from that point of view, the European socialist movements were merely being *used*. While the almost universal conviction in democratic circles, in France as in England and elsewhere, was that the Soviets could be relied upon in any struggle, Maurras was for ever pointing to areas in which the interests of the Germans and the Russians might be the same. So when 1939 came, and the Russo-German pact which brought an appalled astonishment to all liberal and socialistically-minded persons in the west, I felt not dissatisfied with the education I had in the pages of the *Action Française*.

III

If this lesson in the operation of national interests, and in the
secondary place of sentiments, was the most striking outcome of
my apprenticeship with Maurras, as it affected my observation of
practical politics, there were several other strands to his influence,
and it is difficult to distinguish how far they went and where they
led. It was the rich suggestiveness of many pages of Maurras, even
of sentences, and their narcotic mellifluousness, which seduced
me originally, and I certainly did not distinguish the elements of
this charm, or give it a name. He was the proponent and carrier
of a pre-digested Mediterranean culture, and I was the ignorant
Anglo-Saxon lover, even in wintry Paris, of the land 'wo die
Citronen blühen', or at any rate of the un-British lucidities of
the superficies of Latin thought and expression. It was the sort
of illusion which once affected young men before Walter Pater
explaining the Renaissance, but this secret charm spread its ten-
tacles right into the brutal day-to-day world of politics. It was
years later that I came across Maurras's own explanation: 'Notre
nationalisme commença par être esthétique.' Nor did I identify
those more personal poisons of that love of death and emptiness
which lurk under Maurras's devotions. However far back, psychologically, the attraction of Maurras's work began, the direction
of my orientation was towards the open and public world. I saw
Maurras, as he saw himself, as the defender of intelligence and
of 'la cité', the western, ordered, Romanized world of which the
traces round about me, in the 1930s, were already faint enough.
I might say that in Hitler's Germany I had smelt the wind from
the steppes, the great formless wind of the barbarian invaders,
the Attila of romanticism. This was not history but a vision. I had
also read *La Défense de l'Occident* (Henry Massis) as well as dipped
into Spengler. The Maurrasian analysis, which equated civilization with the boundaries of the Roman world, was for the time
being acceptable to me, and I would not pretend that, in spite of
all qualifications, it has not retained a certain hold, or at any rate
a certain meaning for me. I certainly retain a profound conviction,
in spite of all the frivolities we see in that field, that public life
ought to be treated – and conducted – seriously. There is so much
in the Maurrasian conception of these matters which is related
specifically to French history and traditions that a continual work
of interpretation is necessary if one is to understand its implications
for us. It is in the direct *ir*relevance of much of Maurras's work

that its fruitfulness for us lies. It does not so much command assent as work on the mind and provoke reflections.

The *Action Française* movement came to life on the dunghill of the Dreyfus affair. There are pitchforks still turning over that event and I feel no temptation to join them. The significant issues were the innocence or guilt of a particular army officer, in relation to a recurrently hostile foreign power, and the extent to which the considerations of justice to an individual should take precedence over the welfare and safety of the state. The liberal answer to that question is clear. It was not the answer Maurras gave. E.M. Forster put a softer – because imaginary – version of the same dilemma as follows: 'if I had to chose between betraying my country and betraying my friend, I hope I should have the guts to betray my country'. The historical background to all Maurras's political thinking was, of course, the French Revolution and the Reformation. There had been a continuous importing of French notions of abstract right, and social-democratic ideologies, into this country, but the *facts* behind us remain the constitutional struggles of the seventeenth century, with their very different outcome, and the Anglican church settlement which, whatever its defects, did not leave in the centre of the stage a bleak, individualistic Protestantism. And while Maurras brooded with anachronistic relish over Malherbe's admittedly magnificent verses inviting Louis XIII to 'take his thunder' against the Protestants of La Rochelle and destroy them, the most persistent political disruptors in England have been the Papists, who in Maurras's France can be cast in the role of defenders of order. No Englishman can swallow Maurras whole. That whole branch of Maurras's writing, which is concerned with a form of apologetics for the Roman church, is matter for digestion and reflection rather than assent. It consists in praise for her skill in bringing in a Latin discipline to destroy the pernicious judaizing element represented by the gospels themselves. Maurras knew how to give seductiveness to these paradoxes, with his references to Dante's 'sommo Giove / Che fosti in terra per noi crucifisso', and his assimilation of so much that is Christian to the pagan world.

IV

I find it difficult to imagine how far the work of Maurras can retain an interest for my juniors, among the different orientations

of the present day. That it does retain some interest is a matter
of fact, for here as well as in France there are people looking
closely at his work who are young enough not to be blinded by
the emotions of thirties' politics or of the quarrels surrounding
Vichy and the occupation. For me it is as a sympathetic and
wrong-headed figure – as an actor on the scene rather than as a
writer – that Maurras stays in my mind. It was a first visit to his
native Provence, delayed till I was nearly sixty, and a visit to
Martigues itself, which brought him vividly back to mind. He
carried his complex and elaborately-related dogmatisms so consistently through his long life, to the court which condemned
him for treason in 1945 and beyond that to his death, only a few
months half-liberated, in 1952. His life was one of self-abnega-
tion, if you call it abnegation to live toilsomely and simply, and
without wife or family, in order to put your word in at each
day's turn of public events. He founded his politics on his esthetics
and that is a lunacy, and would be even if a man's esthetic were
not, as it is, in the end something more personal and less admis-
sible. I remember how, in one of his daily articles in 1935 or
1936, Maurras followed some even more than usually dashing
excursion into the relationships existing between the then great
powers with the apology: One would prefer to give this advice
in the chamber of the king rather than in a public newspaper.
The whole of his hallucination is there. For if there had been a
king in France in the 1930s, it would not have been Maurras but
Laval, or some similar master of sleight-of-hand, who would
have been advising him. A publicist, even the most brilliant, and
least of all the most honest, is not a politician. What really happens, in the political world, is a matter of the decisions of the
men who, at a particular time, happen to be sitting in the seats
of authority, subject to the pressures which, at that particular
moment, bear upon them. It is not anyone's dream.

Philip Mairet

In 1937 it was still possible to buy journals of small circulation at a station bookstall, and it was thus that I became acquainted with the *New English Weekly*. When I hit on it, at Charing Cross, it was a matter of minutes for me to decide that it was exactly the paper for me – by which I meant, not merely as a reader but, since I was a young man with nowhere to write, and no bearings in the literary world, as a possible contributor. There was a freshness and independence about the *New English Weekly* which struck me at once. There was even an air of amateurism about some of the contributions, though others – including the editorial notes – showed great professional polish. But nobody, either in the articles or the Notes of the Week, appeared to be writing to tickle a political prejudice or to say the right thing commercially. The interest was of a few people – some of them rather odd – speaking their own minds. It was thus that I came to send my first article to an editor. The article was rejected, or rather, suggestions were made as to the presentation of it which amounted to a call for a radical revision. As to the content, not a word, for or against. What I had to do was to confine myself to a single idea, or two ideas at the most. I benefitted from this lesson, and it was not long before I had met the editor, Philip Mairet. He would then have been fifty-one, while I was twenty-three.

Mairet was extraordinary on first as on later acquaintance. Owen Barfield recalls that when he first saw him – which, improbably enough, was 'across the footlights of the Old Vic' when he 'was playing one of Shakespeare's comic low-life characters', for which role 'he had contrived a certain frog-like nuance to his gesture and mien'. There was something of that about Mairet off-stage, and Professor Barfield himself says that 'the image presented itself again whenever I met him'. Mairet was short and slight in stature, with a good deal of bald head and longish grey hair at the back and sides. He had a wide mouth made noticeable by a nervous tic which went with an intermittent stutter. At crucial moments in the middle of a sentence he was likely to hold his mouth open – precisely, like a frog hoping for a fly. His penniless paper – another mark of different times – was able to have a little office off Chancery Lane. Mairet liked this proximity to the city and its goings and comings – which meant for him the man who kept the stock of paper on which the *New English Weekly* was printed, as well as the more nefarious goings-on of more elevated persons. The weekly, which Mairet had taken over from A.R. Orage on the latter's death three years before – he had been Orage's assistant editor – was vowed to the destruction of the overweening powers of bankers and such-like. Despite its general independence, it was an advocate of social credit, though Orage had already looked forward to a time 'in which this particular form of propaganda would no longer be required' and 'his commentary on public affairs would be framed on philosophical and psychological principles, with economics as only a secondary interest'. This, roughly, is what happened, in course of time, under Mairet's editorship and meanwhile there was no question of even regular contributors, such as I soon became, being expected to adhere to any particular view of the matter. A certain scepticism about the credit system was perhaps not out of place in the 1930s, before Keynes's more expansive years, even if one could not make head or tail of Douglas. In fact, in Mairet's hands, such scepticism threw more light on the subject of where Germany would find the money to rearm herself than did the more orthodox economics of the day. Long before the end of the *New English Weekly* Social Credit was, as Mairet said, 'a dead duck'.

The oddity of the *New English Weekly* was not only in its unorthodox economics. There was a whole bundle of connections with what can best be described as some of the more obscure intellectual movements of the earlier part of the century, in a line through Orage or through Mairet himself. None of this meant anything at that time to me as I turned in my little articles of what might be called political criticism. And with Mairet himself, my understanding of his history and points of view came so gradually that it was only after years of a fairly close acquaintance that I began to seize some of the threads. It was some years, even, before I discovered that this immensely intelligent and gentle commentator on public affairs, who wrote his weekly notes so lucidly and elegantly as well as shrewdly, had at one time been an actor. It is only recently, in preparing the material for this volume,* that I have seen Old Vic programmes of 1923-4 in which 'Henry Cohen' – the stage name Mairet is said to have taken from a milk cart, on the way to the theatre – appeared in such parts as the Bishop of Ely in *Henry V* and the Lord Chamberlain in *Henry VIII*, to say nothing of Sir Charles Surface in *The School for Scandal*. Nor did I know, at the outbreak of the Second World War, that he had been a conscientious objector in the First – and I can think of one contribution to the *New English Weekly* in 1939 which I might have hesitated to put to him if I had known. The hesitation would have been unnecessary, for Mairet never doubted that there was no alternative to fighting in Hitler's war; and had he retained some partiality for his own former views, his openness of mind and his sense of the freedom of the contributor were such that he would not have raised an eyebrow.

The fairly accurate sub-title of the *New English Weekly* was 'A Review of Public Affairs, Literature and the Arts'. The paper was well set out, in elegant type, and the relatively small number of books it reviewed included a number which received little attention elsewhere. The contributors were not paid. The Notes of the Week certainly were among the most illuminating appearing at that time. While they started from the affairs of the moment, they looked at things from a longer perspective and with a much greater depth of social and cultural insight than could be found in the other weeklies. How much this owed to the antecedents of its remarkable editor is something few readers can have had much sense of; I as a writer had little enough.

Philip Mairet was the son of a Swiss watchmaker who had settled in London. His grandfather was Sylvain Mairet who was a great name in the history of Swiss horology, a man whose work, his grandson tells us, 'showed a remarkable artistic refinement...' but who was 'above all a scientist, educated in mathematics, physics and chemistry, and, like his uncle' – for the tradition went back further – had 'a particular interest in astronomical time-pieces'. The unfinished memoir gives an interesting picture of the modest and industrious London family. Philip's mother was from Surrey, remembered in the family as a woman of cultivated taste who kept her home in North Islington 'beautiful

* Philip Mairet, *Autobiographical and other papers* (Carcanet, 1981).

as well as spotlessly clean'. There were five sons and two daughters and Philip was the youngest but one of the children.

The story of Mairet's early years is best told in the memoir, a work written when he was in his eighties and intended not for publication, but for circulation to a few of his friends. It is a remarkable piece of writing – perhaps the best starting-point for the newcomer to Mairet's work and, to those who knew the man and his writing, full of illumination. The start was propitious in the sense that Mairet issued from a household full of individuality; he had moderate luck, but no more, with his schooling and later education, which took him to the Hornsey School of Art. But his more advanced education was at the hands of a series of teachers chosen by himself as he went along his irregular course. It is interesting to see him (in a letter to Tom Heron, 20 September 1973) *slightly* regretting the lack of a university training and casting sidelong glances at Eliot, 'the most magnificently educated man I ever met'. He says that he 'was *offered* a university period' when in his twenties, but 'turned it down for reasons which', he thought in retrospect, 'were mistaken'. One can understand that, to someone of Mairet's philosophic cast of mind, the lack of professional academic training did leave certain doors half-closed. In fact, as the memoir relates, he became a draughtsman in an architect's office and then drifted into making stained glass at the tail-end of the craft movement whose ancestry is through William Morris and Ruskin. This brought him early into touch with Ananda Coomaraswamy, and it is certainly not without significance that it was from this quarter, rather than from teachers at Oxford, that he received his 'first real impulse towards philosophic study'. Perhaps it was the early lack of the ordinary western academic disciplines which left him so exposed a few years later to that most extraordinary, and one might think rather menacing, figure in his biography, the Serbian nationalist Mitrinović. The story of the encounter is told in the memoir. The relations with Mitrinović, so it seems to me, take Mairet almost to the frontiers of sanity – but perhaps it is only to the frontiers of my sympathy for him. In the first part of his life he seems to have had a weakness for gurus. Nothing in what is recorded by Mairet as having been said by Mitrinović comes near to accounting for the influence he exercised. Yet the events as recorded do cast light on the nature of Mairet's fundamental orientation, which was certainly far from plain to people like myself who were familiarly but not intimately associated with him in the

1930s and 1940s. With Mitrinović Mairet had, as he says, 'chosen the way of faith and obedience'. I think one has to associate this with the moving account Mairet gives of the effect on him of the outbreak of the First World War. 'I now realized', he says, 'what I had felt only dimly – that to know the truth about man and religion and God was henceforth to be my ultimate concern.' There is another point in the relationship with Mitrinović which perhaps helps to explain the cast of Mairet's mind, and which – when I learnt of it – confirmed the feeling I had long had that, in spite of the charm and lucidity of his prose, he was not a mere writer. This is the patience with which he took Mitrinović's condescending acceptance of his literary gifts, strictly as a means of serving the cause – whatever that was, for the nature of it remains obscure to me. Perhaps all this ties up with the remark Mairet made in a late letter (to Tom Heron again, 22 September 1973) about Adler:

> He was never a very interesting *writer*, whereas Freud was a brilliant one and Jung very fascinating to read. *Adler* didn't *want* to be a writer – didn't much believe in it. To his mind, every fresh spark of universal human understanding has to be struck out between human beings conversing on these things man-to-man. And ultimately, perhaps, we shall have to admit this as the *truth*.

Certainly Mairet's life, as far as one can understand it from these papers, is that of a man the fulcrum of whose life was neither in his words nor his deeds precisely. His work in stained glass came to nothing. He tells, in the memoir, of the moment when he had to recognize this fact – and had to learn it humiliatingly at the hands of the wife some fourteen years older than himself whom he had meantime married. This wife, to whom he came in a state of utter innocence, was herself a considerable craftswoman who achieved notable success as a weaver. When he had first known her she was the wife of Coomaraswamy, so that the whole development took place within a world of slightly exotic relationships. Indeed, the impression one gets through all the turns of Mairet's life is that of a man who is going somewhere – it is not clear where – making personal encounters which are of great significance to him and in time passing beyond them, having learned something, it is not clear what. The fruit of it all was the understanding, so abundantly displayed in the correspondence of his old age, of a realm which one has to call spiritual, because there is no other word for it, and because Mairet himself finally uses that word. In a letter to Neil Montgomery (9 December 1974) only a month before his death, he wrote, surely with exaltation:

> To affirm oneself truly and really as *spirit* is to *be* a spirit and is to affirm God, too, who is the Supreme Spirit – a Unity which is *also* an indefinite multeity, in whom I myself and all individual spirits live and move and have being. It is no longer to be an objective *thing*, an object, but the infinite Subjectivity in and for and by which all *objects* exist *out there*!
> – the total objective *content* of my and of all (including God's, which includes my) subjectivity.

Such language was so far from any discourse I had ever had with Philip Mairet that I felt – as with so many of his other papers – that new layers of the mind of this extraordinary man, whom I had known chiefly as the far-seeing commentator on political and economic affairs, were being revealed to me when I read it. Some indications of the further reaches of his mind did of course come to me, from time to time, even in the days of the *New English Weekly*. He once said to me: 'Of course my real thing was the Adlerian psychology' and although I later came across his excellent little *ABC of Adler's Psychology* (1928), I was far from understanding that he had for some years been closely associated with Adler himself, 'a trusted pupil and colleague', as he says (letter of 20 September 1973 to Heron), 'actually writing his lectures and a book for him, in English – for his English, though effective enough on the platform, was not really suitable to *print*.' Adler even trusted him 'to enlarge a little, in explanation of what he had said in his lectures'. We have here again, of course, evidence of that natural docility which made Mairet look around for instructors and put himself in an attitude of obedience to them. The precise relationship of Mairet to Adler is one of the many aspects of his career which might well repay research. Meanwhile, it is clear that this association, and the formation of the Adler Society, played a part in the development of the specifically Christian, and primarily Anglican, groups with which Mairet was connected in the latter part of his life. There is also a connection backwards in time, for some notes of 1931, in Mairet's hand, make it clear that he saw an affinity between Adler and Mitrinović. 'The respective teachings of these leaders', he wrote, 'are individual and complementary but in no important respect irreconcilable.'

The history of the various groups with which Mairet was connected is a subject in itself – or a series of subjects. There was the Chandos Group, which seems to have arisen out of the General Strike. The instigator was W.T. Symons, and the group attracted several others who became associated with the *New English Weekly*, including Maurice Reckitt and the Revd V.A. Demant, later Professor of Moral and Pastoral Theology at Oxford. This body at one point became in effect (or, in the terms of a stray surviving document of 1928, was to 'find its expression in') the Sociological Group of the Adler Society. The search – continuing the habit of all-too-grand expressions to which Mairet must have submitted rather too readily in the world of Mitrinović – was for 'certain absolute and eternal principles of true sociology'. These principles were to be found, the group believed, 'most clearly in the sociology of the ancient cultures such as India and Greece. They presuppose the truth of e.g. an order of values in social structure, Hierarchy (Aristocracy), Community (Socialism).' No wonder these groups made no impact at all on the industrial organization of the century. Yet one knows that Mairet – and the other distinguished members of the group – must have had some more clearly apprehensible notions in mind. The background of philosophical reflection – in the older sense of the term – was no doubt one of the sources of the acumen displayed in the 'Notes' in the *New English Weekly*, which were written by Mairet and Reckitt alternately. The discipline of commenting week by week on the current events of the world perhaps helped to concentrate their minds. The Chandos Group went on long after the Second World War, and Eliot attended its meetings from time to time, and often sent his excuses. So there is here a link with the (rather tenuous) Christian sociology of *The Idea of a Christian Society* (1939) as well as with the Christendom and Frontier groups with which Mairet was associated in the fifties and sixties. Eliot's debt to Mairet is acknowledged in *Notes towards the Definition of Culture* (1948), which is dedicated to him 'in gratitude and admiration'.

It was no doubt of this book that Mairet was thinking – with a polite cross-reference to *Art & Action* which I had dedicated to him in 1965 – when he said with only the slightest of ruefulness that he would be remembered for the books dedicated to him rather than for those he had written himself. The remark was

delivered with such equanimity, perhaps, partly because his estimate of the writer's role was like Adler's. Whatever truth there
may be in that estimate, I find it difficult to value as Mairet
apparently did the formalized associations and discussions which
played so considerable a part in his later life. I remember saying
to him, *à propos* the Frontier Group of which I attended no more
than the odd meeting but saw much more of in their magazine,
which for a time he edited jointly with Dr Alec Vidler, that I
thought it a fallacy to suppose that people who happened to hold
a job of some professional or public importance, and were Christians, could necessarily *think* about their jobs in any fruitful way
– as the activities of the group rather assumed that they could.
But in all these activities Mairet was carrying out what one might
almost call a predestined function, in accordance with his nature,
and wherever he went he carried his unassuming, lucid and provocative form of discourse, and must have turned all sorts of
people into unaccustomed paths of thought. The slight impediment added to rather than subtracted from the effect of what he
had to say, with its pauses which added to the crucial impact.
The late Dr Neil Montgomery comments on Mairet's 'immense
and recondite stock of learning' and records how he asked Mairet
why 'he, who had considerable skill as a psycho-therapist, having
studied under the personal tuition of Adler, had never yet applied
it to the cure of his stammer. He replied, "I have been at pains
to *develop* that hesitation as a curb to my loquacity. Without it I
should be talking all the time, my knowledge is so extensive."'
The stammer had apparently not interfered with the performance
at the Old Vic: '"I had only to spout Shakespeare then. It's when
I'm spouting *Mairet* that the trouble arises."' Yet whatever his
gifts and persistence as a talker, Mairet did leave a little row of
books which are well worth investigation and contain many clues
to his thought and action. The most significant is the memoir of
Orage (*A.R. Orage: a memoir*, 1936), which anyone interested in
The New Age and the *New English Weekly* and their antecedents
should read. There is the book on Geddes (*Pioneer of Sociology:
the life and letters of Patrick Geddes*, 1957), some of whose early
meetings with Mairet are recounted in *Autobiographical and other
papers*. Both these books – and in a less direct manner, the *ABC
of Adler's Psychology* – are the by-products of Mairet's taste for
gurus, which gives them a high interest in relation to their author
as well as their subject. There is the only moderately satisfactory
little book on *Aristocracy and the Meaning of Class Rule* (1931)

which draws on the remote past as well as current psychology but suffers, as sociology, from its very sweep and remoteness from the contemporary scene. There is also an excellent British Council pamphlet (1958) on John Middleton Murry – and Murry, be it noted, was not one of Mairet's gurus. But for all their varied interest these books certainly contain something less than the best Mairet had to offer and did offer by word of mouth. His best single piece of writing is, I think, the memoir, and a high place must be given to his letters. There is a rich and abundant store of correspondence, much of it not yet collected, some of it, it is to be feared, already lost. It is to be hoped that a selection may one day be published.

The most important of Mairet's correspondents, in terms of the duration of the correspondence and the scope of the subject-matter, was without doubt his old friend Dr Neil Montgomery. The exchanges with most of Mairet's correspondents are more or less incomplete. One important set of correspondence, stretching over thirty years, has happily been preserved more or less in its entirety. This is the correspondence with T.S. Eliot, which comprises some three or four hundred letters, extending from 1932 to Eliot's death in 1963. Mairet was a contributor to *The Criterion*, and Eliot's connection with the *New English Weekly* was close even before the war. The correspondence shows a slow but sure growth of mutual esteem and affection over the years. The common interest in Christian sociology needs no emphasis. There are more unexpected things. Thus we find Eliot (25 April 1955) asking about the origin of a facsimile drawing of Goethe which Mairet had given him some years before and which had since stood framed on Eliot's mantelpiece; and Mairet replying (28 April 1955) with particulars of Maclise's sketch which he had had photographed for him by the Victoria and Albert Museum. 'Where did he ever see Goethe, I wonder?' Mairet asks. 'D M was on 26 when G died. But the drawing of Goethe *must* be a direct impression in a gallery or somewhere, probably unknown to G himself, as in the case of Scott.' (Maclise drew Scott when the latter was browsing in a bookshop.) 'Wonderful suggestion of the old poet as Eckermann knew him; even gives an impression of the remarkable eyes mentioned by almost everyone who knew G'. Or there is an analysis (24 November 1951) of the 'terribly self-elaborated personality' of Gide, with a curious application of Gide's own remarks on Pascal. Some extracts from the corrspondence relate to the work of the French psychologist Henri Benoit – a correspondence which not only evokes Mairet's powers of exposition in these difficult fields but finally brings from the sixty-six-year-old Eliot a letter in which we recognize for a moment the full force of the poet of *The Waste Land*.

There is extant also the correspondence – for the most part in French – between Benoit and Mairet who was at this time thinking about translating him, and this contains a most remarkable and highly personal document, submitted by Mairet to Benoit, which shows how profoundly he could, even at the age of sixty-eight, be moved by what he was reading. The nature of it gives some clues to the attitudes which lay behind his weakness for gurus, and his determination to get to the bottom of his own thoughts and feelings. Naturally Benoit, who clearly recognizes his subject through the pseudonym ('Monsieur H C...' – the old Henry Cohen again, no doubt), does not hesitate to give magisterial judgement. I give Mairet's statement, in translation, both for the reference it gives to his second marriage and much more for its sweeping analysis of the course of his own life. The date is 1954.

Mr. H C 68 years old: approaching the end of a very varied career (artist, designer, farm-worker, etc; then writer and editor for a period of twenty years) without distinction, but with moderate success.

Married at 27 to a distinguished woman much older than himself. Between 30 and 44, given over to the service of a friend from a foreign country, a preacher and teacher of high philosophy and occult knowledge and training ('de haute philosophie et de science occulte de réalisation'). A period of erudition in the teachings of the West and of the East, and the literature and practices of psycho-analysis. Final and painful break with this friend and master, made possible by a second 'marriage' (without benefit of law or clergy) which still continues. Relatively considerable success in the outer world accompanied by growing inner difficulties. This interior condition much relieved on going back to the Church twelve years ago. A régime of celibacy accepted without difficulty by both partners. Decreasing interest in his journalistic and literary work. Reading Dr Benoit's works and the sudden and unexpected fear of being associated with them. Danger of considerable loss of security if he separates from the Church. At the same time, the conviction of a great and important 'truth discovered for the first time, an illumination of everything that had not been understood in the teachings of his old master (who had recently died). It must be indicated here that the teaching of his friend and master was a sort of Christian Gnosticism.

Present domestic situation; very friendly, even an increase of mutual trust; a revival of former Buddhist sympathies on the wife's side. Personal condition: periods of distress *(angoisse)*, often prolonged, marked by pains either in the abdomen or at the back of the neck. Intervals of relative peace. In general, absolute faith in the Zen doctrine, which he had just discovered to be psychologically irrefutable. There remains a great fear (sometimes) of finally rejecting the conceptions of liberty (free-will, sin, salvation, etc). Daily work remains possible, although more difficult.

It is an extraordinary document, on which the best commentary is the correspondence between Mairet and Eliot.

Old age is hardly a time to be recommended, but Mairet was one of those rare people in whom it did involve a certain flowering. He was one of those for whom 'the soul's dark cottage, battered and decayed' really did 'let in new light through chinks that time had made,' and the second section of this book bears witness to this with 'To Death and Back' and a group of letters he wrote to friends after he had had a stroke, at the age of eighty-six. 'Marvellous experience' he wrote to me. 'By far the most deeply instructive I ever knew.' Mairet was much more concerned with the discoveries which this event involved, than with the penalties it brought. His intellectual interests seemed only to have a fresh urgency after his stroke. He wrote to Neil Montgomery on 4 November 1973: 'House-bound and book-bound old recluse that I am...just now and for some time past, my reading has been not only the main occupation of my days but my most absorbing and moving activity.' He had been reading not only Owen Barfield's 'admirable treatise', *What Coleridge Thought*, but the *Biographia Literaria* itself, as well as 'Kant's Critique' and 'The Tempest'. Of the latter he remarks that 'this time, what most impressed me...is the essentially Christian character of his

[Shakespeare's] inspiration.' A year later (30 November 1974, to the same correspondent) he was writing, from his knowledge of the work of Calvin and his contemporaries: 'Nobody in such a "thieves-kitchen" as the 16th century could be what *we* call intellectually honest.' Yet he was too wise to conclude from that to a denunciation of the compromises then reached, and suggests that we should 'not look too censoriously' on the way the Elizabethan settlement was brought about. 'For *in fact and in effect*', he says, 'this settlement poured a lot of oil (non-inflammable) on those raging waves, saved a great deal of life and many people's reason, and it was the envy of the most intelligent people in all the other countries that had been ravaged by the so-called Reformation!' Mairet had been baptized into the Calvinist discipline, and he was received into the Anglican communion in 1943, being confirmed on 31 October of that year by the Bishop of Willesden at St Silas, Kentish Town, of which he afterwards became a churchwarden, as Eliot became a churchwarden of St Stephen's, Gloucester Road. When I saw Mairet after his stroke in 1972, he had a Prayer Book under his pillow and he said: 'It is the words of old Cranmer that come back to me most often'. And even in 1939 he could say (letter of 7 August 1939 to Neil Montgomery): 'But as to having to admit all that the Church claims in its Christology, I came to that conclusion very many years ago... The whole thing formed itself in my imagination as the most amazingly complete system of understanding the human mystery, indeed the *best* conceivable interpretation of it. It is not an exaggeration to say that it has dominated my thoughts for the last twenty years' – back, that is, to 1919 and all the confusions that then reigned about him.

I cannot recall that religion was ever a subject of discussion between Mairet and myself – certainly it was not in any prominent way, and I remember him saying at some stage '... but perhaps you're not very interested in religion' – which I did not dissent from. Long after the *New English Weekly* days – for that paper came to an end in the (as it now might seem) moderate inflation of 1949 – I sent him the little pamphlet which is reprinted in *The Avoidance of Literature* as 'Sevenoaks Essays' (1967). He was then much taken up with domestic duties, 'having to nurse a friend', but he wrote (letter of 11 January 1968): 'Naturally I like it, because I am also both Anglican and Royalist in my allegiances, and I relish many of the reasons you give in defence of those apparently lost causes. And as an old amateur philosopher

of religion I admire the perspicacity – and originality – of your
defence of Theism.' But I was more touched when he returned
to the same subject four and a half years later, after his stroke.
After referring to my book on Bagehot, then about to be published, he added: '. . . although I'm always hoping for you to write
another which will develop at length the *positive* confessions of
faith which occur – or at least are adumbrated – in your little
book of essays of 2 or 3 years ago. All the more because I'm laid
aside and a bit crippled, I seem to hanker for this.' Alas, that
other book was never written, nor is it likely to be, nor have
those 'adumbrations' become any clearer to me, rather the
reverse, I should say. When I saw Mairet in July 1972, he returned
to the subject, adding by way of the gentlest of reproaches, that
he had enjoyed the Bagehot book, but was it really worth while
writing a book about a man who in the end had so little in him?

That was the last I saw of Mairet. The Revd Peter Wright,
vicar of St Michael's, Lewes, has contributed a vivid picture of
him as he was in his last years, and at the end:

> It took me some time before I realized that this old man who
> unfailingly attended the Eucharist Sunday by Sunday, what-
> ever the weather, did so even when he felt quite unwell. He
> looked very old and frail, bent and deaf, short-sighted, very
> often unshaven, shabbily dressed and rather lame; and, when
> one was able to catch him, would, if he were tired, speak
> with a slight stammer . . . His death came actually at a nursing
> home in Seaford, when I was able to give him the sacrament
> of anointing and remember him being quite aware that his
> end was near. He was grateful and courteous and thanked
> me for coming.

He died next morning, 9 February 1975, leaving a letter broken
off at 3 a.m. with the words: 'I am now in *angoisse*'.

III

THE PRACTICE OF GOVERNMENT

The Nature of Public Administration

What is this operation which is the life of the great bureaucracies? The administration which is the *raison d'être* of the multifarious offices clustered around Whitehall has been much denounced, sometimes admired, on odd occasions even studied. But in the main it has been denounced or admired for its effects and studied in its structure. The effects of government administration are an aspect of the history of a people, and the structure is a diagram of the channels of the more formal communications within it. Neither brings us close to the working of the bureaucracies. We are more likely to be brought close by some such personal account as that given by Sir Edward Bridges in *Portrait of a Profession* (1950). There we read of work which provides, 'and provides to a considerable degree, an intense satisfaction and delight in the accomplishment of difficult tasks, a delight which has much in common with that felt by scholars or even on occasions by artists on the completion of some outstandingly difficult work'. We find also an emphasis on the 'strong corporate life' of the civil servant. We find him portrayed as the exponent of a departmental philosophy, 'the resultant of protests and suggestions, and counter suggestions, from many interests', which represents 'an acceptable middle point of view after the extreme divergencies have been rooted out'. Thus we are told two things by Sir Edward Bridges. One is about the affective character of the civil servant's work. A man may take pleasure in it because it is difficult. It is not altogether clear why the pleasure, or the difficulty, should be compared with that encountered by the artist or the scholar, who are certainly not the only other people to be confronted with difficult tasks, or to take pleasure in overcoming them; while the corporate character of the civil servant's work does not give him any obvious affinity with the artist of modern times, or with the scholar *quâ* scholar and not *quâ* member of a learned institution. The second thing we are told is about the opinions the civil servant is likely to hold and to contribute as occasion arises to the solution of his Minister's problems. These opinions

111

are not his own. They are a mediocrity arrived at not because they are likely to be true, though sometimes they may even be that, but because in a system of protests and objections a man may hold them and escape without too many rotten eggs plastering his head. Neither of these two points made by Sir Edward Bridges describes the nature of the intellectual operation, if there is one, that the servant of the state performs. One must in passing note in Sir Edward Bridges, as in other only less eminent authorities, a conviction, natural enough in those who have spent a life-time in the service and have emerged a long way up, that the service has not only changed beyond all recognition in recent times but has improved to an almost equal degree. Emmeline Cohen (*The Growth of the British Civil Service*, 1941) is struck by the improved industry and integrity of the civil servant in the last hundred and fifty years. Sir Edward Bridges sees an abatement of departmentalism. C.K. Munro (*The Fountains in Trafalgar Square*, 1952) sees men less intent on giving orders and more anxious to serve. None of these observations, not even the last, is entirely without foundation. But none of these improvements, most probably, has been without compensating drawbacks. All of them appear to have been in something subsidiary to the operation of administration. The fact that the improvements are supposed to have been so great suggests that they cannot have been in anything permanently essential to the conduct of government. For government has been going on for a long time, and if so much improvement had taken place in its essential procedures we should not have to go far back in history before we came upon a complete anarchy. And looking the other way, we should be uncomfortably near the millennium.

We may take comfort, however. In fact, if we look back three hundred years, we see Samuel Pepys transacting the King's business as aptly as it has generally been done in this century. When we read him our temporary peculiarities, such as the size of our bureaucracies and the quality of our honesty, are seen as such and we catch a glimpse of whatever it is that enables governments to persist at all. The constitutional changes since 1660 have not been of such a nature as even much to alter certain relations of Parliament and the executive. The modern civil servant will recognize himself in this: 'This month ends with my mind full of business and concernment how this office will speed with Parliament, which begins to be mighty severe in examining our accounts, and the expense of the Navy in this war.' He will recognize the tactician's satisfaction at the diversion caused by the Great Fire: 'He says he hath computed that the rents of houses lost by this fire in the City come to £600,000 per annum; that this will make Parliament more quiet than otherwise they would have been.' And he will know the feelings, which are in the very marrow of the profession, described in the words: 'Reckoning myself to come off with victory, because not overcome in anything, or much foiled.'

It has no doubt often been remarked that Frontinus exhibits all the qualities of the good civil servant. It was his task and pleasure, about the year A.D. 97, to reform the administration of the water supply borne into Rome on the great aqueducts. The task had just those characteristics which caused Sir Edward Bridges to reflect that he is almost an artist; but the reflections of Frontinus were different. There were disparities between the records and the facts which no-one had bothered to check; there were false measurements which made it impossible for the authorities to balance their books. In these matters Frontinus set order, and he pauses in his record only to notice the superiority of these works of utility over works of mere beauty such as the Greeks were proud of. *Otiosa sed fama celebrata opera Graecorum.* Frontinus recognized that his modest function was to serve in matters that could be commonly appreciated. He was the man from the water company. But he was not particularly modest about the manner of his performance. He speaks of 'my natural sense of responsibility' and 'my fidelity', and pompously insists: 'Those who sought the Emperor's pardon, after warning received, may thank me for the favour granted' *(De Aquis Urbis Romae)*. His was a typically useful and uninteresting mind.

What are the qualities of mind most needed in the public servant? As his subject-matter must always be a good that is not only common but is commonly recognized, he had better not be in the habit of seeing things with his own eyes, unless he has an abnormal disinterestedness which enables him at once to set aside his own vision. Perhaps it is to be preferred that reality should appear to him exclusively in that form which is capable of preservation in a number, a name, a date – verbal forms which are references and not presentations. His concern, like any philosopher's, is with relationships, but he must avoid all those questions of value to which a philosophic study of relationships is apt to lead. He should have a mind tenacious of his limited sort of fact, and exclusive of other sorts, and such a delight in the play of relationships that the question of value never troubles him. Since great disinterestedness is not always to be found in combination with the primarily required ability to perform juggleries with the rigorously limited fact, he had better be provided with a vanity like that of Frontinus, or one more ignoble. If his most desperate concern is to thrust himself onwards to the top, so that he subscribes in good faith to Montherlant's formula of 'le combat sans foi', he will not be deflected by a temptation to examine values. If he can blow himself up like a bull-frog with thinking of the organization that happens to move under him, he will not seek to inquire whether that organization has any merit apart from the service it performs to his pride.

If Pepys, with his victory over the Accounts Committee, and Frontinus with his pomposity and his virtues display the facts of administration, neither brings us face to face with an explicit theory. They are, however, possibly nearer such a theory than the contemporary writers I have quoted, who seem self-consciously to wish to set on the operation of administration a value which does not belong to it. Miss Cohen, with her moral improvement, and Sir Edward Bridges with his artistic delight, have fixed on matters more relevant to other fields than to the one they profess to be describing. The comments which both Sir Edward Bridges and Mr Munro make about the corporate nature of the civil servant's work look more hopeful. That indeed is a genuine characteristic, but it could not be pretended that it is peculiar to the work of government officials. What J.B. Yeats stigmatises as the 'collective mind, dull as the House of Commons and serious as the Bank of England' (*Letters*, 1944) is common to all business transacted in great organizations. It is by an abdication of the individual vision that such organization is possible. There may of course be an individual initiative within such an organization, as there may be an individual initiative or valour within an army, but in so far as an organization exists by meanings rather than by acts there is little place for the sort of individual adjustment of accepted categories which constitutes thought in a properly intellectual field. The adjustments, and the associations and dissociations, which are made are made to suit the necessities and opportunisms of action and not to fit the truth which, in any philosophical sense of that term, is irrelevant. 'The practical man', to quote J. B. Yeats again, 'cannot afford to be sincere.' He must, not only on all questions of value but even on matters of fact, share the provisional delusions of his fellows. It is a discipline, but it is not a discipline of the truth. It requires the muscles and obedience of an acrobat rather than the patience of a philosopher.

But because these things are characteristic of all work in a great organization they cannot provide us with a description of the characteristic operation of the official. To find that, we have to look at what distinguishes the administration of government from other forms of collective organization. There is a tendency more or less plausibly to blur this distinction. It is sometimes even taught that government and industrial organization are closer together than they ever were before, or that government, as Mr Munro contends, now provides services rather than regulations. No doubt it is true that industry presents certain analogies with government, in so far as it requires, as a subordinate purpose, the government of its employees, but an industrial or commercial organization exists for ends of production or commerce which stamp it with its own characteristics. The suggestion of the kinship of industry and government administration is made with the *arrière pensée* that industry will be less hostile to what is said to resemble itself; and so far as the suggestion is believed we have, not an approximation to the truth, but the success of an act of government comparable to the successive acts by which, throughout history, the governor has claimed kinship with the governed in order to secure that he is himself tolerated – a principle which attains its greatest refinement in a complicated modern democracy. This might be called the sympathetic fallacy. Mr Munro's way of describing certain developments in contemporary administration by saying that the official provides not regulation but a service might be called the philanthropic fallacy. This too, so far as it is accepted, represents a triumph of government but not of the truth. For if a government provides a service, it does so for precisely the same reason as it applies a regulation. It does so because it thinks that that is the best way of governing. If you can keep your kingdom quiet with a few policemen armed with battle-axes, your administration can be of the simplest, but if the people will not be quiet without regulations about how it is to pay for its false teeth then even that detail becomes important for the conduct of government. Administration in the present age is characterized by the necessity the administrator may be under of taking notice, because they may become matters of public concern, and ultimately of public order, of the most personal concerns. That does not indicate any change in the nature of government; it merely reflects the habits of an urbanized and literate population.

The essential character of government, and so of the administration by which alone it is effective, is a process of maintaining the unity of a political group by yielding to the governed enough to keep them quiet and not enough to damage irreparably the fabric of the state. This description covers equally the primitive administration of three policemen and the complicated organization of the welfare state. That is to say, it is a description of the operation of the administrator in both kinds of state as well as in all intermediate kinds of state. Evidently the subject-matter that is put before the administrator may be of the most diverse character, but not the subject-matter but the method constitutes the essence of administration. The administrator steers what may appear to be a craven course among the various pressures of public and still more of semi-public opinion and the opinion of groups, and his concern is to come off with victory, not in the sense that his opinion prevails, for he has no right to one, but in the sense that at the end he is still upright and the forces around him have achieved a momentary balance. Harold Laski regretted that in this country civil servants are not to be reckoned among the experts in the subjects with which they deal, that for example no official of the Home Office 'has ever made a contribution of importance to the study of penology or criminology' (*Reflections on the Constitution*, 1951). That regret shows a mistaken view of the sort of animal the official is. He is, in fact more akin to the criminal than to the criminologist. He is a man who has been trained to a practical operation, not to the exposition of a theory or a search for truth. The operation, in his case, is nothing less than the preservation of the state. He is, no less than any soldier, a man who must give his life to the Crown. That is what gives his task a permanent sense amidst the mutations of party policies.

There is no need for the administrator to be a man of ideas. His distinguishing quality should be rather a certain freedom from ideas. The idealisms and the most vicious appetites of the populace are equal before him. He should be prepared to bow before any wisdom whose mouth is loud enough. It is the negative character of the official's rôle which makes him, while admitted to be honest and trustworthy, an object of distrust. It is clearly undesirable that his cynical method, beneficent in its proper field, should be applied beyond that field. People who, from the official's point of view, are mere trifling forces at the periphery of things may, from the point of view of the truth, be at the very centre. The fact that to the administrator they may be of less weight than some well-organized pack of fools should strengthen and not weaken their determination. The acts of the administrator are, in effect, mere acts of recognition. It is the business of those who think they hold the truth on any subject to make themselves recognizable to the administrator's deliberately commonplace vision.

Anything alarming there may be in this description of the administrator's work is due to the generality of the description. Governments differ as countries differ, because the facts to be recognized by them are different. It is the state of society which colours the government much more than the reverse. Yet government has a certain positive role, and those who understand what is being done should use their efforts to secure that the officials aree men who might, in the last desperation, exhibit a scruple.

Administrator and Law in France

The emphasis which both the school in Speyer and the *Ecole Nationale*, in spite of the more comprehensive conceptions of the latter, put on legal qualifications and training, reflects certain characteristics common to the French and German Civil Services and, indeed to European Civil Services in general. These common characteristics are in part a consequence of the prevalence over most of Europe of the traditions of Roman Law and consequently of the passion for codification. More immediately they are due to Napoleon, and one cannot travel around Europe looking at her bureaucracies without receiving the strongest impression of Napoleon's administrative force, even though one may also reflect on the different thing his works became when that force had departed. Perhaps it would not be putting too sharp a point on the matter to say that one sees the importance, for the British Civil Service, of the Battle of Trafalgar. Certainly the French Civil Service is in some sense the type and pattern of modern European bureaucracies, and there are important differences in kind between most of those bureaucracies and our own.

The typical guide-book to the British Civil Service is a descriptive work which sets out at more or less length what the various Ministries are supposed to *do*. The starting point for the study of the French service, on the other hand, is almost inevitably a legal text-book. It is no longer permitted to say that we have no administrative law, but most British administrators would find it difficult to say what it is.

> With cow and plough and barley mow
> We puzzle all our brains.

The merest aspirant to the French service could tell you precisely:

> It is merely a branch of public law. It is concerned with the state and the state's relations with individuals. It is made up of the whole body of rules relating to the organization and working of the public services and the relations of those

118

services with private persons. (Louis Rolland, *Précis de Droit administratif*, 1957, 1.)

Though the present French administration derives much of its form from the Napoleonic reorganization of the year VIII, its spirit is distinctly not that of the Consulate, and the relationship of the *administré* to the state is very different from what it then was. The First Consul made use of the revolutionary principle of the subordination of the administration to the law because such principles were part of the material of government in his day, but the *administré* had no guarantees against arbitrary treatment and the state was irresponsible. The administrative law on which French Civil Servants are now nursed, and which they spend their days manipulating or complicating, is by contrast a tissue of rights and privileges accorded to the citizen. It is explicitly conceived of as setting limits not merely to the actions of officials, but of Ministers who, it is feared, might without this restraint 'let party considerations prevail in the execution of their administrative tasks'. Its characteristic organ is the *Conseil d'Etat*, the most prominent function of which now is to act as a supreme administrative court to which the *administré* may have recourse in his battle against administrator and government. The evolution of the last hundred and fifty years, which has brought the *Conseil d'Etat* to this position, has likewise effected a fundamental change in the position of the official. In the system of the year VIII, officials were conceived of as performing only preparatory and executive work; it was the Minister who took the decision. In time the officials came 'to want to be something else than subordinates without guarantees and without initiative'. Louis Rolland's explanation of this change conveys in few words weighty indications as to the nature of the French system:

> The officials had reason to complain of arbitrary treatment and favouritism on the part of the Ministers at the head of the services. The abuses became all the more apparent since the number of services and, consequently, of officials continually went on growing, the suffrage was extended and the parliamentary régime was installed. A Minister, whose position depends on the votes of a majority, is inclined to secure the votes of the deputies by satisfying the demands they make regarding the officials in their constituencies.

To remedy or mitigate these abuses, and for more general

social reasons, the officials were in time given important guarantees. The status of French officials is regulated by a law of 19 October 1946. Alain Plantey, in his *Traité pratique de la Fonction publique* (1956), says that 'the situation of the members of the French service is now thought of as objectively determined by the legislative and regulatory dispositions taken by the administrative authorities...' and that 'these rules being fixed, once for all, do not need the agreement of those concerned before they are applied... The theory most generally applied is that of the statute: officials, established or not, are in an objective legislative and regulatory situation.' That is magnificent language: its practical meaning is that the legal definitions of the official's position place him in an artificial position of great strength. His rights have been written up in such complicated fashion that it is difficult for those who would otherwise be in a position to manage him to do so. Plantey himself puts the matter almost as brutally:

> the statutory character of the legal régime... has as its principal consequence the rigidity of the administrative structures, automatic working, the absence of new methods and outlooks. Indeed, the object of the statute is to protect the official and the service against the arbitrary intervention of political power; but that object is soon over-reached; the authorities in the hierarchy are thus deprived of their power; responsibilities are watered down, rewards no longer go by merit, and the permanence of the employment, for all but the highest officials, makes way for all kinds of negligence...

For the official himself, the statutory basis means that he has a legal vested interest in whatever benefits come his way, whether they be in the matter of promotion, establishment or leave. It is not always understood, says Plantey, that officials 'invoke the rights they have acquired under existing regulations against any new regulations which may be less favourable.' No doubt that is, in principle, what British officials do, when they get the chance, and the employees of private enterprise as well. But there is one basic and vital difference. The rights of the British official are, in general, not guaranteed to him by law. Even where the right has a statutory basis, as is the case with superannuation, the law in fact merely gives a discretionary power to the Treasury. It is the Treasury who determine the amount of the pension, if any, which is to be granted, and no one has any reason to doubt that they will do so in accordance with the rules promulgated. But the retiring Civil Servant dissatisfied with the amount, alleging, perhaps, that not all of his reckonable service has been taken into account, cannot seek redress either in the ordinary courts nor before any special tribunal such as the *Conseil d'Etat*. The *rights* of the British Civil Servant are minimal, while his duties are clear. In place of rights he has, however, two advantages – a reasonable confidence that the Treasury, although mean, will not actually try to cheat him of his due, and a deeply ingrained habit of negotiation.

In speaking in general terms of the administration, Plantey lays stress on its spirit of hierarchy and centralization. He quotes in the introduction to his book certain words of Michel Debré: 'The administration of modern France was thought out twice, first by Richelieu and then by Napoleon.' Napoleon set out to create a civil hierarchy analogous to the military power, and to the ecclesiastical power which impressed him so much and which is, after all, the pattern of bureaucratic power in modern Europe. The traces of his aspiration remain. Plantey says a little wrily that the duty of obedience to superiors 'is indispensable even in political *régimes* where the accent is not put on hierarchy'. Naturally this duty is written into the statute at several points. Just as naturally, no such thought has ever troubled the heads of British legislators. In spite of the insistence of the French statute on obedience, and in spite of the fact that 'from the year VIII and throughout almost the whole of the nineteenth century, the accent was put on the duties of officials and their narrow hierarchical subordination to the government', the principle of hierarchic obedience 'has however acquired an increasing number of limitations which' – and there is, to a foreigner, a touching faith in certain popular French abstractions behind this last phrase – 'are to be taken for granted in a legal system which, like ours, demands a refined solution of the problem of conciliating the supremacy of law and the exigencies of the public service, which are bound up with the ideas of the political régime.' The refinements in question are very largely the work of the *Conseil d'Etat*. 'All decisions effecting the official's career' may be brought to that august body. Nominations, promotions, reversions, disciplinary penalties, 'can all be attacked in this way'. Judging by the volume of business before the *Coseil d'Etat*, a very large number are so attacked. One has the picture of officials watching one another's careers like lynxes and at each suspicion of an arguable irregularity in

effect going to law about it. It was not always so. At the end of
the last century little besides certain disciplinary penalties could
be treated in this way.

The *Conseil d'Etat*, this most symptomatic of French administrative institutions, has found a brilliant student and an enthusias-
tic admirer in C.J. Hamson. It is hardly too much to say that the
book in which he records his findings and his admiration,
Executive Discretion and Judicial Control (1954), is a masterpiece.
It is brief and lucid, and presents a vivid picture. It is however
to be suspected that it was intended to be, not merely a study of
a foreign institution, but a blow struck in a domestic quarrel.
For Hamson believes profoundly in the justice of the quarrel
which many British lawyers have long engaged in against the
administration in this country, and Hamson sees in the *Conseil
d'Etat* a control of an effectiveness undreamed of here. The lectures were given under the terms of the Hamlyn Trust, and Hamson has had to impart an irony, for which he makes an ingenious
apology, into the words of the deed, for Miss Hamlyn's intent
was that 'the Common People of the United Kingdom may
realize the privileges which in law and custom they enjoy in
comparison with other European peoples'. The privileges in this
field turn out, in Hamson's view, to be, in comparison with
those enjoyed by the French, negative.

Hamson is concerned with 'the judicial business of the *Conseil
d'Etat*, the *contentieux administratif*'... and within the judicial
sphere what interests him most is the *'recours en annulation pour
excès de pouvoir'*. In effect he is concerned with the blows which
the *Conseil d'Etat* is able to strike against the bogey of lawyers,
the executive. Hamson is anxious to assure us that what the
Conseil d'Etat does in ensuring 'a decent standard' is 'as much in
the interests of that administration as in the interests of the individual', and that the work is in fact carried out by what is in
effect and administrative *corps d'élite* so that there is no question
of rulings being given without knowledge of the needs and
rigours of the administrative game. It is no doubt the case that
the members of the *Conseil d'Etat* are better equipped for incur-
sions into the administrative field than the generality of lawyers
who have learned their trade in and around the courts. The question of interest, however, is not *who* fulfils the peculiar rôle of
the *Conseil d'Etat*, but what that rôle is and how it looks from
the administrator's, as distinct from the lawyer's point of view.

Marcel Waline, one of the great authorities on administrative

law at whose feet Hamson sat, so described the procedure of
recours pour excès de pouvoir: 'any interested party can ask the
administrative tribunal to annul any illegal decision taken by the
administrator... the appellant simply asks for the disappearance
of a record... any administrative record which has the character
of a decision being susceptible of being annulled' (*Traité élemen-
taire de droit administratif*, 1950, 105). The disappearance of an *acte*
of the administrator! Second best, no doubt, to the final disappearance of the executive, but still a conjuring trick to please a
lawyer. Waline, from whom Hamson no doubt takes his line,
insists that this trick is 'in the interests of good administration',
and an ingenious Spanish theorist, the Marques de las Marismas
makes out that it is itself a kind of administration – a special sort
to which he gives the delightful title of '*la Administración vigilante*',
in contradistinction to '*la Administración actuante*', which is what
most people think administration is (*La Institución del Consejo de
Estado en la Actualidad*, 1952). Marismas admires the 'exquisite
care' French jurisprudence is said to show in delimiting the scope
of these two activities, in that the *Conseil d'Etat* limits itself to
annulment and does not seek to fill the gap thus created by a
positive direction as to what is to be done. This is an example
of a legal nicety which is effectively a bludgeon; does not every
actuante know that an administrative negation, an annulment or
a mere failure to act, can resound every bit as loudly as the most
positive and constructive decision?

Hamson illustrates the working of the *Conseil d'Etat statuant
au contentieux* by reciting at some length the proceedings in a
certain *affaire de l'Ecole Nationale*. Certain young men presented
themselves as candidates for a Civil Service competition. They
were excluded from the list of candidates by the appropriate
Minister who was acting under authority delegated to him by
the Prime Minister. Each of the young men appealed to the
Conseil d'Etat and there followed what was, in effect, a long
'public dialogue between the *Conseil d'Etat* itself and a Minister
at its bar'. The dialogue was, in accordance with the normal
procedure, in writing, and the production of documents was
demanded. The Minister at first tried to refuse to produce what
was required, but he was ultimately obliged to do so. It is hardly
too much to say that to Hamson this spectacle of a Minister
publicly eating humble pie is little short of delicious, the more
particularly, no doubt, because lawyers in England sometimes
find themselves up against difficulties when the Crown claims

privilege and declines to produce certain official documents. In the *affaire de l'Ecole Nationale* the Minister had ultimately to rescind his decision and the candidates were allowed to have their names restored to the list.

A Minister may well be wrong, and when he is it is in general well that he should be brought to admit his fault and to reverse his decision. What is of interest here is not the mere fact that the Minister's decision was in fact reversed or even the frivolity of the lawyer's pleasure at seeing him brought to this pass, but the criteria by which the Minister's actions are judged. The claim is that the administrator and his act are by the *Conseil d'Etat* brought to 'the test of reason', and the gravest charge against the Minister is that he 'failed to make known the grounds of his decisions'. No doubt it is in general a good thing that a Minister should explain what he is up to; it is an important part of government, and not only in a democracy, to do so so far as is necessary for the actions of the government to be effective. But the 'test of reason' is by no means a self-evident one. Nor is it by any means self-evident that that other reason, which Hamson dislikes so much, the 'reason of state' is altogether nefarious. Certainly the courts in this country are right to watch critically to see that the Crown's right to withhold the production of documents is not used excessively. Certainly the highest vigilance is justified in maintaining the right of *habeas corpus*. But the proper functioning of the machine of state, which, and which alone, justifies the refusal to produce certain documents, is a long term interest of everyone in the country, and although Hamson apparently regards the late Regulation 18B with great horror and shares the scandalized feelings of his French interlocutor in this matter, people at large in this country and not merely the government almost certainly felt that, however repugnant arbitrary imprisonment might be, in a time of war its moderate use ought to be preferred to the risk of a treason which would endanger all. It is not altogether irrelevant to the substantial merits of the argument that France was defeated and we were not. Hamson, however, is not much concerned with the substance of affairs. Like a good lawyer he is a man of forms. Even the admission that the activity of the *Conseil d'Etat* has kept in being 'an obsolete and sometimes corrupt administrative machine' does not damp his enthusiasm for it. It must, however, damp ours. We are concerned with how in practice an effective government machine should be run, and a mere glance at the progress of pure reason is a poor consolation for the growing debility of the state. The progress of the *Conseil d'Etat*, in certain directions, has proceeded *pari passu* with the decline of the French state. One may imagine the chagrin of Napoleon, its founder, at the present scope and nature of the activities of the *Conseil d'Etat*. Hamson records how in 1822 in *l'affaire Lafitte*, the *Conseil d'Etat* refused, for reasons of state, to entertain a claim that was good in law. He adds that this *'théorie du mobile politique'* was rejected at the outset of the Third Republic and has never since been revived. *'La théorie des actes de gouvernement est fort simple'*, he quotes with approval, *'il n'y en a pas.'* And he might have added that there was no government either, the Third Republic having proved its incapacity to survive. One should at least entertain the possibility of a connection, of a nature less strong, no doubt, than direct cause and effect, between the developing theory of administrative law and the general strength or weakness of the state. The views of 1822 on the 'reason of state' did not preserve the régime of those days; the laws of survival are much more complicated than that. But it is hardly to be denied that a certain weakening of the conception of government has played a part in the troubles and disasters of the French state in recent years. Already in 1851 Rouget is saying: 'In days gone past the *Conseil d'Etat* probably did recognize a *pouvoir discrétionnaire* which was practically equivalent to an *acte de gouvernement*. But this is now merely of historical interest.' What has taken its place? The conclusion of *L'affaire de l'Ecole Nationale* was that a man holding a lawful political opinion could not be excluded from the Civil Service, 'the "could not" turning on a *principle – l'égalite de l'accès etc.'* This principle is constitutional in France, going back beyond the preamble to the Constitution of 1946 to the Declaration of Rights of 1789. In view of that principle, the *Conseil d'Etat* could, no doubt, not have decided *l'affaire de l'Ecole Nationale* otherwise than it did, and it is clearly no business of an outsider to comment on that decision itself. Of more general interest, however, is the scope of the work of the *Conseil d'Etat* as exhibited by this case, and the spirit in which it operates.

As regards the latter, the high manner in which Hamson and others speak of the rôle of the *Conseil d'Etat* is very remarkable. Hamson speaks of the sovereign power of Parliament being 'recognized' rather as if that were a generous concession, and even Plantey, himself an *auditeur au Conseil d'Etat* speaks of Parliament and the *Conseil* in one breath as, so to speak, peers. There is, in this conception, the power of parliament and the power of reason represented by the *Conseil*; what is missing is any conception of government as such, and of its powers and responsibilities. The popular voice, supposed to be heard in the Chamber, is good, the voice of reason, for all true Frenchmen, is good, but the power of the government is an iniquity. No state can stand on such foundations. It is hardly too much to say that Hamson's view of the matter puts the *Conseil d'Etat* in the last resort, above the state. 'It is in no sense a rival or superior administration', he says. But is it not? At least it is the conscience of the administration, which in this country is in the keeping of Parliament, and in a sense, of the Ministers themselves who have, however, to maintain a dialogue with Parliament as Hamson describes Ministers doing, in France, also with the *Conseil d'Etat*. The *Conseil d'Etat* is 'the incarnation of the republican and revolutionary spirit'; while governments come and go it has a continuity and a unity, 'the continuance of a temper of mind'. In a remarkable passage Hamson speaks of the working of the *Conseil* as a 'quaker's meeting' and says that its corporate sense depends more on a 'state of mind than on any text or regulation'. Some such guiding spirit there must certainly be in a state; but is it certain that an administrative court is the proper repository of it?

The habit of legal thought represented by the attribution to the official of a status which gives him, as it were, an existence in his own right, dresses him with certain privileges and regards him as holding a little parcel of the authority of a notional thing called the state, is very much of a piece with the habit which is content to see a Minister brought to a shadowy 'test of reason' before the subtle experts of the Palais-Royal where we would have him answerable to the patience or impatience of the inexpert and commonsense Members in Westminster. These things reflect profound constitutional attitudes. British government and British administration are in a sense merely things that go on here, whereas French government and administration, with their written constitutions and juristic refinements, aspire as it were to a theoretical status. It must not be thought that these differences date back merely to 1789, or are merely revolutionary habits of thought, as certain words of Hamson might seem to suggest, though undoubtedly the failure of institutions may lead people to seek a certain solace in theory. Justinian had a hand in the matter and his influence in modern Europe, like the secondary influence of Napoleon, was not confined to France.

The Judge and the Administrator

The classic British criticism of continental systems of administrative law has been that by its association with administration the law loses its independence, that it is, so to speak, perverted by proximity to the seat of power. Once the British lawyer is satisfied, as Hamson was in the case of the *Conseil d'Etat*, of the effective independence of an administrative tribunal, his distrust may turn, as Hamson's did, to admiration. The administrator's point of view is different. He is concerned – and it is surely a legitimate professional concern – at the damage which may be done to the administration by the inept intrusion of the law. The slowness of legal procedures, and the stiffness which excessive prescription may introduce into the practical business of government, are what interest him. What repels him in the continental systems is a certain Byzantinism. French law as contrasted with English law, French administration as contrasted with British administration or, for that matter, the Roman Church as contrasted with the English Church, have characteristics which are observable in Justinian's code. 'A preference for abstract standards, referable to definite and conscious ethical conceptions, ... and a taste for logical arrangement which sometimes degenerates into the multiplication of unreal and practically useless distinctions' (H.F. Jolowicz, *Historical Introduction to the Study of Roman Law*, 2nd edn, 1952). The application of the words Jolowicz uses to describe the *Corpus Juris* is clear. We may not unreasonably think ourselves nearer 'the practical spirit of the true Roman law', to which 'the subsequent development of generalizations and classifications' was 'alien'. Justinian's cap fits exactly the French laws on the status of the *fonctionnaire* or the Austrian Law of Administrative Procedure as showing 'a taste for excessive regulation by statute of matters to which fixed rules can hardly, by their very nature, be applied with success'.

It may be said that the British administrator on the whole avoids law-making when he can, though it may be thought, from the look of the bulging statute-book, that his efforts have been singularly unsuccessful. The extent to which legislation can be avoided is strictly limited, because a Minister who is to embark on any new line of action is likely to need parliamentary authority to do so. But, although there have been exceptions, the administrator's general practice, in this country, has been to shun legislation where other means can achieve his ends. He prefers to see things taking shape in the real world before he invents an elaborate legal construction, because he knows that with such a construction, devised *in vacuo*, nothing may ever correspond. In an obscure way, he is not unfriendly to the old concèption of law as custom, and where the subject-matter of the business allows he may try to stimulate a habit of behaviour and recommend legislation only when the habit is widely enough diffused to bring effective enforcement reasonably within sight. Where the nature of the business does not allow of such a proceeding he likes, by consultation with the parties most immediately affected, to ensure the viability of what is to be proposed. This conservative and realistic habit of mind is very different from that found in a number of countries where the traditions of the lawyer-administrator prevail. In France the administrator's thoughts run very early to a draft law, embodying an ideal conceived *in vacuo*, the execution of which, in the form proposed, may prove impracticable. A similar habit of mind accounts for the edifying nature of the reading matter which is to be found on the statute-books of many primitive or ill-governed countries.

The British administrator, in short, likes to see the law growing out of practice and crowning it, but he is far from any prejudice against the state taking a proper initiative. Indeed, the only distinction that interests him is that between the practicable and the impracticable, and a flood of legislation which gives Ministers new powers is unsatisfactory only if he feels that it is coming at a pace which puts in doubt the effectiveness of the execution. This practical concern may be due in part to tradition and to the national habit of mind. It is also due to the fact that, under our system, the administrator who plans the content of the legislation on particular topic is normally also the man who, even though the government should change, will be responsible for seeing that the machinery it sets up works properly, and for drafting the briefs, letters and replies to parliamentary questions in which the Minister of the day will be forced to demonstrate the effectiveness of his administration. The *politics* of a measure, in the sense in which parties use that term, genuinely do not exist for the

British administrator, but the practicality of the thing is something of which he has daily cause to be even agonizingly aware. An amending bill which follows, after some years of working experience, a piece of established and accepted legislation, is likely to be the fruit of practical experience of administration and will be presented by the administrator to his political chief of the day in the knowledge that so far as the pure practicality of the thing can be demonstrated it is likely to be welcome to a British government of either political colour. To the making of the estimate of practicality there goes, of course, an estimate of the reactions of the special publics concerned or of the general public. That is the concern of both politician and administrator. The mechanical practicality of the thing is not likely to be in question where the legislation has grown out of practice.

The British administrator who has cast a look in the direction of continental systems of administration will moreover become aware that the lawyers brought up in the empirical muddling of the common law are nearer his own way of thinking than are his fellow-administrators on the continent, brought up under entirely different legal systems. His attitude none the less differs in important respects from that of the British lawyer. The lawyer in England, unlike his colleagues in the Roman law countries, has behind him a professional history which tends to separate him from the administrator. He is not accustomed to think of justice, as they do in France, as a 'government service like the provision of education or roads' (G.R.Y. Radcliffe and Geoffrey Cross, *The English Legal System*, 1954). He is conscious of belonging to a kind of independent corporation, knowing that 'Parliament only passes statutes affecting the organization of the courts on the advice or suggestion of the legal profession'. He is haunted by the ghost of Sir Edward Coke, and is inclined to believe in the common law as in a power independent of the state, forgetting that in so far as Parliamentary supremacy was established in 1688 the standing of the common law fell with that of the Royal prerogative. The administrator thinks of the law as an instrument for getting things done. His legal outlook is formed entirely by the conception of statute law, and it may be said that on this account his view of the law is at once more up-to-date and, in certain reaches, shallower than that of the lawyer. Above all, and as compared both with the British lawyer and the foreign administrator, he regards law as secondary, and in this he is at once modern and affiliated to traditions of government which are anything but modern.

In recent times administrators in this country have been the object of severe criticism, one might say of violent attack, from the lawyers. Hamson's book (see p.122 above) may be regarded as a by-product of this hostile movement. The most famous protagonist in the lawyer's quarrel was the late Lord Hewart. *The New Despotism* (1929) was written – to use a phrase Hewart quotes from North's Plutarch – to pull down the pride and stomach of the clerks. The lives of Cato and the late Lord Chief Justice of England were not quite parallel. The former was more like an energetic Minister raising hell in his department; he 'made great alteration amongst the clerks and officers of the Treasury'. The latter was not convinced that Ministers could have such power, and he was concerned to abate the power of the executive lest the liberty of the subject and the standing of the judiciary should themselves be abated. To this task Hewart brought a partiality not altogether judicial, and only a moderate respect for the High Court of Parliament. In his anxiety to save the House of Commons from the officials he did not scruple to suggest that it did not know what it was about when it delegated to Ministers power to make certain statutory orders and that it was the helpless victim of a plot 'intended to produce, and in practice producing, a despotic power'. The Lord Chief Justice was not called to the Bar of the House and made to purge his contempt, but he might have been. The new despotism 'gives Parliament an anaesthetic'. Its strategy is 'to render the will, or the caprice, of the Executive unfettered and supreme'. The language is not moderate.

The evidence for this plot Hewart found in enactments passed by Parliament itself. Parliament was 'being outmanœvred' by being persuaded, apparently by officials, to pass such legislation as that Rating and Valuation Act (1925) of which Section 67 was entitled – 'pleasantly enough' as Hewart says – 'Power to remove difficulties'. The fact that the public departments were in the charge of Ministers, and that Parliament, having specified with some precision how the rating and valuation system was to work, chose to leave some of the details to them, was indifferent to Hewart. He evidently did not believe that Ministers had the energy of Cato, or that they would 'thoroughly understand what the clerks and registers should be'. He was one of those who, in the words of Mr Justice Eve which he quotes, 'were convinced that the best Government was that which governed least'. Many people, and certainly many Civil Servants among them, have the same sentiments. But 'less government' is not what Parliament has judged fit for the times and assuredly since 1929 the electorate have not wanted to be saved, even by judges, from officials with power to run effectively a socialized state. What they have wanted is parliamentary control of the direction of government, and of the measures introduced, and the power to protest, through their Member of Parliament, if they thought the laws were ineptly administered. Mr Justice Eve's remark, however true in some contexts, is in the context of an England where the main policies are popularly determined, simply not true at all. It is no more good government to govern a socialized democracy with two proctors and a policeman than it would have been to govern pre-industrial England with a Civil Service of the size we have now. Hewart's thesis, like Eve's, is based on a preference for the common-law world where the upper class and a prosperous middle class gave work to lawyers by much litigation *inter se*. It is amusing to see that Hewart is inclined to forgive the lawyers in the government service. 'The Law Officers of the Crown, the Treasury solicitor, and the Parliamentary draftsmen have from time to time used all their influence to prevent, or mitigate, acts which they could not approve.' Parliament is blamed for not seeing things with a lawyer's eyes, and the non-legal officials, the real villains, are contrasted unfavourably with the legal gentlemen employed by the State. The very notion which Hewart attaches to the idea of 'responsibility' is one which belongs to a world of substantial burgesses the passing of which one may well, from certain points of view, regret. The official is anonymous and removable; he will do anything for pay. His answerability to his superiors, to his Minister – on which after all much, even from the basest point of view, depends – and his Minister's answerability to Parliament on which, in turn, much of the Minister's reputation and future depends, do not constitute 'responsibility' for Lord Hewart. His notion, and it is well grounded – it is indeed, basically the notion of responsibility before God – is that the judge, unlike these others, is responsible precisely because he is answerable to no man. He gives reasons for his decisions, which are taken after public argument, and whether or not his decision is liked he can scarcely be called to account for it except by a superior court, unless it be by the improbable and extreme remedy of a petition by both Houses of Parliament. In the popular view, it is the difficulty that there in fact is in removing the ordinary official which may tempt him to irresponsibility because people have a parliamentary notion of responsibility and think that responsibility means, in some form, responsibility to them. Hewart is in fact turning his back on this and saying that judges are responsible in much the same way as was Charles I, who did not regard himself as responsible to the people. One is entitled to think that Hewart was not altogether wrong in his conception and that the democratic notion of responsibility needs, in a sane constitution, to be supplemented by some other, different in kind. But the idea is not one for which, in the present way of the policy, much popularity is to be expected.

Hewart was the defender of 'a polity wherein the people make their laws, and independent judges administer them', but although he imagined that in so doing he was defending the present liberties of the subject he was in fact looking back, for that polity is the same in which most of the administration of the country was in the hands of magistrates. The respective territories of administrative and judicial activity are by no means clearly defined. W. A. Robson, who could hardly be suspected of partiality for the official's side of the quarrel, has spoken clearly on this matter. 'It is very difficult to discover any adequate method by which, in a highly developed country like England, judicial functions can be clearly distinguished from administrative functions. Mere names are of no avail, for...judges often administer and administrators often judge' (*Justice and Administrative Law*, 3rd edn. 1951). And Maitland, in reference to Montesquieu's assertion (*Esprit des Lois* XI, ci) about the separation in this country of administration and judicature, comments that 'in England, of all places in the world... the two have for ages been inextricably blended'. Decisions, such as whether the child should be brought up as a Papist, or about the suitability of a marriage, which may arise in connection with a ward of court, are essentially administrative decisions. They are questions of what in the circumstances, and within the law, is the sensible thing to be done. These are decisions taken by judges. On the other hand, the official has often to determine questions of right, and to administer the law is, inevitably, to interpret it. The question of the distinction between a judicial and an administrative act often comes before the courts, because 'orders of prohibition and *certiorari* will lie only in respect of judicial acts, and not for those of an administrative or ministerial character', but Robson concludes that the decided cases 'disclose no coherent principle' and merely demonstrate, 'by the very confusion of thought they present, the difficulty of arriving at a clear basis of distinction'.

Formerly it was convenient to give a number of administrative functions to justices of the peace, which in a loose and rudimentary administrative system was well enough. But for the last century or more the government has, in general, had to look elsewhere for the machinery of administration. Although it is obviously of the utmost public importance that certain matters should be dealt with in an open court, and the foundation of our liberties would be irrevocably weakened if they were not, yet in respect of some matters it may be said that it is largely a matter of historical accident whether they are dealt with by the judiciary or the executive. As Robson puts it, 'plenty of administrative acts are performed by judges arrayed in scarlet and ermine and surrounded by all the pomp and circumstance which for centuries has attended the administration of justice by the King's judges. And many an obscure Civil Servant, sitting bespectacled in a quiet office, is engaged in activities which partake of a judicial character.'

The lesser pomp is not necessarily undesirable. Provided that the public can make trouble if things go wrong, as in fact, through their Member of Parliament, that can, there is something to be said for going to discuss something with men in an office rather than submitting to all the formalities of a court. It will probably take you less time; it will almost certainly be cheaper to your and to the public purse. The price of ermine and scarlet, and even of wigs and black gowns, is high, and Hewart shows some sensitivity on this point. Moreover, it is the nature of much of the business to be decided that it involves a detailed knowledge of a great organization and of a particular subject-matter, which the courts will not take tacitly.

The relationship between judicial and administrative proceedings is dealt with at some length in Roscoe Pound's *Administrative Law: Its Growth, Procedure and Significance* (1942). The first of these lectures is entitled 'The Place of Administration in the Legal Order'. That is a legitimate and useful subject of inquiry. No less useful, and surely no less legitimate even if less acceptable to the legal mind, would be a study of the place of the legal order in administration. If in classical and medieval theory administration holds a subordinate place and is, as it were, a mere dependency of *suprema lex*, it is a matter of fact that only in a society with administration enough to hold it together can there be any question at all of a lawyer's law. And even in our own time we have seen that the failure of government which permits the irruption of hostile forces into a territory may, if the invader be a barbarian, result in the failure of the law. The law, in any refined sense, is in fact protected as the consciences of those who refuse to fight are protected by those who do.

The exercise of justice is, indeed, a part of the attributions of the supreme authority which only a fortunate history has taught us to regard as separable. From this separation has sprung a liberty which we are right to guard jealously, but if the means we choose to defend it were to result in the destruction of the administration we should, in fact, be going abut to destroy justice itself. It is one of the merits of Roscoe Pound's book that he is aware of the close link between justice and administration. He is very much on the lawyer's side of the quarrel that must always go on between these two, but he realizes that there is a price to be paid for the liberty that he defends. 'We must pay a certain price for freedom; and a reasonable balance between efficiency and individual rights is that price.' In any particular historical situation, it has to be decided how much efficiency can be afforded in return for the goods of justice. Roscoe Pound was giving his lectures in the autumn of 1940, in the security of Pittsburgh. On this side of the Atlantic the price of the full measure of our freedom had become a bit high, and we had Regulation 18B as in the last resort any nation which has the will to live will fall back on the Roman formula: *Salus reipublicae suprema lex esto*! The area of judicial justice changes with the times, and what is lost or gained by the courts may be gained or lost by administration. For not only do these two methods or institutions depend from the same source; they are different forms of the same activity. To hold that they are the same by no means necessarily implies acceptance of the Marxist view in which, as Pound says, 'there is no room for law'. It may instead imply the view that all government should be subject to a law which is anterior to the state's and to which those who govern as well as those who judge are answerable. In any case, the identity of the two activities may be studied without reference to any justificatory theory. 'To this day, in the Roman-law world, the judiciary are thought of as a part of the administrative hierarchy.' It is we and the Americans who are odd. It is interesting to see how far the descriptions Roscoe Pound gives of judician activity are, in fact, equally applicable to a competent administration. 'Judicial interpretation postulates that a formula prescribed by statute was meant to cover certain definite areas of fact discoverable and to be discovered.' The judge has to decide how the particular case falls within those areas. But that is precisely the work of the administrator in so far as the latter is concerned with determining or adjudicating. In most cases the answer is so plain for all to see that there is no question of recourse to the courts. In a few difficult cases a more elaborate and expensive procedure is thought to be justified, and because of the doubt as to the outcome it is felt that all the steps by which a solution is reached should be public and so open to criticism. Roscoe Pound's description of administrative action is much coloured by the peculiarities of the American system. The lay administrators, he says, in contradistinction to the man of law 'are prone to act, in deciding, as very likely they properly may in directing, as if every case were unique'. This surely reflects the outlook of the business man turned official. Nothing could be less like the procedures of the wary professional bureaucrat, for whom precedent is so important and whom the anxiety to secure uniformity is always gnawing. The defence of 'administrative determinations' which Pound quotes in order to destroy is likewise one which would not have occurred to an official in this country. One of the points of the defence is that the process of administrative determination 'as distinguished from the judicial process, moves in a narrow field' so that 'the administrative is not open to the broad range of human sympathies to which the judicial process is subject'. This extraordinary defence, the validity of which Pound rightly calls in question, would be as repugnant to a British Civil Servant as to the American lawyer. Similarly as to the second point of the defence of administrative determinations', 'that singleness of concern quickly develops a professionalism of spirit – an attitude which perhaps more than rules affords assurance of informed and balanced judgements'. The British Civil Servant would be less likely to see himself in that than in Roscoe Pound's reply which sets out what are said to be the advantages of the lawyer's outlook: 'But does the professionalism which grows from preoccupation with a single type of controversy afford the check that is to be found in long continued occupation with controversies of every type?' That, certainly, as well describes the type of general administrator which the British system seeks to produce as it does the lawyer or the judge. The guarantee of impartiality which Pound sees in the permanence of judges as contrasted with the doubtful tenure of 'boards' is also one which has more force on his side of the Atlantic than on ours.

The respective areas of administration and the judicial process are not something to be determined *a priori*. They are matters to be determined by the joint light of tradition and the needs of the time, the object being always to maintain that 'balance between general security and the individual life' of which Pound speaks. More generally, one may say that if the continental conception of the lawyer-administrator involves too close an identification between legal and administrative processes, an attack such as Hewart's involves much too sharp a view of the singularity of the legal process. But if there is a similarity, in certain respects, between what the judge does and what the administrator does, there is also a difference in their points of view. A judge's own sense of what is good for the country may well enter into certain of his judgments, for example in the matter of obscenity. The administrator, on the other hand, has as his main and ultimate concern, what is good in terms constitutionally appropriate: what will keep his Minister going. He looks at the thing from the point of view of Ministerial responsibility, a matter which lies at the root of our liberties but of which neither Hamson nor Hewart shows much understanding. The judge has his sense of continuity; the administrator has his, not less acute but different, looking towards the future more than towards the past, and concerned with the persistence of the Queen's government, as such and without regard to its political complexion, and more remotely with the continuance of the realm itself.

The Administrator as Governor

If a concern for the coherence and continuance of government is implicit in what the British administrator does, it is a characteristic of the British system that no official is explicitly charged with these matters. In many European countries things are different. There are, in addition to the numerous officials who, like their British counterparts, have their particular charges, a small number of trusted men who, in some sense, act as the general overseers of the country. The central government feels the need, as ours does not, of having at key points throughout the country men whose function is to act as their general agents and representatives. These men are, in some sort, provincial governors.

In Spain the officials who answer to this description go frankly by the name of *Gobernadores civiles*. A Spanish writer on administrative law lists a number of more or less remote precedents of this office showing, as he says, 'that the central power has always needed its representatives in the various regions of the country'.* The praetors of Roman times were the first of a long succession known at various times as *corregidores asistentes, intendentes, jefes politicos*. The *Gobernadores civiles* have the general duty of carrying out the laws and policies of the government; they have responsibility for public order, with all that this can imply; and they are the heads of the central administration in the province they govern. They provide a link – to put it no more strongly – between the central government and the local authorities, for they act as heads of the local administration and have a general oversight over those authorities. In Italy each province has its *prefetto* 'the highest authority of the state in the province, representing the government in its unity... the only local authority recognized as having a certain power of a political nature' (Aldo M. Sandulli, *Manuale di Diritto Amministrativo*). The general attributions of the *prefetto* are not dissimilar from those of the *gobernador civil*.

* Sabino Alvarez-Gendin, *Manual de Derecho administrativo español* (1954), 55 ff.

The official of this general type who is most familiar to people in this country is the French *préfet*, who, owing to the influence of Napoleon and the prestige of the French service, is in some sense the model for Europe at large. It is not the custom among French writers on administrative law to boast of the ancestry of the *préfet* as Alvarez-Gendin does of that of the *Gobernador civil*. It would not be in accordance with the revolutionary mythology which hangs about north of the Pyrenees. None the less, it is generally recognized that in establishing his hundred overseers, to whom he gave, as a First Consul understandably might, a name formerly given to Roman provincial governors, Napoleon was in a manner resuscitating the system of *intendants* which had prevailed under the *ancien régime*. There had been thirty-six *intendants*, each managing the business of a province as the direct agent of Paris, and just as the British traveller nowadays will find in the *préfet* a governing official of a type unknown in this country, so the eighteenth-century traveller must have remembered, as he extolled the superior liberties he enjoyed at home, that in his county the central power was represented by nothing more permanent or arbitrary than the judges or circuit, unless it were by the Lord Lieutenant or by himself and his friends holding commissions as justices of the peace. Like other offices and institutions created by Napoleon, that of *préfet* has undergone significant changes in the last hundred and fifty years, but the *préfet* remains, like the *intendant* before him, solidly and unmistakably the central personage of his district, and he holds that position as being, explicitly, the direct agent and general representative of the central government. He can be sacked by the government at any moment, though the cadre of *préfets* is in fact considerably more stable than is suggested by this rule of formal dependency.

It would be hard to imagine an official with a more comprehensive load of attributions than those which rest upon the *préfet*. He is *'dépositaire dans le département de l'autorité de l'Etat'*, and he is the chief representative of all the Ministers. He supervises the execution of laws, orders and government decisions. He represents the national interests in general and as the chief Civil Servant of the department in theory directs the activities of all the others. He keeps an eye on various local government activities, acting as a sort of permanent secretary to the elected *conseil général* of the *département* and having, besides, the power to suspend and replace mayors and to approve or to withhold approval of certain deliberations of municipal councils. No British official has anything like this range of duties; above all, none has this kind of responsibility. In case of a break-down of public order, Frenchmen would be likely to turn to their *préfet*, if they turned to anyone, for a lead. In Britain people in trouble do come in great numbers to seek the help of the officials of the several ministries, but if any kind of public lead were required they would expect to find it elsewhere, even though the figure-head provided in fact contributed little that did not come out of the official advices he received. It was on this principle that the government, during the war, took the precaution of appointing Regional Commissioners who could have taken over the administration of their areas in case of a breakdown. It would never have done to suggest that free-born Englishmen should submit themselves to the judgement of a Civil Servant. The Regional Commissioners, whose effectiveness as co-ordinators and directors was happily never fully tested, and who stood much further out of the ordinary cadre of officials than do the prefects, were the nearest approximation we have known to the French officials who do, effectively, and in spite of the misgivings that one cannot but entertain on a close acquaintance with the system, form the backbone, in a sense the whole skeleton, of French outstationed administration.

The British administrator, and indeed the British Civil Servant in general, tries to be as far as possible invisible. The *préfet* is professionally prominent. Not only has he a sort of admiral's uniform which he puts on when he unveils a memorial or takes the salute at a march past of the local garrison; he enjoys a certain modest luxury. He lives in the prefecture, and he and his lady hold a little provincial court, in which gather from time to time the leading members of the *conseil général* and other local notables. Among British Civil Servants, one would have to go to the Foreign Office, which is remote in spirit and function from the Home Civil Service, to encounter officials who made it their business to glitter in any but the dimmest way. None the less, the British administrator may feel himself in some respects more at home in a prefecture than with certain of the legal contortionists in Paris. While he cannot but be impressed by the skill and learning of the *Conseil d'Etat*, the outlook of the *préfet* is certainly nearer his own. The *préfet*, like the British administrator, is trying, with the help of or in spite of the law, to get something done. Moreover, the range of business which passes before him is wide – wider, indeed, than that which falls in the way of the

British administrator – and he has therefore something of the amateurishness which is a professional requirement in Whitehall, a knack of picking up any business, whatever it may be, and turning it into the way of government. But the British administrator's trimming of the business to fit the requirements of government is of course the trimming that is required for preparing it or dispatching it on behalf of a single Minister on whose doorstep he lives and to whom he is responsible. It is also that of a man who stands at the centre of an administrative machine the working of which is conditioned by the notion, or rather by the effects in practice, of Ministerial responsibility. The *préfet*, as the servant of all Ministers, the chief man of his *départment*, but a subordinate point in a number of nation-wide administrations, is in a different and in some ways more complex position.

The *préfet* has as immediate assistants, a sort of private office, with a *chef de cabinet* who is a junior member of the Prefectoral Corps, various *bureaux* which do the main routine work of the prefecture, and a *secrétaire général* who ranks as a *sous-préfet* and is, under the *préfet*, the chief administrative official of the prefecture and generally ensures its smooth internal working. By no means, however, are all the officials of importance in the *département* to be found in the prefecture or the *sous-préfectures*. The prefect lives surrounded by a variety of administrations. The British system is, by comparison, of a Napoleonic logic and simplicity. It is often said that in the eighteenth century France had become a confusion of authorities with overlapping areas of control. A hundred and fifty years after the Revolution she is certainly in that position. Every Frenchman is bound to tell you sooner or later that his country has *l'esprit cartésien*, one of the implications being that she has a passion for making a clean slate and designing a logical structure to replace what has been erased. Nothing could less accurately convey the spirit of French administrative reform. It is indeed impossible to achieve radical reform without more power and coherence than French governments have had for many years. If Napoleon approached the Cartesian ideal, there have been too many little Cartesians since for the result to show much of the logic on which the French pride themselves. The idea that the prefect could, by the exercise of mere authority, make good the deficiencies of the administrative system, is one not likely to appeal to the student of administration. Napoleon's more orthodox idea was to put the right men in place in a good system. A man of parts can get something out of a bad system, but a lack of simplicity and intelligibility is inadequately compensated by individual talent. The administrative systems which surround the prefect hardly enable him to exercise his abilities to the best advantage. They certainly do not enable him to live up to his theoretical rôle as the general representative of the government in his area.

It is not that the prefect has any competitor for this post. No one in the *département* has his finger in so many pies. The prefect's *chefs de division* appear between them to control everything. In fact, however, most of these divisions are concerned with legislation which is not only made in Paris but is designed to be administered on a national scale. As the representative in the department of all Ministers, the prefect is theoretically empowered to deal with it. It can even be argued that, in view of the excessive specialization which characterizes the central administration, a man of the prefect's general experience can inject a little common sense into what is proposed or commanded from Paris. If that were true it would merely show the prefect as an inadequate brake on a bad system, or as one of two wrongs which still do not make an administrative right. In practice the men at the centre are generally working on more rational or, what passes for the same thing, more modern lines. The prefect can, in many matters, do no more than meddle. He may take things out of straightforward day-to-day administration for reasons irrelevant to the responsible Ministers, whose real representatives are the senior local officials of their own Ministries and the specialist staff responsible to those officials. A prefect might well intervene to stop the prosecution for fraud of a local notable whom the central administration and its servants would certainly have pursued; he will hardly intervene to ensure that the intention of certain legislation is being properly carried out. He may, occasionally, by using his prestige, that 'touch of authority' supposed to be dear, bring to a conclusion, in the right sense, a negotiation with which the specialized services have struggled without final success. This can happen in industrial conciliation, where the determining factor, it can safely be said, is not a nostalgia for a vanished authority but the well-known habit of hagglers not to give in before the highest authority to which they have access has been reached. If the prefect was not there, someone more expert would be the highest authority.

The prefect may, of course, play a useful rôle in problems which are of a local character but which involve various Ministries.

For these matters he is the natural chairman. In this country the chairman would be determined – and generally quite without difficulty – by the subject matter of the problem. The Ministry most concerned would take the chair. It may be that such arrangements are facilitated, with us, by a somewhat greater readiness to agree among ourselves than the French can generally show, or a greater readiness to be bored by the argument to which disagreement can give rise. The consultations in this country would, on any important question, be regional rather than more narrowly local. This brings us to one of the *cruces* of the prefectoral problem. It is evident that, for most of the major problems of government, the department is an altogether inadequate unit. Most of the Ministries which need an organization in the provinces in fact work on a larger scale. Their regional territories do not have the same boundaries; the Ministries do not all have the same number of regions. A modest reform to be hoped for would be some alignment between them. That, however, would leave unsolved the problem of the relation between the Ministries and the prefect. It was the reactionary government of Vichy which first tried to put the prefectoral system on a regional footing. Like other works of Vichy, it had to be undone. In 1948 posts of inspector-general of the administration were created with a competence extending over several departments. This reform, like that of Vichy, sprang from a concern for public order, and the regions of the inspectors-general are aligned with the military areas. The inspector-general could be and occasionally is of great utility. The inspector-general is, in the language of the people, a *super-préfet*, and the people is no doubt in the right of it as compared with the Ministry of the Interior's more discreet term. The *super-préfet* is better able to deal with the regional officers of the Ministries than is the prefect. He is more nearly the right size. But the same general objections hold good against him as against the prefect. There is no system or logic about the relationship between the frontiers of his territories and those of the Ministries; he cannot do anything that the representatives of the Ministries, agreeing among themselves could not do. He has not the advantage the prefect has of being *dans les mœurs*, with the force of tradition behind him, but there is no doubt that he is potentially the more useful official, an official more suited to the needs of the time. His very success, however, might lead to the continuance of a prefectoral system which can hardly be said to be an administrative necessity. It might prevent the decay of the prefect who, with a long period without the obsession of public order, might well attain the status and dignity of a Lord Lieutenant.

In a sense, the whole question turns on the preoccupation with public order which has, for reasons which the recent history of France make only too plain, been obsessive. The constitution of 1946 envisaged the department as run by an elected official, as it might be by the chairman of the county council. The laws applying this provision of the constitution have never been voted, and the reasons for this failure include a legitimate fear that, under a communist chairman, there might be danger even of a departmental separatism. There is a lack of confidence among the French in the possibility of a political solution of any such difficulty, and a preference for relying on an administrative solution. A long history of inadequate political direction, combined with a tradition inherited from an absolute monarchy, had led the French to look to the *fonctionnaire*, and above all to this strange half-political *fonctionnaire*, the prefect, to secure the coherence of the state. It is hardly for a foreigner to call in question the efficacy, in this matter, of the sober building in the *chef-lieu* of the department. There is no doubt that that building does represent, for the ordinary Frenchman, public order. And yet one cannot help wondering whether this conception of public order is not a trifle parochial, an affair of *gendarmes*, having little relation to economic forces that move the country.

The presence, in the Departments, of officials whose job is to carry out the will of the central government, is no more than is essential if there is to be any government at all. The prefect, however, like his opposite number in Spain and elsewhere, is something different in kind from the merely necessary official of a central administration. He is an official who, to use Gambetta's distinction, is *quelqu'un* as well as *quelque chose*, a politician as well as an administrator, and one may wonder whether an official of this type is altogether suited to the needs of a modern democracy. He is embedded in the administrative machine, and with the recruitment of a proportion of the prefectoral corps through the *Ecole Nationale d'Administration* he may well come to feel himself as more and more of it. But in reality he is a bit of the political mind of the country, a bit of political grit in the administrative machine. The mere fact that his appointment is revocable at any time and that his continuance in office is dependent on his political acceptability will separate him from the permanent officials. The fact that he is equipped, like a Minister, with a sort of private office which is apt to take a hand in matters as soon as they begin to smell slightly political, will ensure that the political aspect of the affairs dealt with by the administrative divisions is not lost sight of and may even cause it to be exaggerated. In this country the politics of any new legislation is generally lost sight of in the execution. This is probably largely true in France, where the social legislation, for example, is now *dans les mœurs* and accepted as much as the habit of political intervention is accepted. But the prefectoral system does in a measure keep the politics of things alive in the heart of the administration. Above all, it provides a ready opening for interventions based, as such things generally are, not on political principles but on political associations.* The French, particularly in the south, are passionately interventionist, and a great deal of time must be wasted in explaining the inevitability of administrative decisions, even when the intervention does not secure its object of effecting a deviation in the exercise of authority. This could of course be called educating public opinion.

It is unlikely that the cruder manifestations of the presence of a political official are much in evidence or extremely deleterious. The prefect has to please a lot of people, almost everyone except perhaps Poujadistes and Communists, and the more people he has to please the more nearly his circumspection will approach that of the ordinary administrator. Even so, the prefect will hardly be open to influences of the same generality as the pure administrator under the control of a central department would be. It is here that the local character of the prefect appears. The fact that he has so many masters – the fact that he is the representative of all the Ministers and not merely of the Minister of the Interior who no doubt has his first loyalty and to whom he sends a monthly report – must give him more independence than an official who has only one. His pressing concern is that all should go well, and above all that nothing should seem to go wrong, in his department. *Pas d'histoires!* His first impulse will be strangle at birth any project likely to give trouble to powerful local interests, and he will be tempted to abet the latter when they

---

* It is amusing to recall, in this connection, Tocqueville's remarks about those who, under the *ancien régime*, demanded of the *intendant* 'that in their case the rules should be waived, and demand it just as imperiously as if they were asking that the rules should be followed.' Tocqueville (Paris, 1952), 135.

find themselves opposed to a national policy, a situation which puts a new gloss on the monarchic formula: *'Ordonne en outre Sa Majesté que toutes les contestations qui pourront survenir sur l'exécution du présent arrêt, circonstances et dépendances, seront portées devant l'intendant.'* The instrument of Napoleonic centralization has become in a manner a focus for a kind of discreet decentralization, for a propping up of the departmental unit much as the individual citizen seeks to prop himself up against the ravages of the tax collector. Above all the prefect, while jealous of his rights as the first official of the department, does not want to do anything unpopular, or unpleasant to the influences that matter. If anything unpleasant has to be done he would rather some less public figure took the responsibility. *'C'est la politique du parapluie.'*

Viewed from the point of view of British *mœurs*, it is absurd to have an official in an admiral's uniform to get the work of the government done. Admittedly a prefect does not normally wear these garments when he is talking business, but in this country the mere knowledge that an official had such a get-up hidden away in his wardrobe would tell against him. The Lord Lieutenant is allowed to dress up because he has no authority to speak of. We have retained the splendour at the centre of loyalty but prefer not to be dazzled by those we are going to talk to. The French, having abolished the crown, are said by some Frenchmen to like a touch of authority. One may always suspect those who make assertions of this nature of liking themselves to exercise authority. There are however those who see in that exercise the most legitimate function of the prefect. It may be, in the vicissitudes France has known, that it has been; and it may be that some local stiffening of this sort is still required in a democracy so much less strongly led than ours, and with a general administration less integrated and more in love with its own academic and legal inventions. The hundred little men of authority in the *départements* may be thought of as battling against the fissiparity of the French party system and the subtilizings of the logicians at the Palais-Royal.

The Politician as Intruder

It is possible for the political and administrative authorities in this country to act as effectively as a single power for the very reason that there is so sharp a differentiation of function between them, because, in short, there are no administrative *authorities* but only administrative instruments used by the political power. This differentiation is by no means to be taken for granted. It is least marked in those régimes which have a tradition of the Civil Servant as governor, and it is precisely in the case of such officials as the *préfet* that the danger of their being at cross-purposes with the political power is most feared. An English authority on the prefectoral system, speaking of 'the events of 1940 and 1944', says that they 'confirm, if that was necessary, that the Prefect's place in the administration of the country is of such importance that a real change in political direction must be accompanied by a profound modification in the composition of the corps. This, to the French, appears reasonable.'* Both 1940 and 1944 were years of revolution and it is natural that, at such times, the governing politician should be alarmed about what the governing official might get up to. Although the possible dichotomy of the political and administrative powers, resulting from the imperfect differentiation of their functions, gives most cause for anxiety in times of violent change, the anxiety is not confined to such times and is indeed endemic in the system. Hence, of course, the special insecurity of tenure of such officials as the *préfet*. Chapman's comment, which is illuminating, is no doubt intended to have a wide application: 'The selfless administrator', he goes on, 'without clear or profound convictions is of little use either to a Government or to a society when called upon to deal with matters so fundamental as the control of education, police and industrial conflict.'

This comes very near to equating 'clear and profound convictions' with the specific differences of opinion which are the stock-

* Brian Chapman, *The Prefects and Provincial France* (1955), 157.

146

in-trade of politicians; an administrator might reply that there are national terms of reference, the common ground of parties, which may be held to not less firmly than the items of a party programme, though admittedly they are less clearly seen in a country which has undergone frequent changes of régime than in one which has been more fortunate. The British, anyhow, do not pay their officials to 'control education' nor to exercise their own opinions in the conflicts, industrial or other, that are played out upon the national stage. And it may be added that, in these matters, it is far from certain that the play of opinion is more effective than a long patience.

The British system rests on the obedience of the official or, if all systems may be said to do the same, one may fairly characterize our own as exhibiting a remarkable degree of mutual confidence as between politicians and officials. It is not suggested that French Ministers do not, in general, trust the officials in their Ministries to carry out the policies imposed on them from on high, but it is probably true that the relative instability of French governments gives high officials in that country a somewhat strong sense that the government rests on them and a consequent predisposition to nurse their private policies. It is hard for an outsider to judge such matters. A certain distrust of 'the selfless administrator' is, however, openly written into the administrative system of France, as into that of a number of other countries. The French Ministry is, in effect, divided into two interacting parts, a large neutral part and a small part of high political voltage. The neutral, stable element is made up of the *bureaux*, divided up, much like a British Ministry, into what in France are called *directions* and *sous-directions*. The political part is made up of the Minister's *cabinet*, and one might say that that institution is there to ensure that the permanent structure of the Ministry is sufficiently responsive to his direction. Up to 1940, there were really several *cabinets*: an office which received and registered correspondence and shared it out among the *bureaux*; sometimes a technical office made up of specialists; and finally the private secretaries doing a mixture of political work and routine office work. The *cabinet* consists of people of the Minister's own choosing. Their number is fixed by law, and, if the law does not prescribe their functions it is at least at pains to give each of them a general description. There is a *directeur* and a *chef du cabinet*; there are assistant *chefs*, a chief private secretary, and two people who in some sort act as specialist advisers – normally nine people in all. The appointment is a formal one, announced in the *Journal Officiel*. The members of the *cabinet* may be ordinary officials, but the law lays down only the minima of qualifications, or rather of disqualifications, namely that they must be people who have not been deprived of their civil rights and that their military service papers must be in order, and anyone may be chosen. They are, collectively, the dynamite with which the Minister, in the course of his peregrinations, enters a new establishment. But more gently, one might say that they are supposed to form a link between the Minister and the permanent administration. The scheme must be supposed to have some advantages in the contexts in which it is used, but it is probably better administratively not to interpose a body of trusties between the Minister and his Ministry. A Minister commands loyalty by virtue of his office, but it is difficult to believe that a band of wandering hangers-on does not arouse something more like suspicion and jealousy, and make the ground more fertile for intrigue. However that may be, the system inevitably creates a class of officials who follow the personal fortunes of Ministers in a way which is unknown in this country and which can hardly contribute to the smooth working of the administration. There are certain safeguards in the law. Public officials called upon to serve in a Minister's *cabinet* may be promoted only in accordance with the rules governing promotion in the class to which they belong, but the situation is not without possibilities and the placing of ex-members of Ministers' *cabinets* in the prefectoral corps does not pass without jealous notice from their colleagues.

The British administration enjoys an extraordinary degree of freedom from political intrusion, and there is no doubt that this freedom greatly facilitates the responsiveness of the administration to the purposes of cabinet government. The British administrator is able to be genuinely indifferent to the political colour of the government he serves because politicians accept constitutional limitation of their field of influence in a manner which is by no means to be taken for granted in countries outside Britain. The forbearance of British politicians is systematic, resting on the critical force of the opposition and on public opinion. It gives us, in contast with what might fairly be described as the general system in Europe – or indeed in the world at large – permanent heads of Ministries who owe nothing to political connections and whose status is such that they can as a matter of course, without reference to political connections and subject only to

Treasury concurrence which prevents more than a limited amount of departmental idiosyncrasy, determine the *personnel*, or as the scarcely less inelegant usage of Whitehall has it, the establishments policies of their Ministries.

The German Civil Service of the Bismarckian Empire, which in some respects must have been exceedingly unlike the present service in Whitehall, is said to have enjoyed an independence of political influence in its internal workings somewhat similar to that we still enjoy. Such independence is possible only under the shadow of a strong political *régime*. Theodor Eschenburg says of the old German service that it was 'socially one-sided, but it operated as a unity and in accordance with firm standards of quality. The much exaggerated class consciousness of this service corresponded to a high professional ethos and standard of performance. Neither political nor economic groups had influence on its establishments, not even the agrarian organizations' (*Herrschaft der Verbände?* 1955). One has not to wander long in the corridors of Bonn to discover that things are not like that now. It is a long time since they have been exactly like that. Eschenburg puts the beginning of the modern patronage of office in 1921, when the political parties began to press for a quota of posts as a means, though it would seem an inadequate one, of securing a bureaucracy sensible of the needs of the new times. Hitler hated the bureaucracy and tried to secure its dominance by *one* party, partly by planting or promoting sympathizers, partly by employing agents, sometimes among the messengers and drivers, who could keep an eye on their nominal masters. If the new politicians suspect the Civil Service, they are not in a particularly good tradition in doing so, nor in a particularly democratic one. And if the personnel has changed, so that one could say that something a little different was being suspected by each of the three régimes, the changes as between consecutive régimes have affected only a small, though admittedly important, proportion of officials. A modern state has need of its bureaucracy and is hardly more likely to lose the lot in a revulsion of public feeling than it is to lose the whole of its hospital or newspaper staffs.

The German official is still, in his way, a proud creature. His preserve (as distinct from that of other employees or workers in the state service) in general includes all those administrative and executive posts which carry with them a bit of the authority of the state or of a public corporation, as well as all those more modest positions of trust, such as those of the postman, the railway-driver and the signalman, in which public safety is involved. The generic name for the tasks carrying with them a morsel of public authority is *'hoheitsrechtliche'* activities. The etymology of the word *'hoheitsrechtliche'* is no doubt significant: *Hoheit*, 'Highness', *'Hoheitsrecht'* 'royal prerogative'. The official is the successor of all those advisers and executants who flourished around the German courts of former times. This touch of what was once magic is probably, in these times, more damaging than helpful to the official's reputation with politicians and public. And yet if in one sense the politician may be said to distrust the officials and perhaps tends to be a little too desperately anxious to prove that he is commanding and not taking advice, in another sense there tends to be, from our point of view and indeed from that of some German critics, an insufficient gap between officials and politicians. No single feature of the arrangement is, to an Englishman, more striking than the fact that the *Staatssekretär* (the equivalent of the Permanent Secretary) can and does deputise for his Minister in the House. When he does so he may get into trouble either for not putting forcefully enough all his Minister might have said or for taking upon himself more than becomes a mere official, or both.

The *Staatssekretär* is of course a political official, nominated by or at any rate pleasing to his Minister. So are the *Ministerialdirektors*, his lieutenants, who may be regarded as the equivalent of our Under Secretaries. It is not to be supposed, however, that political influence on establishments policy ends there. It is of course impossible for an outsider, and perhaps not always easy for an insider, to say exactly how far it does go and what is involved in it. One cannot fail, however, to notice a certain uneasiness in German officials on this point; either urging that the extent of political influence has been much exaggerated or openly regretting that it is there. The influence is not only that of the parties directly but of other outside bodies which, generally, make their influence felt through the politicians. One instance, taken from Eschenburg who offers a varied selection, will show not merely outside influences at work considerably below the level of those appointments admitted to be political but working in a manner which we should regard as the grossest interference with a question of conscience. The case is one of a candidate for promotion to a rank below the rank of our 'principal'. He was a Roman Catholic, married to a Protestant, and he had allowed his children Protestant baptism, in defiance, of course, of the

Roman rule for mixed marriages. The Minister was also a Roman Catholic and, it was expressly said, could not answer for such a promotion. It is as if, in England, an Anglican Cabinet Minister should stop the promotion of an Anglican on his staff who had married a Roman Catholic and given way to the Roman rule that the children should be baptized into her branch of the Church. The considerations involved in an appointment or a promotion would, happily, rarely be of this intimate character. More often it takes the form of looking for a candidate with the right combination of connections, political, confessional, and other. There is no doubt that the confessional question is a very live one, and the situation is dominated by an inextricable mixture of politics and religion which can be paralleled, in what were once the British Isles, only in Ireland. To listen to an impassioned sermon, in a packed cathedral, telling the congregation that they were *'das Volk Christi, das Reich Christi'*, with the Pope at the head, is involuntarily to recall that one had heard those words *'Volk'* and *'Reich'* resounding with an equal but different passion on ground not very remote some twenty years before, and to reflect that a priest is not precluded, even during an exposition which is textually orthodox, from invoking evil spirits.

The examples given by Eschenburg of the interests of outside groups being brought to bear on establishments include cases involving the peasants' group and the refugees. Eschenburg points out that the importance attributed to groups in 1945 was virtually inevitable owing to the disarray of the political parties, and he says: 'Even today there are Ministries where the key positions – not always marked as such – are occupied by high officials who in the bottom of their hearts think of themselves more as commissars of their interest groups than as the advocate of the state. The view that certain Ministries in Federation and *Länder* are state-organized and maintained strong points in the service of the interest-groups, is fairly widely held.' In a more exuberant mood Eschenburg declared that every organization would like if possible to have its own Ministry – 'the doctors a health ministry, the middle class block a Ministry for the middle classes' and so on. 'All that is missing from the claims to date is a Ministry of Midwives.' Claims of this nature are not unknown in other democratic countries, and are perhaps not to be avoided in the modern mass state, for which Eschenburg also has the names the 'group state' and, more comprehensively, *'der Gefälligkeitsstaat'* the state that tries to please. One can, however, usefully distinguish between claims for the setting up of special ministries and other bodies, which are public acts and can therefore be the subject of public discussion, and the more private business of interfering with appointments and promotions inside the ministries. The latter is a truly sinister phenomenon of which this country has happily almost no experience, though there is something of the sort in the claims that are made that certain posts should be reserved for Scotsmen, Welshmen, or women.

The working of political and (through the political) of other pressures on recruitment and promotion is limited, so far as federal officials are concerned, by the operation of a government order, and it would be misleading to suggest that the outside pressures play more than a subordinate – though it is by no means a negligble part – in establishments policy. The rules laid down are applicable to all officials including those of the rank of *Ministerialdirektor* (Under Secretary) and above, which, in the German system are the properly political offices whose holders have not the same security of tenure as the rest. The rules are, as is inevitable with such things, limiting rather than determining. That is to say, they lay down certain general minimal qualifications for recruitment and promotion, but cannot determine *who* is recruited or promoted. They are comparable to the conditions of eligibility for a Civil Service competition, and the choice in the hands of the particular ministry is, broadly speaking, as wide as that which, with us, is, in the matter of recruitment, open to the Civil Service Commission, though the shortage of qualified candidates has in fact meant that the freedom of choice is, at the recruitment stage, very restricted. In the matter of promotion, the British establishment officer has no regulations of any kind to guide or restrict him, though, for all but the higher posts, there are agreements with the staff which effectively govern procedure, though they leave the choice open to the authorities as in Germany.

There is little doubt, however, that the choice is not exercised in Germany in quite the same way as in England. Leaving aside the procedural differences which affect the middle and lower grades only, and leaving aside the question of political influence, the German official lays greater stress than we should do on specialist knowledge, and the career of the typical administrator is made in a narrower field than is the case with us. People tend to specialize and to be promoted within the speciality. The high official faced with an awkward question feels for a specialist as

Goering felt for his revolver when he heard the word 'culture'. The passion for specialization, so characteristic of the Germans and betraying their desperate hope for certainty and their basic wobbling, may increase the size but certainly cannot increase the homogeneity of the service or the facility of communications within it.

The service has, of course, already a basis for homogeneity in the academic training of the entrants. We have seen that the general administrative cadre is, in accordance with the general European pattern, an affair of lawyers, though with some who have done something less than the full course, in addition to those who have done the full course of legal studies leading up to the second state examination and others who have pursued some other supposedly utilitarian studies such as economics. There will also be a small number without university training. The academic training is never forgotten as it cheerfully is in England. It is recalled when people are moved from one job to another and is a factor in limiting movement. We are free of this sort of thing in our general Civil Service classes, but not outside them, where a man of fifty may still be classified as a chemist on the basis of a not very good degree he took thirty years before.

The pride in their legal training and in their specialization strengthens among German officials an *esprit de corps* which tends towards exclusiveness. It might be said that the official feels himself not only separated from the people but from his Ministers, neither of whom, he likes to think, can really appreciate the complicated laws he weaves for them. It might be said that in a blundering way the injection of political influence is an attempt to put this right. It is a blundering way, however, for it increases distrust and so makes the service a less sensitive instrument of the popular will. Only a service where there is no fear or favour, or so little as not to matter, can respond in a ready and integrated fashion to governmental control and the feeling of the country. Such steadiness is not to be found in the Germany that has known 1919, 1933 and 1945, and a bureaucracy is, after all, a secondary thing, sick or well as the country is sick or well. As to popular feeling, the German bureaucrat probably never had any antennae.

Changes of political habit in Germany would be needed if the defects of her bureaucracy were to be remedied. 'It is notable', to quote Eschenburg again, 'that the Opposition in Germany frequently restricts itself to control of the direction of policy...

A pre-condition of public control is not only that it succeeds in forensic criticism, but that it finds an echo in public opinion.' Eschenburg is not the first German to regard his country (somewhat mistakenly one may think) as a kind of England *manqué*.

The Mind of the Administrator

A comparison of one national administration with another inevitably involves much more than a confrontation of techniques. It involves a confrontation of cultures. History pops up her head. As one walks across the courtyard of a modern prefecture certain pages of Tocqueville come to life, and as one watches the *fonctionnaire* wrestling with the evasions of his countrymen one sees Rousseau's peasant hiding his wine and his bread from the tax collector. A Spanish official, whom one has met before in a gleaming modern office, suddenly appears beside one in an ancient palace. As, folded in his gown of black and crimson, he leans across the table to expound the business his sheaf of papers contains, one is faced with the deadly reasonableness of the Inquisition. These recollections have something of the fortuitous in them, but one must be deaf and blind to all tones and colours if one's gaze is not troubled by some such evocations. So sober a matter as the style of official utterances and enactments has in it something not to be accounted for in theories of organization or the science of administration, if there is one. The whole habit of French scholastic discipline, with all that is behind that, may be apparent in the text of an order or of an *Exposé des Motifs*. It is not, to say the least, obvious that British officials are writing in the language of Shakespeare until one observes that French officials are, by contrast, using the language of Racine. It is amusing to compare the 'Plain Words' Gowers recommended to the British Civil Servant with *Le Style administratif* of Robert Catherine. The very titles indicate the difference – so characteristic of the two cultures – in the authors' points of view. For Gowers, the thing is a practical exercise. He is bent on improvement as much as any organizer of a society for the suppression of vice. He has a righteousness which he is burning to impart. For Catherine, the starting point is a simple reflection on the existence of an administrative style, leading, so appropriately for a countryman of Descartes, to 'an embryonic essay in the metaphysic' of the style in question. It is only after a comparatively complicated evolution that Catherine reaches the point of putting the bias 'on the pragmatical side of the subject'. The lack of any metaphysical foreground, so to speak, almost of any spirit of pure inquiry, in the work of Gowers gives it a smugness which is, one must sadly admit, in the surest British tradition. The new righteousness is every bit as right as the old righteousness which is relegated to the dustbin. Yet, in spite of that, it is curious that Catherine, for all the superiority of his intellectual tone, succeeds in the end in seeing less of his subject than Gowers. He is almost wholly unaware that the administrative style is an instrument of government or rather, he is aware of the governmental function of the style in so far as it relates to the powers and proprieties of the hierarchy but the governed, for him, scarcely exist, whereas the constant concern of Gowers is that the words used in government should do their job which, means, in the first place, their being understood by ordinary people. It is true that Catherine is not wholly content with the French style as it is practised, and he devotes some space to 'le choix des termes'. He can underline the inelegance of a phrase, or note that an adverb may conceal an inadequacy in a thought, but it is with the complaisance of a mandarin whose empire might be crumbling unobserved before his eyes that he notes the relationship between the administrative sentence and the sentence of Proust, or observes the use of the imperfect subjunctive which tends more and more to make the official style an exception in the epistolary style of our day. This subjunctive may be said to characterize the French Civil Service as plain words do the British.

Yet in spite of national differences, there are undoubtedly important similarities to be found in the cast of mind and the outlook of administrators at home and abroad. The administrator is everywhere, and in spite of Bridges's remark about the near-artistry of his task, essentially an inartistic person. This does not mean that officials are, as a class, less sensitive in their private tastes than men of other professions. Indeed, as one migrates among the Whitehalls of Europe one has the impression that those places contain no bad samples of the civilizations of the countries they administer. It means that the administrator cannot be content with the partial and individual view of the world which, whatever general truths may be hidden in his work, are the starting points of the artist. Barrès notes in his *Journal*, that he and France and Zola all had bad memories, but that each had his own peculiar memory. It was that peculiarity, Zola suggested, which constituted the originality of each of the three. 'Abstractions of failing attention to the outside world,' says Ford Madox Ford, 'are not necessarily in a writer signs of failing as a writer' (*Some Do Not*). The artist makes his work out of *his* world, a world he has invented or formerly observed. The official, on the other hand, looks as if he is claiming an impartial and general view of the world. So far from congratulating himself on having forgotten what bits of the world are like, and happily leaving them to other people to remember, he has to claim that all the facts which not he, but the world at large, think to be relevant to a particular subject, are within his grasp. By this claim he sets himself over against the individual; for many people, who have forgotten what the word used to mean, he appears to be claiming to be God. In fact the official mind, is far from opposing any kind of universality to the artist's individuality; what it does oppose to it is a kind of impersonality. The official may voluntarily exclude a large part of reality, but he does not, like the artist, do so because he can in this way give play to his personal vision of some other part. If the artist imitates nature, the official averts his eyes and makes the picture out of bits of other people's. He cannot pride himself, like Zola, on what he forgets, having to obey other people's impulses and not his own. It is characteristically the mechanical faculties, memory, logic and the power to apprehend certain set patterns, *esprit mathématique* rather than the *esprit de finesse*, in Pascal's distinction, which are required of him. For most of his purposes an electronic brain would be better than his, but the complexity of it would be such that, whatever the progress of cybernetics, the traditional type of official is likely to remain considerably cheaper.

The official may be said not to have vision at all, except in the drabbest sense. The world he is looking at is not the same kind of world that the artist sees. Although the artist modestly admits to have forgotten much that passed outside him, the chunks he remembers and represents are solid. Even if he uses only a few lines of pencil, or a few rhythmic words, he is concerned with something which is unmistakably whole enough to live. Things are far otherwise with the official. A whole reality is no good for the work he has to do. God might, as Berkeley says he does, hold the entire universe, with all the physical variations of its appearances, in his minid, but the official is always in search of the *relevant*. The criteria of relevance are the very definition of his job. It is here that national and in particular constitutional differences begin to appear. There is one set of criteria for the French administrator who may have one eye on his Minister and one on the *Conseil d'Etat*, and in the back of his head a calculation about the possible effects, on the policy he is advocating, of pending changes in government. There is another for the official in Bonn who, because he is singularly cut off from the administration in the *Länder*, must often have to give his advice with only a vague sense of what the detailed consequences of it will be. The head of a Swedish agency will give play to his aristocratic status as an official responsible directly to the crown as well as to his practical subordination to a democratically controlled Ministry. For the British administrator the criteria of relevance which usually appear to him in clear and compelling form, are determined by what is necessary, at a particular time, to help his Minister to ride the waves of criticism in the House, and the necessary includes what may happen at Land's End as well as what has already happened in Westminster.

The official must no doubt know more than he finally uses, in order to be satisfied that he is selecting the best for his purposes. One may say of the British official that, if he is engaged on a job with no immediate outlet to Minister and Parliament, he will still be working tacitly with the sort of notions of relevance that would mean something to them; he must try so to order things that, of all that can happen, only those things happen which are susceptible of explanation in the parliamentary context. Of the limitless number of atomic facts of which reality is made up, and out of the whole range of which the artist is free to make his pattern, only a threadbare few could possibly come into play in public discussion. The official knows so well of what kind these are that he may in time begin to think that reality is indeed constructed of them; he will call them the facts. Sometimes new kinds of interest break through into the public and parliamentary world, usually long after they have been known in the world of books, and the official may be caught off his guard, so deserving the appellation of 'hide-bound' from business men who for forty years have been thinking exclusively in terms of an even more limited range of merchandise.

The independence of the criteria of relevance employed by the official from any convictions, as distinct from habitual preconceptions, of his own, can be made out to be extremely noble or extremely ignominious. There is indeed an element of genuine self-discipline in it. The inter-connection of government, and the width of the field of public discussion in which any action of his may become embroiled, mean that he must continually be testing his logic and opinions against those of others. The luxury of the snap decision, or of the smart or good-natured bargain with the favoured customer, are not for him. Naturally, among all the situations his career will bring him into, he will encounter a wide variety of moral relationships, but his characteristic stance must be that of the man not concerned as to what is to be done, but only that what is done shall be acceptable. This can be called disinterestedness; more often it is called indifference or worse. The popular view, in other words, is rather that the official's activity is ignominious than that it is noble. Unless one takes a very optimistic view of human nature there is no occasion to quarrel with this. But if the point of the criticism is that the official is sold to a master, it is fair to inquire whether the position of his critics is in general much different, and whether something of the sort is not implied in all working for money. If one is seeking to differentiate the official from others, it is necessary to inquire for what master he works.

The notion of the ignobility of the official is implicit in Churchill's description of Sunderland: 'the zealous official, who does not care what is done so long as he is at the centre of it' (*Marlborough*, vol. I, 1933). It is a confrontation which is not agreeable to the official's self-esteem. It warns him of the final perils of his profession. Some German officials certainly encountered those final perils; and one cannot forget the reproach of one of them, 'that it is too much to expect heroism of everybody'. But again, the possibility of an encounter with evil is not to be removed by choosing another profession. What is peculiar in the official's position is merely that he is called upon to serve in turn masters who present themselves, as dramatically as they can, as the protagonists of opposed convictions. The tenability of the official's position rests, in the end, on the depth and nature of those convictions and the secret of their opposition. The party politician, is surely, almost as much in danger of moral distortion through being professionally bound to exaggerate differences as the official is through being professionally bound to ignore them? There is a value in the emphasis on difference, and without the dialogue between the two sides of the House the administration could not show even as much life as it does. There is, however, also a value in ignoring the differences, and the British official need not be ashamed that his profession requires him to care more for the continuity of the realm than for the success of party. Balfour had it that the Crown is above party, and the official below it. This is somewhat a *grand seigneur's* way of putting things, and it implies a rather grand notion of party to suppose that one could easily be below it. There is of course an operational sense in which Balfour's way of putting it is exact, but in the longer strategy of government the official is a dependency of party only within limits, and of the Crown, in the last analysis, without limits. That the official is a Crown servant is one of those commonplaces which, for want of active reflection upon it, many people have come to regard as a fiction, but it is indeed the truth. For here is the official's master or, as it at present turns out, his mistress. It is no mere chance of nomenclature or technicality of the law which puts the British Civil Servant in that relationship to the Queen; it is because his task, like that of the Crown, is to maintain continuity.

The heartless character of the official is of a kind with the ultimate heartlessness of all government. One of the grand debates since the Renaissance has been on the question moved that princes may be compelled, like Machiavelli's, to all unscrupulousness to keep themselves in power. That ultimate unscrupulousness is not, however, the peculiarity of princes. It is the characteristic of all government which is determined to go on without regard to anything but survival.* In fact, while a puritan fastidiousness might refuse to have anything to do with government, or trade, or anything but solitude in a desert, neither Queen, politician nor official commonly face situations in which the turpitude of one course shows up grimly against the radiant goodness of a practicable alternative. No doubt such choices come unexpectedly, and Pontius Pilate was perhaps taken off his guard. The steps he took to still a particular local clamour were

---

* In current American theory of administration, the conception of the prince whose actions are determined by his supposed need to survive has reappeared in the context of the business world. Thus Herbert A. Simon, seeking to differentiate the objectives of the entrepreneur from those of the employee and the customer, describes them as being 'closely related to the survival of the organization' *(Administrative Behaviour)*. Chester Barnard's lecture on 'Mind in Everyday Affairs', appended to *The Functions of the Executive*, compares the intellectual activities of the executive to those of a climber who, in an emergency, takes a rope between his teeth. The lecture describes illuminatingly, but with a relish which suggests an imperfect appreciation of them, the Machiavellian horrors which lie at the very centre of the life of action.

more or less what the service required, and he washed his hands with a civilized regret. The practice of government has its risks, but what practice has not? According to the standards of our ordinary sleepwalking, the cynicism of the official is, like that of the politician, limited by the context in which he works. The debate between the two sides of the House is far from being a debate *à l'outrance*, and although some logicians might think that a bad thing it is in fact an excellent one. For the debate in the House is as to the conditions which will or should govern the further existence of this country, which would already have ceased to exist if there were no common ground in the debate. It is like a consultation between doctors, who have to decide what is best for the health of the patient but are not authorized to kill or maim him. Such a consultation could become loaded with malevolence if the standard of health within the context of which they advise became distorted, as is not inconceivable. So with parliamentary government, the decisions of which are good only in so far as it works in a context of good sense. The Member of Parliament normally has to choose not between black on the one side and white on the other but between alternative ordinary mixtures of good and bad. The official works under the same broad terms of reference. He does not invent criteria of acceptability for the means he proposes; the rules of the game are that he shall take what he finds in the country at large.

'On a peu de volontés', says Antoine Rivarol, 'et c'est pourtant alors qu'on a la tête politique' (Maximes et Pensées). It is in our system of government that the official should learn to discount his own opinions, and if he were thereby committed to becoming the instrument of any opinion whatever, however grotesque or barbarous, it would indeed be the case that he had become inhuman. His face would become, as Theodor Haecker noted of the faces of German generals, 'metaphysically empty'. One could not say that the metaphysically empty face would seem altogether out of place in Whitehall: there have no doubt been able men who would hardly have noticed a translation to the Wilhelmstrasse. But the terms of reference in fact in this country have not become such as to demand metaphysical emptiness, and democracy, though not infallible, is not likely to demand this particular pattern. It is of course in the logic of democracy not to declare what it will in the future demand, and in so far as its terms of reference are thus unlimited it is no doubt a dangerous institution. But declared terms of reference are usually worse, because, without being able to guarantee that the good that is in them is not in the end sacrificed to the requirements of survival, they provide excuses for oppression. Nothing will guarantee a reasonable and humane environment. To those for whom the device can have any meaning it may seem a shift as good as any that sovereignty should rest with a Christian Queen in a Parliament less specifically committed.

It is the absolute nonentity of the British administrator that is his chief merit. Without making extravagant claims one may safely suggest that as much practical ability is collected in the acres around Whitehall as in any comparable area elsewhere in the world, but it is, to revert to Gambetta's phrase, if not quite in the sense in which he intended it, the ability of *quelque chose* rathern than of *quelqu'un*. That is not to say that the ordinary human foibles, what is called force of character and the various colours of personality, are not to be found there as elsewhere. But the enterprise is in its nature impersonal because it is constitutionally subordinate, and it is in its constitutional subordination, completed by an utter lack of pretence to arcane qualifications, that its characteristic merit lies. It is true that the British administrator, like indeed the administrator everywhere, is suspected rather of being insubordinate and of being rather full of *volontés* than otherwise. To the suspicion naturally attaching to people whose work is done near the centres of power, there has been added since the days of Max Weber, and *a fortiori* since the days of James Burnham, a suspicion, of a rather more shadowy kind, that historical forces are somehow working to put power in the hands of the bureaucrats and managers in general. Burnham was, however, not particularly brilliant as a judge of historical forces. Writing about 1940 (*The Managerial Revolution* was copyrighted in the United States in 1941) he boldly stated that 'the localization of sovereignty in parliament is ended save for a lingering remnant', and that in England it might 'not last the next few months'.

The Managerial Revolution may be regarded as a vulgarization of Max Weber, and in defence of that it could have been said, to be sure, that if ever a man needed a little vulgarization Max Weber did. It was intended as a philosophy of revolution, the revolutionary element consisting of a large injection of Karl Marx and a tone of menacing prophecy, accompanied, of course, by an assumption of scientific objectivity which is forgivable since it was accompanied by a confession that, in general, 'the socio-

logical and historical sciences have not yet reached even the level
that the physical sciences held in ancient Greece'. Burnham supposed 'that the conclusions reached' in his book would be 'dis-
pleasing to most of those who read it'. Perhaps this was a joke
or a manifestation of the author's flair for publicity, for Burnham's own theory must have told him that a large public of
managers was in fact waiting to be told how important they
were. Some of them, it is true, might not like the crude simplifi-
cations as to the nature of society, but it was obvious that a
sufficient number of people would raven down the theory with
the flattery. What Burnham in fact had concocted was a sort of
opium for the managerial middle classes. The people his theory
reassures are 'production managers, operating executives,
superintendents, administrative engineers, supervisory techni-
cians; or, in government (for they are to be found in governmental enterprise just as in private enterprise)... administrators, commissioners, bureau heads, and so on... these who already for the
most part in contemporary society are actually managing, on its
technical side, the actual process of production, no matter what
the legal and financial form – individual, corporate, governmental – of the process.' These people were not those engaged in
tasks 'which need elaborate training in the physical sciences and
in engineering', but those engaged in 'direction and co-ordina-
tion'. They might, however, sometimes have to have 'an acquaintance with the physical sciences or the psychological and social
sciences since human beings are not the least among the instruments of production'.

Burnham understands by a ruling class 'a group of persons
who, by virtue of special social-economic relations, exercises a
special degree of control over access to the instruments of production and receives preferential treatment in the distribution of the
product of these instruments'. The question of who rules in that
marxist sense is of somewhat limited interest. On this view of
the matter, the fact that what a man achieves has no relationship
to what he aims at does not matter. In the classic case, he fights
for freedom of conscience and wakes up, it is alleged, with political power. This comedy will no doubt continue to be played as
long as there are human beings with mixed motives and muddled
heads, but the deluded victor cuts a poor figure as a ruler. He
may indeed be the man who has permission to eat most, but
when one has taken a bored look at this prodigy one is still left
with the question as to who, if anybody, rules in the sense of

understanding what is happening and, with a full sense of the limitations of effective action, being able at an appropriate moment to give a directing touch. Whether or not the administrators with whom this book has been concerned count as 'managers' in Burnham's sense – and it would seem that he would clearly regard them as one with the commissioners and bureau heads – they undoubtedly appear to some people as a ruling class in this other sense. It is the fear that they are, that the official may originate something – naturally something unpleasant – and by virtue of his position impose it on the rest of society, which leads people to try to control him in a legal straight-jacket and to inject a little more political influence under his skin. The remedies are superficial but the anxieties they are meant to cure are deep. Notions of what is meant by originating something differ not a little.

The British official is undoubtedly a powerful person in the sense that he occupies an influential place in the system of our government and that his advice is always listened to and generally taken; and 'power', says Professor S.H. Beer, means 'the ability of someone to get his decisions accepted by others' (*Treasury Control*, 1956). No doubt if the person making the 'decision' were in fact in a position to decide what he liked you would have there a definition of absolute power. The American professor, however, was writing about the British Treasury, and it is certainly not the case that Treasury or any other officials in Britain can get accepted by the government or the country at large any decision they care to make. The context is so powerful as to be almost everything. Government is by opinion, and the official's power is limited by the necessity he is under of accepting the opinions as well as the facts of the day. Indeed, it may be said that the extent to which an official feels that he is exercising real power is a measure of his lack of originality or even of individual perception, at the very least of his contentment with the preconceptions of the age. The official is a kind of second-hand merchant; the only ideas of direct use to him are those that are vulgar and current. He may be thought of as a walking *Dictionnaire des Idées Reçues* or, at the most daring, of ideas which are receivable by the world at large. To be brilliant, he has to be one move ahead of Bouvard and Pécuchet, but only one move. If the real powers in a society are those who get their ideas accepted by others, he is in no better case than the bus conductor or the barber, and his not inconsiderable wisdom, like theirs, comes from having had to listen to so many clients.

The official is of course not ordinarily conscious of the restrictions of his habits of thought, any more than is the member of a primitive tribe who none the less seems to the visiting anthropologist generally to be pounding around in a narrow circle. Moreover, Whitehall like the primitive tribe is an ordinary human society, in which accordingly almost anything can happen. The official assuredly does not feel tongue-tied, and the discussions that go on in these offices certainly show no unusual degree of respect for successful personages or received ideas. Indeed it might rather be said that the constant preoccupation with other people's ideas and importances produces an attitude of scepticism and irony, which is prevented from becoming dominant only by the constant and imperative need for action which must be in terms of publicly acceptable ideas. The relations between Ministers and Permanent Secretary, or of the member of a commission or committee with the principal who acts as its secretary, are not restricted by the constitutional limits. The decision, or the recommendation, is unequivocally the responsibility of the Minister or the committee, but all manner of things may have been said by the officials before they are arrived at. Clearly it is desirable that Ministers, and chairmen and members of committees, should be people both patient to listen to advice and firm in drawing their own conclusions. It is, however, also desirable that the officials nearest to them should be, not merely well-informed on the subject in hand but intelligent and willing to speak their minds. At any rate it is difficult to see any advantage to the public in these people being either stupid or timid, and no Minister or committee member worth his salt will be intimidated by some marks of ability. Of course those for whom any advice is bad if it come from an official are appalled at the risk that the political decision may be more exclusively the work of an official than it should be, and it is no part of the thesis of this book to pretend that the official should have his way against the proper authorities. On the other hand it can hardly be contended that it is a very great evil that the advice of officials who, by the nature of their job, are likely at least to be acquainted with the pitfalls surrounding a particular decision, should play a part in the making of that decision. The advice the official gives, if he finds even too ready a listener, is very unlikely to be merely a good idea of his own. He will have had too much experience of affairs to believe that an individual good idea is of much value in action.

His error is more likely to be relying too heavily on what Bridges calls the 'departmental philosophy', which is nothing else than the resultant of previous experience in the field in question.

The administrator is likely to remain sceptical of any general theory as to the source of the ideas which in the end determine his action. They seem to him to come from here and there, from one corner of the kingdom or another, from one group or organization or another. He deals with them as rising forces and not as ideas. If this holding the ring is ruling, no doubt he has a hand in it. If to rule is to generate the ideas, the vulgarizations of which turn the course of history, no doubt Shelley is in the right of it, and the rulers are not men in Whitehall, or even men who badger Whitehall but people who stay at home writing surprising sentences or drawing unexpected lines on paper.

A Note on the Monarchy

There is no danger of our forgetting that we live in a democracy. The fact is repeatedly mentioned, usually in the course of a reminder that the democracy we live in is one of a number. Moreover, it is usually supposed that the common elements by virtue of which the democracies constitute a nameable class are more important features of the governments concerned than are the elements by which they differ. Although every literate person must have had cause to doubt this in particular cases, the ordinary supposition so far has force that the patently undemocratic elements in these governments, and most of all in our own, are obscured. It is true that, in a democracy we suddenly have cause to dislike, the undemocratic elements will as suddenly walk abroad like skeletons from a cupboard. In the case of our own country, certain undemocratic elements are inescapably visible even to the most friendly eye; they have to be laughed off or explained away as 'survivals' (as if democracy itself were not that) enjoying, in comparison with the real works of government, only an inferior degree of reality. So the Trooping of the Colour must be regarded as a leg-show of Guardsmen, the crown as a bauble, and the Coronation itself as something for the illustrated papers.

It is a common state of mind to suppose that, in matters of government, the more obvious a thing is the less it is to be believed. Bagehot was of this mind. He was a publicist, and the dearest professional hypothesis of such people is: Things are not what they seem. The outward show, what you, poor fool, take to be real, is something they whip away to show you the cleverly constructed machinery behind. The typical publicist is like Berkeley's minute philosopher, putting a logomachy in place of the visible world. With such people, the very patency of the monarchy tells against its significance being recognized. Bagehot attributed importance to the monarchy, but it was an importance of an inferior kind. The Queen was 'dignified', in his phraseology: that meant she was not much good. She was for fools to goggle at. As there were a lot of fools, that counted for something. Indeed, Bagehot seems to have estimated the number of those who were not fools as being, in his day, not more than ten thousand. These read *The Economist* and formed a freemasonry of republicans.

Bagehot has had a prolonged success, so that one might be tempted to think that the Constitution, so sensitive to everything that is said about it, has adapted itself to him. At any rate we find Ivor Jennings, whose book *Cabinet Government* (2nd edn, 1951) is so sober that it might have appeared as a serial in *The Times*, saying without turning a hair that 'the existence or absence of a monarch does not in itself make a fundamental distinction in a Constitution'. This outbids Bagehot's statement that it is a 'fiction that ministers are, in any political sense, the Queen's servants'. Jennings can even say: 'The functions of the head of the state, be he King or President, are ancillary.' For Jennings, as for Bagehot, the cabinet is really the head as well as the guts of the commonwealth.

Observe that the place assigned to the monarch is a matter of theory. It is not directly dependent on the facts about the day-to-day exercise of her powers. We can accept what Jennings says on that point. He says, among other things, that in that matter Bagehot was wrong, and that the monarch may in fact have considerable influence on the decisions of the government. For all that, his view of monarchy is, in principle, the same as Bagehot's. The monarch is ancillary, she is not part of the main function of government. Bagehot and Jennings agree in this matter in spite of their differences as to the facts because such general conclusions are the children of faiths, valuations and pre-dispositions as much as of observation. Do not be deceived by Bagehot's boasting that he looks at the 'living reality' and not at the 'paper description'; that he is for 'rough practice' and not for 'the many refinements of literary theory'. All that is merely a flapping of the robes of the wizard and the diviner. It is a glimpse of the role Bagehot liked to think of himself in. The author of the biographical note prefaced to his *Literary Studies* says that 'it was a satisfaction to him to show that he understood the world far better than the world had ever understood him'.

Against Bagehot and Jennings we can set Clarendon, for although 1688 may have altered some practices of government (even if to a less extent than is sometimes supposed) it could not alter the principles. Clarendon says: 'Kings having still all the power remaining in them, that they have not themselves parted with, and released to their subjects, and their subjects having no pretence to more liberty or power than the King hath granted and given them' (*A Brief Survey of the Leviathan*, 1676). It is a weakness of writers on politics in our days that they have to pretend that what they write is pure observation. Clarendon's remark is pure theory. It contains an assertion or principle about the final source of power. What the kings have 'released to their subjects' is of course a variable matter of fact, but a variation, as between Clarendon's day and our own, in the quantity of what has been released, does not affect the principle. If we start with an unlimited power, whatever is given away something will remain. To quote an authority more likely to be tolerable to modern opinion than is the historian of the Rebellion, here is D. Lindsay Keir: The king's 'prerogative, however circumscribed by convention, must always retain its historic character as a residue of discretionary authority to be employed for the common good' (*The Constitutional History of Modern Britain 1485-1937*, 1946). The monarchic principle is not that the king should have all power, but that he is the legitimate source of all power.

Look at our present constitution by the candle of this principle. We shall deny Bagehot's assertion that it is a 'fiction' that 'ministers are, in any political sense, the Queen's servants'. We shall say, on the contrary, that the Queen rules through her Ministers, and that she does not rule any the less for that, just as Ministers are not the less Ministers because they exercise their functions in the main through officials. But the Queen, you will say, does not attend to the details of her country's administration. The Minister does not attend to the details of his Department's administration. It would be a true anachronism for him to do so. It would be a true anachronism for the Queen to express her preferences in the million and one topics that come before her government. The Minister has one inalienable function, which is to secure the coherence of his Department. The Queen has one inalienable function, which is to secure the coherence of her country. The Minister performs his function more by taking advice and bowing before facts than he does by giving advice and making facts bow before him. And so with the Queen. Her quiescence is the very principle of order. In the course of her duty of securing the coherence and continuity of her realm, the controversies which overturn parties are of no account. 'The Queen's service must be carried on', now this way, now that, to please the whim of party and populace, but that is only because, if those whims are not appeased, there will be disorder and the service will be broken or at an end. The Queen's duty perhaps demands any submission except what will break the realm.

In this scheme of things, the reins of authority meet in the Queen's hand. All the other authorities are subordinate and derivative from her. If the Commons unseat a Government, she takes other advisers because her duty is to govern in a manner that will be tolerated. Jennings makes much of what he calls a new principle. He says that a fundamental change came with the Reform Act. Before it, the government reposed in the Sovereign's confidence; afterwards, on the people's. There are historical refinements, evidently, in the position before the Reform Bills and after. But there never was a time when a Government had not to be tolerable if it was to endure. James II's popery made his power crumble under his feet. It is not the Reform Bills themselves, but the urbanization and literacy which produced them, which made it necessary latterly for the monarch to listen as attentively to the murmurings of the people as formerly to the growls of the nobility. It is the notorious complexity of a modern administration which has caused the monarch to 'release to his subjects' (in Clarendon's phrase) so many powers.

The maxim that the Queen's service must be carried on means, among other things, that it is of greatly more importance that there should be a government in England than that its complexion should be that of one or another party. It is of the nature of party politicians to exaggerate and exacerbate their differences. They present their policies, which are merely an aspect of things, as the thing itself. The thing itself is the great *res publica* whose continuance the Queen wills. She wills, all the time, all those laws which, by and with the advice of the Lords Spiritual and Temporal, and the Commons, she or her predecessors have enacted and have not repealed. She wills the continuance of all those rights she has protected without enactment. While she broods over this body of laws and institutions, and her servants daily perform the acts which constitute the life and continuance of that corpus, the party managers come along with their medicines and their scalpels to purge or trim some corner of it. The activity of the most fevered session of the House amounts to no more than that. Much is made of these adjustments, and much ought to be made; but more ought always to be made of the great work of time which is the subject of these meddlesome but necessary treatments.

It is recognized by all theorists of government that their problem is to find and define the executive, and it is recognized by Bagehot and Jennings that recent times are (to put it no higher) not marked by any weakening of the executive's powers. Bagehot and Jennings, however, have in effect chosen to place the head of the executive at an intermediate point in the chain of command. They have said virtually that the Cabinet is the beginning and end of government. They have done this partly, no doubt, out of a Whiggish or Progressive horror for the supreme though not for the penultimate heights. Partly, however, they are motivated by an inability to admit a principle of government to which the most exalted advices on our day-to-day affairs would be subordinate. They both have the publicist's touch, and for the publicist day-to-day affairs have a final dignity. Moreover, these matters are those which the popular will, whether of ten thousand or ten million, is supposed mainly to busy itself about and by which it is mainly evidenced. And the Cabinet, even if at a couple of removes, reflects what the people are supposed to think about these matters.

But if the recognition of the importance of the executive means anything at all, it means that the fact that the Cabinet reflects in some measure a popular will of some sort is the least important thing about it. The Cabinet is a government not because it is an outcome of certain electoral procedures but because it governs. It is a government not in so far as it obeys the people but in so far as it constrains them. What a government loses when it ceases to be regulated or modified by an electoral procedure is not the power to govern but a certain advisory force which tells it what the people will stand. It can go on governing, but henceforth it has to rely exclusively on other means of informing itself when the worm will turn. Politicians are apt to make something tragic out of the electoral procedures which may result in their losing their jobs. But an electorate which votes in such a way that an existing Cabinet is overthrown is not saying that it will not continue to be governed substantially according to the same laws as before. It is, in effect, not objecting to the things that in general are done, but in a greater or less measure to the way in which some of them are done. The Crown in short remains; the Constitution remains; the officials, who are the Queen's servants and not the politicians', raise their eyebrows and continue as before, only noting that certain emphases must be slightly changed – and in general Oh how slightly!

The constitutional developments of recent times, and still more the spread of literacy and the frequent allusions to acts of government in even the most widely circulated of the papers called news-papers, have obscured the fact that the so-called popular character of our modern governments is an historical accident. Popular institutions are – to use a word which Jennings misapplies to the head of the State – ancillary. It would be perfectly possible to govern England without Parliament or elections. At first there would be merely a prolongation of the administrative peace of the parliamentary recess. Then, when new legislation was required, it would take the form of Orders in Council. The Departments, carefully consulting the outside world, would produce the material for these enactments as they do for enactments of any kind. Ministers, appointed by the Crown at its own full choice or on the nomination of the Civil Service Commissioners or the Treasury, would come to their offices to decide important matters. Briefed by the officials, they would continue to explain things to the press, to their correspondents, and to those who came to see them in deputation. They would meet from time to time in committees, which would be the Cabinet and its committees. There would be a chief among them, who would be Prime Minister, and they would look through him to the head of the State who would give unity and continuity to their miscellaneous acts. Elections, and an elected House of Commons, do not produce a government. They merely modify it. They inform it with life and even with information, and it would be, in the strict sense, an imbecility for a government to dispense with these resources. None the less, a government conducted without them would be less ill-informed than is commonly imagined about the impact of its proposals. Even at present, with the extra-parliamentary consultations that take place, 'many wills', as Keir rightly says, 'mingle with that of Parliament in the making of a law.'

Plain words about the nature of government have always been offensive to the people and to all but the most intrepid of those whose career depends on being elected by them. Whatever Charles I may have meant by the phrase, there is a sense in which the assertion that government is 'nothing pertaining to' the people is not controversial but is a statement of inescapable principle. A government must be a compact body with a central point and capable of rational communication between its parts. It must be capable of acting as an entity on the larger body of society and compelling that larger body to act as an entity, but an entity more loosely knit than the government, and not necessarily with any rational communication between its parts, so that the government may divide and rule, cajoling one section of its society with one argument and another with another. It may of course try to persuade the governed that it is so responsive to their wishes that it is really hardly a government at all. But that is a kind of ballyhoo, practised, incidentally, with most thoroughness by governments like Hitler's or Stalin's, which enforce their wills most ruthlessly and in the most intimate departments of their subjects' lives. The essence of a government consists in being obeyed, and we learn this quickly enough if we refuse to pay our income tax or decline to present ourselves for military service. The part of the people, in contradistinction to that of the government, consists in obeying. Naturally the fact is not much advertised by politicians who are allowed to share in the governing only on the pretext that they represent us. Charles I, who was not interested in this aspect of the matter, could speak more freely, even if only at the price of his head.

The general horror with which the pure theory of government has always been regarded – well illustrated by the *succès de scandale* of Machiavelli – is by no means without foundation. It is obscurely felt that to talk too openly of these matters is likely to have an unfortunate effect on the way in which government is in fact conducted, just as it is felt that too public a recognition of our private lusts may end in an intolerable disorder. But just as it is salutary not to deceive ourselves about our sexual appetites it is salutary to remember that, politically, we live in a system of force modified, as the expression of our appetites is modified, by traditions as ancient as our race. It is, roughly speaking, the claim of political parties that they stand for this modification and not for the system of force that is modified. In our own Constitution, there is a certain truth in this. If the elected elements influence and inform a permanent executive rather than themselves constitute it, and influence and inform it in such a way as to render it more tolerable, they may plausibly claim to be on the side of civilization rather than of the naked appetite. None the less, in so far as they tend, through the necessities of the electoral system, to exaggerate their own benign influence and to conceal the extent to which the executive is not so much changed as given new force by their election, their influence is obscurantist. There is a tendency to contrast a wicked past, when terrible things were done behind the back of Parliament, with the present Golden Age in which, because actions of State are in general the subject of a vote in the House, nothing really wicked can be done. It is as if the executive had been touched for a sort of King's Evil by this formal contact with the public will. This way of looking at things is a little less than honest. As to the nature of what happens in Parliament, one must at least take into account such views as those of a very perspicacious observer who wrote: 'Members carry on a ceaseless mock debate with one another, inside and outside Parliament – a debate that has little relation to any of the real issues of the day, and all real political discussion is outside Parliament and between people who are not members. It is only the man who is not handicapped by the letters "M.P." after his name who is free to tell the truth about politics.'*

While the politician, by his insistence on his *representative* character, tends to obscure the fact of the separateness of government and people, he tends also, by suggesting that his is the only legitimate creative role in the State, to denigrate the State which exists independently of the politician's role. The orthodox theory may be said to be that the State, starting with the Queen at its head and descending to the humblest clerk behind a government counter, is neutral. In a certain limited connotation of the term, that is true, and is, moreover, an excellent thing. Neither the Queen nor her officials are to be associated with any political party; they work independently of all, because their functions demand that they take a view in which the most hotly-contested policies of parties can be see as parts of a longer perspective. But the neutrality of the Crown neither is nor should be absolute. An absolute neutrality would involve a policy of individual self-interest in which the State itself would quickly dissolve. A less absolute form of neutrality, such as is much more likely to develop, and may be said in some measure actually to have developed, would consist of making a religion of bowing before *force majeure*. The forces would be assumed always to be tolerable on the grounds that the permanent State must always look outside itself for its regulative force. This view of things has a certain charm, because it seems to promise a government responsive to the changes in society, and if a State is to endure it must show a large responsiveness. None the less, there are evident limits to the

* Christopher Hollis, M.P.: *Can Parliament Survive?* (*Everybody's Weekly*, 12 January 1952).

tolerance the State can properly exhibit. The most obvious limitation is that it cannot tolerate, to a point at which they become a real menace to its existence, suicidal tendencies in its society. It cannot tolerate treason. That will in general be readily conceded, and it may be said to fit into the logic of *force majeure* if one assumes (what may, however, be doubted) that treason can only be of the minority. But that is surely not all. Unless one maintains the right of an executive to exercise any bestiality on its subjects, it must not evade the responsibility of making a positive contribution to society. For all the horror of what is called ideological government, a government having no principle but self-preservation must surely, in the last analysis, be worse.

The limitations of the tolerance of the State are expressed primarily in the sovereign. There are no doubt persons who can recite the Oath of Allegiance and regard it merely as a form of words conveying a reality which they might not well explain but which they vaguely hope is more popular. None the less, any conception of treason as being something other than, in the last analysis, infidelity to the Queen, is bound to prove a form of evasion. The final safeguard of our unity is a point of unity in a single Person present on the throne by hereditary right and form of law. If we depart from that, we admit the legitimacy of faction. No doubt it is only in the most desperate troubles, such as we pray we shall be preserved from, that that Person would present herself to us so directly. But it is well that we should not allow sloppy ideas to obscure what would be our duty in such an emergency. We have in our generation seen in Europe such national divisions as can leave no doubt that it is not desirable that, in a final crisis, the choice of a guide should be left to our individual whims. What Keir calls the monarch's 'final responsibility for the national interest' can mean only, in the last desperate case to which no precedent is equal, that the Queen must be the judge of the fate of the nation. And if treason is not the only thing the State should decline to tolerate, other positive elements must find expression in the Queen as head of the executive, and in appropriate, more partial, forms in her various servants. No doubt, in the public mind, the conception of the Queen can contain no more than that mind contains. That is to say, the monarchy will be seen through the only explicit ideas that the largely secularized and press-fed populace has access to. But the sovereign of England is an Anglican, and only those ignorant of the superior force of a coherent and comprehensive body of ideas over an incoherent and partial, can suppose that this fact is without a national signficance which will end only with the monarchy. The Queen adheres to the only religion possible in the West, and to that form of it which is most surely embedded in our millennial English traditions.

The ultimately religious character of the monarchy is to many a matter of derision. We have Kingsley Martin sneering at the suggestion that the Coronation 'would in some way be rendered inefficacious if it were not exclusively solemnized by an Archbishop' (*The Magic of Monarchy*, 1937). Such persons should distinguish between their own incredulity and the nature of the thing. Their smiles are in imitation of Voltaire who, after all, lived before Frazer and even before Fustel de Coulanges. Do what we will, religion moves our secularised society as the appetites of sex move none the less the man or woman who denies them. If we deny our ancient motives, it is out of a will to frustrate ourselves and bring our country to ruin. The monarchy, perfectly adapted to the needs of a modern society, is so in part because it can draw its loyalty from the deepest well. So long as we have the Queen, her heirs and successors, England could remain conscious of herself and give play to her deepest energies even after the most appalling national catastrophes. If the mechanical civilization of the West should one day break down, and we can no longer ignore the possibility, that nation will most readily reassert itself which can immediately re-establish, around the indubitable leader to whom a thousand years of history point, a compact and simple administration.

IV

A TOUCH OF WHIGGERY

An Enlightened View of Government

The English Constitution (1867) is the work by which Walter Bagehot is best known; it is, so to speak, the reason for Bagehot. Without that he would have been in the memory of economists as the author of a clever book on the money market and in that of general readers who browse in the second-hand shops as an essayist sensitive up to a point. The idea of his greatness – of his being, even, 'the greatest Victorian', rests on this book, for such an idea must rest on something. It has had other than literary supports. Not only have a lot of people read *The English Constitution* but influential people have had cause to remember it. Most classics are put out of mind, by most men of affairs, but one that purports to explain their own activities will not be lost sight of. A book which insinuates, as this one continuously does, that these activities are incomparably important and to be criticized by no standards but those of the actors themselves, is sure to be dear to them. And the actors are now very numerous, including all those lesser figures, who as journalists, officials, commentators or academics somehow contrive to make a living out of the conduct of the *res publica*. Bagehot's book has also the advantage of being readable, which is unusual in this class of literature, once the flutter of contemporary interest has gone. It is at any rate unusual, as Balfour pointed out, that a constitutional treatise can be regarded as light reading. Bagehot's book is certainly that. It is light, like so much of Bagehot's writing, with the style of a man who is letting you into a secret, or revealing something perfectly obvious which you, poor fool, have missed. Bagehot is not a very well-bred writer, and the herd of knowing commentators we now suffer from have a real affinity with him.

Descriptions of the Constitution, as Bagehot himself remarked, may exercise an immense influence. If the description is erroneous – which Bagehot naturally thought was the case with other people's descriptions – people may begin to act as if they were true. And indeed it is the nature of the subject that it is not easy to establish what is a true description. If one confines oneself to the legal forms in a state, it will no doubt be possible to say something reasonably accurate. Bagehot's claim, however, is to describe a reality behind the forms, which indeed he makes very light of. The bare legal forms certainly give an inadequate notion of the mechanism. Any constitution is custom as well as the more explicit proprieties. And custom – it may be, all behaviour – involves ideas, those enemies in practical affairs which Bagehot so derided. It is not enough to say, as Bagehot does in the *Letters on the Coup d'Etat*, that 'rigorous reasoning would not manage a parish vestry, much less a great nation'. That is true, but it is not what is in question. Nor is it enough to speak of getting hold of 'some large principle' as if it were merely the habit of some deluded people like the French. The human mind will produce reasons – often very sketchy ones – for its actions, and those reasons will be related to its conception – necessarily even sketchier – of reality as a whole. There is not even much hope, except provisionally and in a narrow field, of restricting the notions in play to a few of the kind that are called positive, based on ascertainable and confirmable fact. That is rarely possible even in those statistically supported memoranda which are so much used in the conduct of business, public and private, and which often conceal more intentions than they reveal. In discussing something so radical as an inherited constitution – and even the newest constitution is based on inherited ideas – it is quite impossible. The whole body of our conceptions and preconceptions is involved. Bagehot conceived of his approach as being that of a reasonable man, and we know what an array of prejudices that figment may conceal. 'In discussing any Constitution,' he had said in looking at the one the French were currently giving themselves in 1851-2, 'there are two ideas first to be got rid of. The first is the idea of our barbarous ancestors – now happily banished from all civilised society but still prevailing,' he adds for the benefit of his liberal and Unitarian readers, 'in old manor-houses, rural parsonages, and other curious repositories of mouldering ignorance.' This is the notion that foreigners ought to have Kings, Lords and Commons like the rest of us. The second 'old idea' is 'that politics is simply a sub-division of immutable ethics'. Of this misconception Bagehot gives a curious and rather revealing illustration – the idea that you have no more right to deprive a Dyak of his vote in a 'possible Polynesian Parliament, than you have to steal his mat'. Politics was a field in which morals did not come into play, especially when all that was involved was the rights of

Polynesians, Frenchmen, or perhaps more generally, the non-banking classes. Bagehot's description of the English Constitution, when he came to that, did not lack the colouring of his own preconceptions.

Indeed the *Letters on the Coup d'Etat* form an excellent preface to *The English Constitution* because they reveal Bagehot's ideas so nakedly. His sympathy for Napoleon le Petit was not superficial. 'Of course you understand,' he says, again in the tone he adopted when he was intending to astonish the Unitarians, 'that I am not holding up Louis Napoleon as a complete standard of ethical scrupulosity or disinterested devotedness.' That is old Langport stuff, not to be regarded by a young man, however cautious, in Paris. But Louis Napoleon's 'whole nature is, and has been, absorbed in the task he has undertaken... he will coolly estimate his own position and that of France; he will observe all dangers and compute all chances'. He is indeed a man of business such as Thomas Bagehot would have approved. But of course he belongs to a wider world visible only to Walter – and to him, it might be said, only from a distance. How is a man like Louis Napoleon, 'by circumstances excluded from military and political life, and by birth from commercial pursuits, really and effectually to learn administration?' Not by reading Burke, Tacitus and Cicero. None of that old stuff! 'Yet take an analogous case. Suppose a man, shut out from trading life, is to qualify himself for the practical management of a counting-house. Do you fancy he will do it "by a judicious study of the principles of political economy" and by elaborately re-reading Adam Smith and John Mill?' The 'analogous case' was precisely Bagehot's own, and the fancy he rejected was exactly his own method of preparation. But in this little fantasy Bagehot pours scorn on such notions. 'He had better be at Newmarket, and devote his *heures perdues* to the Oaks and the St. Leger... Where too did Sir Robert Walpole learn business, or Charles Fox, or anybody in the eighteenth century?' His ideal is that of the speculator. The shadow of Victorian morality has passed, to reveal the sunny smile of the successful gambler, though in practice Bagehot always hedged his bets with some caution. It is with regard to the fortunes of the winning classes that Bagehot sets out to examine the working of politics.

The famous distinction between the dignified and efficient parts of government is made at the very outset of *The English Constitution*. The dignified parts are 'those which excite and preserve the reverence of the population' and the efficient parts are 'those by which it, in fact, works and rules. There are two... every constitution must first *gain* authority, and then *use* authority; it must first win the loyalty and confidence of mankind, and then employ that homage to the work of government.' It is like a bank, in fact. It took the barges on the Parrett, the local reputation of Samuel Stuckey, the enterprise and London connections of Vincent, and the grave face of Thomas Bagehot, to provide cover for the transactions on which Walter Bagehot flourished; others had to be dignified so that the author of *Lombard Street* could be clever. And it was the cleverness that mattered. Bagehot was always preaching the merits of stupidity, but he meant that smart-alecry could not survive without it. If there is contempt, in Bagehot, for the 'inferior people', there is an equal if more uneasy contempt for all that was above him. That is why his book has so been taken up by the managerial classes; it teaches admiration of themselves. Bagehot himself points out that the two parts he describes in the constitution are not 'separable with microscopic accuracy'. The Queen *could* be useful, when she was helping the managers; a cabinet might even be dignified, though this could not happen very often. The respect for the higher powers was not respect *for* anything. Indeed the only thing worth the respect of an intelligent man was what went on inside the counting-house, but the vulgar would not understand that – better for them that they should not, perhaps. And the efficient people were busied about being efficient; they were above being respected except so far as there was something to be got out of it. So loyalty had to find another peg, which would be no more than a peg. It was no more than a confidence trick, managed in the end by the banks. The matter was not put as plainly as that. We have to wait for *The Monarchy*; Chapter I, in the original edition, is *The Cabinet*.

Another preliminary sophism stands at the beginning of *The English Constitution*. This is that there are classes of society which correspond respectively to the states of development characteristic of various ages of history. 'We have in a great community like England,' Bagehot says, 'crowds of people scarcely more civilised than the majority of two thousand years ago; we have others, even more numerous, such as the best people were a thousand years since.' He is wary of identifying these groups too precisely with the social classes which were usually recognized. It is certain that his highest group is not meant to correspond

with the highest social classes, though it is a well-placed group
he has in mind. 'The lower orders, the middle orders, are still,
when tried by what is the standard of the educated "ten thousand", narrow-minded, unintelligent, incurious.' This is the
sceptical *élite* who are at the core of Bagehot's social theory. The
rest of the population are more or less contemptible. When
Bagehot invites the reader to test his theory, it is with a remarkably narrow reference. While a member of the landowning or of
the manufacturing classes might have suggested looking at the
farmers and farm-labourers, or at the foremen and mill-hands,
the banker's son can think only of going into the kitchen. 'Those
who doubt should go out into their kitchens. Let an accomplished
man try what seems to him most obvious, most certain, most
palpable in intellectual matters, upon the housemaid and the footman, and he will find that what he says seems unintelligible,
confused, and erroneous – that his audience think him mad and
wild.' One can imagine the servants at Herd's Hill: 'Mr. Walter .
do say some things.' His is not the voice of the country gentleman, speaking with respect of some special knowledge or skill
among his retainers. The things he said were evidently not of
the kind which struck his less sophisticated listeners as being on
the bottom of reality. He was convinced of his superiority; he
was less sure about what the lower classes had to offer. His social
class, indeed, represents the beginning of the disjunction of management from which industry so notably suffers in our day.
Bagehot was thorough-going about his theory of the retarded
classes. 'Great communities are like great mountains – they have
in them the primary, secondary, and tertiary strate of human
progress; the characteristics of the lower regions resemble the
life of old times rather than the present life of the higher regions.'
A certain time-lag in the diffusion of habits is, certainly, characteristic of the old, agricultural, society. But Bagehot's theory of
the co-existence, in different classes, of the *mores* of different
historical epochs goes much further than that. He is quite sure
that all that does not belong to banking is appropriate to a more
primitive age. 'The ruder sort of men – that is, men at *one* stage
of rudeness – will sacrifice all they hope for, all they have, *themselves*, for what is called an idea – for some attraction which seems
to transcend reality, which aspires to elevate men by an interest
higher, deeper, wider than that of ordinary life.' It is for this
gullibility that the dignified parts of the constitution are designed,
or at least preserved. One could hardly have a more complete

identification of the dignitaries with religion and the ancestral voices, or a more complete dismissal of all such things as 'adjusted to the lowest orders – those likely to care least and judge worse about what *is* useful'. The old dignitaries are, however, not entirely without relevance to the conduct of the better sort of men. Luckily such people are not inventive all the time, and the traditional parts of the constitution so to speak keep them together while they make their money. But the sole merit of the 'historical, complex, august, theatrical parts' of the constitution, 'which it has inherited from a long past' is that it 'takes' the multitude, and the ten thousand intelligent people benignly go along with it. It is not only the ancient and dignified that 'takes' people and carries them along, however. The novel and undignified, of which Bagehot was the advocate, have an attraction scarcely less, and when, as in our day, the accepted ideas are those which lay claim to novelty and modernity, the 'carrying along' of people at large becomes a torrent. It is certainly not liberal ideas which lack apologists, in our day. Nor does anyone need to defend Bagehot's famous distinction between the 'dignified' and 'efficient' parts of government. It is regarded as self-evident, the truth itself. 'We have in England an elective first magistrate as truly as the Americans have an elective first magistrate. The Queen is only at the head of the dignified part of the constitution. The prime minister is at the head of the efficient part.' This is doctrine children take in with their mother's milk. It is a new separation of powers, only one of the two is not a power at all, but a sort of consumer luxury. Bagehot of course would not admit that. For him the merit of the monarchy is 'that it is an intelligible government. The mass of mankind understand it, and they hardly anywhere in the world understand any other.' It could hardly be said, however, in Bagehot's day, any more than in our own, that the idea of a committee – a cabinet – deciding things was beyond the understanding of a country which had watched the French Revolution and had itself had, more than two hundred years before, a Long Parliament, and Standing Committees in every county expropriating and otherwise putting down all who inclined too much to the King's cause or indeed tried to use the Prayer Book. Bagehot did his best to make the notion of 'efficient' government sound difficult. Of course the details of any government will be boring and comparatively difficult but this has really nothing to do with the question whether people have wit enough to understand that the Queen is unimportant, and the cabinet important. 'The nature of a constitution, the action of an assembly, the play of parties, the unseen formation of a guiding opinion, are complex facts, difficult to know, and easy to make. But the action of a single will, the fiat of a single mind, are easy ideas: anybody can make them out, and no one can ever forget them. When you put before the mass of mankind the question, "Will you be governed by a king, or will you be governed by a constitution?" the inquiry comes out thus – "Will you be governed in a way you understand, or will you be governed in a way you do not understand?"' Bagehot makes it sound very pat, but the illustration that follows shows the absurdity of what he was saying. 'The issue was put to the French people; they were asked, "Will you be governed by Louis Napoleon, or will you be governed by an assembly?" The French people said, "We will be governed by the one man we can imagine, and not by the many people we cannot imagine."' But in fact not so many years before they had beheaded 'the one man they could imagine' and run through a series of democratic devices until they settled on Napoleon I, not because they found assemblies unintelligible but because Napoleon had settled on *them* and because he was *efficient*, in the way the assemblies were not, as well as having, perhaps, his own style of dignity. Indeed the notion of separating the efficient and dignified parts of government is very corrosive. It is a way of discrediting part of the apparatus, and when people seek to discredit a bit of the machinery of government one should ask who they are and what they design to put in its place. There should be no doubt that, so far as the monarchy is concerned, Bagehot's book is intentionally subversive, and that, so far as his description of it is correct, he is describing a decayed polity.

The insistence, in *The English Constitution*, that the monarchy is merely a trick which clever men of affairs play off against the common people, is repeated. It is a symptom of Bagehot's contempt for those below him as well as for any who might be presumed to be above him. He is the middle-class man who *looks after himself*; he had not even children to deflect him from his complacent self-admiration, or to spill his resources. The 'labourers of Somerset' have a special disapproval reserved for them. Their sincerity when they touched their fore-locks was perhaps not all that he might hope for and even the pre-1867 voters of Bridgwater – themselves an *élite* – had refused to return him to Parliament. The Greek legislator, fortunate enough to have 'slaves to keep down by terrors', 'had not to deal with a community in which primitive barbarism lay as a recognised basis to acquired civilisation. *We have,*' he said, 'We have whole classes unable to comprehend the idea of a constitution – unable to feel the least attachment to impersonal laws.' There is a prim shockedness about this, a horror of this race which knows about hedging and rabbitting and cider but does not care about the clever gentlemen who read the *Economist*. Yet Bagehot certainly did not wish to rouse these people to any too acute sense of their political rights and he was against any reckless extension of the franchise, which might lead to the banking classes being under-represented, as he thought. The stupidity of the helots was really Bagehot's excuse for the monarchy. 'So long as the human heart is strong and the reason weak, royalty will be strong because it appeals to diffused feeling, and Republics weak because they appeal to the understanding.' *Mutatis mutandis*, this might be an extract from one of the Sunday sermons preached by Thomas Bagehot in the drawing-room at Herd's Hill, on the rationality of Unitarianism and the mysteries practised in the church on the hill opposite.

Bagehot indeed goes on from these generalities to discuss the relationship of the monarchy with religion in a manner which shows little sympathy with either. What he gives us is a rather shoddy version of Whig history. A superstition of sanctity, holding up the march of constitutional progress, is all that remains of the other side of the argument. 'In former times, when our constitution was incomplete' – this 'incomplete' must have been inadvertent from one who believed that his subject was 'in constant change' – 'this notion of local holiness in one part' of the constitution, namely in the Crown, 'was mischievous. All parts were struggling, and it was necessary' – there is another kind of mystification here, that of the Progressive – 'that each should have its full growth. But superstition said that one should grow where it would, and no other part should grow without its leave. The whole cavalier party said it was their duty to obey the king, whatever the king did. There was to be "passive obedience" to him, and there was no religious obedience due to anyone else. He was the "Lord's anointed", and no one else had been anointed at all.' How unfair that was! 'The Parliament, the laws, the press were human institutions; but the monarchy was a Divine institution. An undue advantage was given to a part of the constitution, and therefore the progress of the whole was stayed.' It is remarkable how much is jettisoned, in this argument. It is not only the comedy of Bagehot's regret that the press, which after all had at this time hardly been invested with its later beatitude, had not been 'anointed' as the King in fact had been. The solid, one might say incontestable, legal argument that the 'parliament' had no authority to legislate without the king, and that the 'laws' were in fact not laws without him, is thrown aside. This is indeed the crux of Bagehot's method of description. There is no objective, legal situation to be explored. That sort of reasoning, which might allow of legitimate differences of opinion and even of rational solutions, is discarded. The great, objective *res publica* is pushed aside to enable the critic to start from his own prejudices. The 'diffused feeling' of the traditional Whig is where Bagehot starts from, and the pretensions of law and religion are ignored because 'they appeal to the understanding'.

Bagehot follows the Whig course of history in some detail, making great fun of the fact that the legitimate succession was deflected, to a greater or less extent, in William III, in Anne, and the Georges. It was as if all this had not been argued out, in principle, by Sir Robert Filmer and his critics. It is still supposed, in some quarters, to be extremely funny that Filmer derived all monarchy from Adam. He was not, however, such a fool as is sometimes made out. It is evident enough that crowns and thrones have been upturned, and that this did not happen for the first time in English history with William III. There is a vestige of the patriarchal notion in monarchy, and that our political notions should have a link with our more intimate psychology is not necessarily absurd. 'A *family* on the throne is an interesting idea also', as Bagehot said. For him it was interesting because 'it brings down the pride of sovereignty to the level of petty life'. Another way of saying this would be that it ties monarchy to something more interesting, for the mass of mankind, than the doings of politicians and the leaders in the *Economist*. Bagehot is determined in his rejection of anything which resembles an incarnation. He is so highly evolved, in the direction of economics and banking, that certain modes of thought escape him altogether. 'The nation is divided into parties, but the Crown is of no party. Its apparent separation from business is that which removes it both from enmities and from desecration, which preserves its mystery, which enables it to combine the affection of conflicting parties – to be a visible symbol of unity to those still so imperfectly educated as to need a symbol.' This idea that superior men think wholly in abstractions – symptomatic of the turn of mind which accounts for the drift, in Bagehot's career as a writer, away from literature and towards business – is connected with his emphatic disjunction from the primitive, and more generally from everything which does not bear the mark of urban, and preferably banking, civilization. The artist, and indeed the orthodox Christian, cannot fail to find in himself a kinship with primitive peoples, or to regard the accidents of the last few thousand years as making small difference in the essential nature of man. Faced with the caveman's drawings, or the crafts of some tribe surviving from the Stone Age, his attitude will be one of awed deference. Not so with Bagehot. 'If we look back to the early ages of mankind, such as we seem in the faint distance to see them – if we call up the image of those dismal tribes in lake villages, or on wretched beaches – scarcely equal to the commonest material needs, cutting down trees slowly and painfully with stone tools, hardly resisting the attack of huge, fierce animals – without culture, without leisure, without poetry, almost without thought' – he might have said, without drawing-rooms – 'destitute of morality, with only a sort of magic for religion; and if we compare that imagined life with the actual life of Europe now, we are overwhelmed at the wide contrast – we can scarcely conceive ourselves to be of the same race as those in the far distance.'

It is only after a whole chapter on the dignity of the Queen that Bagehot turns to the work she actually does. At the outset of this part of his study he exposes 'two errors' in 'the popular theory of the English Constitution'. The first is that the sovereign is 'an "Estate of the Realm", a separate co-ordinate authority with the House of Lords and the House of Commons'. In the tone of supercilious patronage which is really Bagehot's main contribution to the theory of the monarchy, he says that the Queen 'must sign her own death-warrant if the two Houses unanimously send it up to her'.

It is to be doubted whether the Whiggery of the English at large even now goes as far as that. Bagehot's argument is, of course, that because the Royal Assent to parliamentary bills is automatic, the idea that she has any legislative power belongs to the past. But this is not so. Acts of Parliament are still, without doubt, acts of the Queen in Parliament. With the complexity of modern government, and its dependence on consultation and opinion, it would obviously be folly for her to press her opinion, on a particular measure, and an attempt to do so, in normal circumstances, would lead immediately to a constitutional crisis which the ruling party of the day would almost certainly win. Consider, however, the situation which might occur in war and might indeed, had things gone worse for us, well have occurred in the war of 1939–45, in which rival 'governments' are established. There could be no doubt that the legitimate government would be the one whose advice the Queen took. It is equally certain that so-called Acts of Parliament made without her assent would have no more force than opinion cared to attribute to them. They would certainly not be the law of the land. Nor, at any other time, would a piece of paper which had not, in due form, received the Royal Assent, be an Act of Parliament which could be recognized in the courts. In asserting baldly that the Queen has no legislative power Bagehot is 'trying what seems to him most obvious, most certain, and most palpable in intellectual matters, upon the housemaid and the footman'. One may be unpersuaded as they seem to have been at Herd's Hill.

The second 'error' which Bagehot exposes is 'that the Queen is the executive'. He is afraid that people may not have noticed the Prime Minister. It is evident that the Queen is not the equivalent of the American president – a point on which he finds it necessary to insist – and that many of the functions of the latter are analogous to those performed by our Prime Minister. The Queen is a passive head; she is also a permanent one. The Prime Minister is active and impermanent; his impermanence is the price of his activity. Bagehot is right in saying that 'in most cases the greatest wisdom of a constitutional king would show itself in well considered inaction'. In the complexity of a modern administration it could hardly be otherwise, and what is called a decision, at any level in any organization, is more often than not nothing but a recognition of the facts. Bagehot cannot concede the good sense of Queen Victoria and Prince Albert without some gratuitous remarks about the abilities and education of princes. It is evident that no hereditary system can guarantee a succession of outstanding men, and that any such system should be so devised to make allowances for this. Bagehot however feels bound to assert not only that 'the education of a prince can be but a poor education' but even that 'a royal family will generally have less ability than other families'.

Once more one feels on the side of the footman who thought his talk 'mad and wild'. In spite of the disparagements he utters, Bagehot goes on to say that he thinks 'it may be shown that the post of sovereign over an intelligent and political people under a constitutional monarchy is the post which a wise man would choose above any other'. One cannot but feel that he has his eye on the job. It is thwarting – and many editors seem to feel it – to go on year after year commenting on public affairs without being sure anyone is listening to you. The English people, we have seen, were in Bagehot's view far from being wholly 'intelligent and political'. They were not all fitted to read the *Economist*, by a long way. The job of a constitutional monarch in this country could not therefore be all agreeable discussion, like theology. It was, however, the job in which the wise man – and certainly Bagehot is thinking of himself – 'would find the intellectual impulses best stimulated and the worst intellectual impulses best controlled'.

Bagehot's evident inclination – if only his circumstances had been more favourable – towards seeking a post as a constitutional monarch, and more particularly the reasons he gives for his choice, are eminently characteristic of him. He was a man who liked to amuse himself, in a prudent way. He does not think of a job in terms of what he could produce in it; he is a member of the banking and not of the producing classes. He is a dilettante and not an artist or a man of action. He thinks of the job in subjective terms. He would be king in order to enjoy a flutter of intellectual impulses, rather as Walter Pater fancied getting a little 'high' on the drugs of art. His 'best' intellectual impulses were to be stimulated; there is no direct indication which they were, but one may guess from the indications he gives about the 'worst'. The worst were those which would be checked by a knowledgeable Prime Minister who had done the work and knew the facts, and so prevent King Walter making a fool of himself. Perhaps this distinction carries some recollection of occasions when his exuberance as a leader-writer had got ahead of the facts, and he had felt a little foolish afterwards. It would certainly be a bad impulse that made a fool of Walter Bagehot.

'To state the matter shortly,' Bagehot goes on, 'the sovereign has, under a constitutional monarchy such as ours, three rights – the right to be consulted, the right to encourage, the right to warn. And a king of great sense and sagacity' – this is Bagehot himself, and this is why he changes the sex of the sovereign – 'would want no others. He would find that his having no others would enable him to use these with singular effect. He would say to his minister: "The responsibility of these measures is upon you. Whatever you think best must be done. Whatever you think best shall have my full and effectual support. *But* you will observe that for this reason and that reason what you propose is bad; for this reason and that reason what you do not propose is better. I do not oppose, it is my duty not to oppose; but observe that I *warn*." Supposing the king to be right, and to have what kings often have' – a slip-up surely this, for he is talking of a poorly-educated class, from families with less ability than other families – 'the gift of effectual expression, he could not help moving his minister. He might not always turn his course, but he would always trouble his mind.' This is, no doubt, to some extent, the voice of experience. Bagehot, in a state of semi-detachment from the bank in order to pursue his journalistic interests, must often have treated his trembling managers to much this sort of discourse, *mutatis mutandis*. He goes on to liken the position of the constitutional monarch – and there is some truth in the comparison – to that of the permanent official who can warn and advise his minister from long-standing knowledge. He also points out the difference. The minister is the permanent official's superior – and no one who has watched the process would be disposed to deny that the relationship often deflects the course of the advice, in an official at once weak and ambitious – while in the sovereign the minister has 'to answer the arguments of a superior to whom he has himself to be respectful'. There is nothing except the ordinary politenesses of conversation, and the need for tact in handling his man, to induce the sovereign to conceal his opinions. Bagehot fairly comments that permanence gives the king 'the opportunity of acquiring a consecutive knowledge of complex transactions, but it gives only an opportunity. The king must use it. There is no royal road to political affairs: their detail is vast, disagreeable, complicated and miscellaneous. A king, to be the equal of his ministers in discussion, must work as they work; he must be a man of business as they are men of business . . . An ordinary idle king on a constitutional throne will leave no mark on his time; he will do little good and as little harm.' Rather less fairly or at least less certainly, Bagehot follows this comment with another '*corruptio optimi pessima*. The most evil case of the royal form is far worse than the most evil case of the unroyal.' The evil case is of the meddling or corrupt constitutional monarch. But the worst case of the non-royal form is probably something different in kind – the passions roused by popular selection and the uncertainty of the succession from which monarchy is a protection. When he goes on to discuss the House of Lords, Bagehot reverts to the notion of *dignity* of which he had made so much in relation to the Crown, and of which in his day peers still had some. Once more he deplores the 'incredibly weak' fancy of the mass of men, which needs a visible symbol, and what he says has perhaps a touch of personal recollection about it. 'A common clever man' – though Bagehot was certainly never exactly that – 'who goes into a country place will get no reverence; but the "old squire" will get reverence.' There is surely a touch of personal indignation here. Though Mr Bagehot's clever son got some respect, no doubt he will have had less than the stupid landowners. 'Even after he is insolvent', he goes on revealingly, 'when everyone knows his ruin is but a question of time' – when the bank is going to close on him, in short – 'he will get five times as much respect from the peasantry as the newly-made rich man who sits beside him.' Really it is most unfair. Ah, the 'coarse, dull, contracted multitude, who could neither appreciate or perceive any other' form of distinction, and did not care whether the bank got its money. But the banker is, after all, just as visible to the simple clown, or to anyone else, as the genuine squire, so that it cannot be visibility alone that determines who is taken as a symbol by the populace.

Bagehot has, however, some sobering things to say about the use of a nobility – in his day, for in ours of course family is something to apologize for. A nobility 'prevents the rule of wealth' – for Bagehot is far too subtle to recommend that. The merely rich had to defer to traditional society. 'As the world has gone, manner has been half-hereditary in certain castes, and manner is one of the fine arts. It is the *style* of society; it is in the daily-spoken intercourse of human beings what the art of literary expression is in their occasional written intercourse.' One is almost in the world of Madame de Sévigné. 'In reverencing wealth we reverence not a man, but an appendix to a man; in reverencing inherited nobility, we reverence the probable possession of a great faculty – the faculty of bringing out what is in one.' The tone is striking, after the incivilities to the Royal Family. It may be that Bagehot, on the fringes of public life, was prepared to be benevolent to the aristocracy for the sake of being preserved from the 'third idolatry'. This was perhaps the 'worst of any', the idolatry of office. 'In France and all the best of the Continent it rules like a superstition. It is to no purpose that you prove that the pay of petty officials is smaller than mercantile pay; that their work is more monotonous than mercantile work; that their mind is less useful and their life more tame. They are still thought to be greater and better. They are *décorés*, they have a little red on the left breast of their coat, and no argument will answer that. In England, by the odd course of our society, what a theorist would desire has in fact turned up. The great offices, whether permanent or parliamentary, which require mind now give social prestige, and almost only those. An Under Secretary of State with £2,000 a year is a much greater man than the director of a finance company with £5,000, and the country saves the difference. But except a few offices like the Treasury, which were once filled with aristocratic people' – and with which Bagehot had a sort of connection through his father-in-law, James Wilson, as well as, more remotely, through the early activities of his uncle Vincent Stuckey – 'and have the odour of nobility at second-hand, minor place is of no social use.' Bagehot had not attained office himself and he was glad to have the nobility to keep down the pride of those who were in office.

A good deal that Bagehot has to say about the working of the House of Lords was applicable in his day but is not in ours, for the House of Lords, that most fashionable of institutions, is always changing. It is of general interest that he remarks that, even when the authority of the peerage was at its height – which was of course before Bagehot's day – the House 'was a second-rate force'. This was because greatness of rank could not guarantee proficiency in the business of the House, and those who were proficient naturally took the lead. Before the Reform Act, however, the peers, with so much influence in the country, were able powerfully to influence the House of Commons, so that there were never two antagonistic chambers.

Nobody now supposes that it would do to have the two at odds. If the Lords in 1832 gave way because of the threat to create new peers, the House of Lords now has been so bludgeoned with threats of reform that it is in no doubt at all that its best defence against the more stupid of them is a reasonable concurrence with the House of Commons. As Bagehot says: 'With a perfect Lower House it is certain that an Upper House would be scarcely of any value. If we had an ideal House of Commons perfectly representing the nation, always moderate, never passionate, abounding in men of leisure, never omitting the slow and steady forms necessary for good consideration, it is certain that we should not need a higher chamber.' It is far from certain that we are even now in that happy position.

As to what might be meant by representing the nation, Bagehot's ideas are not ours. He was writing before the Reform Act of 1867 when, according to Coventry Patmore, 'the false English Nobles and their Jew' were 'by God demented' (*Poems*, vol.II, 1886) to the extent that they extended the franchise in the boroughs even to working-class householders. Bagehot was in favour of the erosion of the power of the Crown and of the land-owning nobility; he was not so extreme as to wish to see a similar fate overtake the banking classes. He saw that, in 1872, when he wrote the preface to the second edition of *The English Constitution*, it was still too soon 'to attempt to estimate the effect' of the 1867 Act, because the 'people enfranchised did not yet know their own power'. The difficulty of a long foresight did not prevent him, when he was writing his book in 1865-6, confidently foretelling the doom which various schemes of electoral reform then current would bring. 'The scheme to which the arguments of our demagogues distinctly tend, and the scheme to which the predilections of some most eminent philosophers cleave... would not only make parliamentary government work ill, but they would prevent it working at all; they would not render it bad, for they would make it impossible.' The scheme favoured by the demagogues, 'the ultra-democratic theory', proposed nothing less than 'that every man of twenty-one years of age (if not every woman, too) should have an equal vote in electing Parliament'. Under this preposterous arrangement, 'the rich and wise' were 'not to have, by explicit law, more votes than the poor and stupid'. It is, certainly, very stupid to be poor and Bagehot, who had taken precautions enough, seems to have had a strong conviction that there is a close association between wisdom and riches. The second scheme, favoured by the philosophers (Mill is meant by this plural designation) was a form of proportional representation. It was an objection to a Parliament elected on manhood suffrage under the 'ultra-democratic scheme' that it 'could not be composed of moderate men' and if there were equal electoral districts, 'the scattered small towns which now send so many members to Parliament, would be lost in the clownish mass', that is to say, would be swamped by the agricultural interest. Langport itself, as Bagehot liked to recount, had petitioned in the Middle Ages to be spared the expense of sending a member to Parliament. The objection to the philosophers' scheme is more interesting. It is that it would lead to 'the return of party men mainly'. This, to Bagehot, was highly objectionable. 'You would get together a set of members bound hard and fast with party bands and fetters, infinitely tighter than any members now.' The voters would keep altogether too close a grip. 'The members,' he says, 'will be like the minister of a dissenting congregation. That congregation is collected by a unity of sentiment in doctrine A, and the preacher is to preach doctrine A; if he does not, he is dismissed. At present a member is free because the constituency is not in earnest: no constituency has an acute, accurate doctrinal creed in politics.' Geography is a better basis for representation than principle. Against our sort of democracy Bagehot saw no protection except the monarchy, or rather the illusions which monarchy could produce in ignorant persons who had not read *The English Constitution*. 'The mass of uneducated men could not now in England be told "go to, choose your rulers,"; they would go wild; their imaginations would fancy unreal dangers, and the attempt at election would issue in some forcible usurpation. The incalculable advantage of august institutions in a free state is, that they prevent this collapse.' But 'if you once permit the ignorant class to begin to rule you may bid farewell to deference for ever. Their demagogues will inculcate, their newspapers will recount, that the rule of the existing dynasty (the people) is better than the rule of the fallen dynasty (the aristocracy). A people very rarely hears two sides of a subject in which it is much interested; the popular organs take up the side which is acceptable, and none but the popular organs in fact reach the people. A people *never* hears censure of itself. No one will ever tell it that the educated minority whom it dethroned governed better or more wisely than it governs. A democracy will never, save after an awful catastrophe, return what has once been conceded to it, for to do so would be to admit an inferiority in itself, of which, except by some almost unbearable misfortune, it could never be convinced.'

With *Physics and Politics* Bagehot moved on to the sort of essay in modern thought which such a man was sure to attempt some time. The first part appeared in the *Fortnightly* in 1867, though the book did not come out until 1872. The sub-title is *Thoughts on the Application of the Principles of 'Natural Selection' and 'Inheritance' to Political Society*. It starts with the sort of invocation which has since become the stock-in-trade of popularizers: 'One peculiarity of this age is the sudden acquisition of much physical knowledge. There is scarcely a department of science or art which is the same, or at all the same, as it was fifty years ago. A new world of inventions.' But it was, of course, Darwin above all on whom he was drawing for his new excitement. 'The problem is, why do men progress? And the answer suggested seems to be that they progress when they have a certain sufficient amount of variability in their nature.' 'We need not take account,' he says elsewhere, a trifle exuberantly, 'of the mistaken ideas of unfit men and beaten races.' The sentence shows how limiting, as well as liberating, may be the sudden sideways waft of the latest ideas from one science into another, or into a study which hopes to become another. With a flourish of Huxley's *Elementary Physiology* and Maudsley's *Physiology and Pathology of the Mind*, Bagehot lays down the dubious but to him clear proposition 'that there is a tendency, a probability, greater or less according to circumstances, but always considerable, that the descendants of cultivated parents will have, by born nervous organisation, a greater aptitude for cultivation than the descendants of such as are not cultivated; and that this tendency augments, in some enhanced ratio, for many generations.' There is science for you. The book had a great success, but is very slight.

Taking his grand scientific look around the peoples of the earth, Bagehot sees war as making them into nations, customary law drilling them until they became genuine 'co-operative groups' and finally, in a few favoured cases, the 'age of discussion' liberating them and making progress possible. It is the modern world's view of itself. The servants and the peasants have dropped from view. It may be thought that something else has dropped too. A 'progressive' view of society can hardly fail to place emphasis on the differences between one age and another to the point at which the similarities are almost lost from view. It is true that Bagehot says, in his most generalizing vein, that 'unless you can make a strong co-operative bond, your society will be conquered and killed out by some other society which has such a bond' and that co-operation 'depends on a *felt union* of heart and spirit; and this is only felt when there is a great degree of real likeness in mind and feeling', but he is thinking mainly of an earlier stage than that of the fully industrial society. He is thinking of the stage at which societies are formed by 'the most terrible tyrannies ever known among men – the authority of "customary law".' And he notes that this process goes on 'far away from all distraction'. 'All great nations have been prepared in privacy and in secret.'

So it was with Greece, Rome, Judaea, which 'were framed each by itself, and the antipathy of each to men of different race and different speech is one of their most marked peculiarities'. In this horrible condition 'trade is bad because it prevents the separation of nations'. Bagehot hardly faced the implications of this for modern societies. Does it mean that, despite all 'progress', they are in inevitable decay? Perhaps he found a consolation, cynical enough, in the passion all societies have for uniformity. 'A new *model* of character is created for the nation; those characters which resemble it are encouraged and multiplied; those contrasted with it are persecuted and made fewer. In a generation or two, the look of the nation becomes quite different.' Those distressing squires and peasants give place to the more enlightened characters on Herd's Hill. 'A lazy nation may be changed into an industrious, a rich into a poor, a religious into a profane, as if by magic, if any single cause, though slight, or any combination of causes, however subtle, is strong enough to change the favourite and detested types of character.' But if he applied this to contemporary industrial societies, he certainly failed to show how this ever-renascent conservatism could prevent them from sinking rapidly into the 'mummy-like' condition he scorned in societies still subject to customary law. 'It was "government by discussion" which broke the bond of ages and set free the originality of mankind.' But there can be no doubt that such discussion tends to be conducted within a circle of prejudice which is itself limiting. Bagehot himself had, in *The English Constitution*, something to say about the unwillingness of democracy to hear any ill of itself. In his delight at the passing of an order which demanded a certain subordination of himself he forgot this. 'Once effectually submit a subject to that ordeal' – discussion – 'and you can never withdraw it again; you can never clothe it with mystery, or fence it by consecration; it remains forever open to free choice and exposed to profane deliberation.' It does not, however, and the question remains what is to be a mystery, and what is the nature of the consecration.

Bagehot of course had answered that question. He had chosen one of 'the better religions' which 'have a great physical advantage'. Truncating a problem which he could not solve, as he said, adopting a phrase of Sir William Hamilton, he opted for 'verifiable progress', 'that is, progress which ninety-nine hundredths or more of mankind will admit to be such, against which there is no established or organised opposition creed, and the objectors to which, essentially varying in opinion among themselves, and believing one thing and another the reverse, may be safely and altogether rejected'. Obviously opponents of that model were to be 'persecuted and made fewer' without mercy, so far as Bagehot was concerned. The model was provided by 'the plainer and agreed-on superiorities of the Englishman' as he then was. It was 'the development of human comfort'. With such a religion, many fripperies could be put aside.

The Art of Money

Having misdirected his youth towards the study of literature, for which he had no talent, and then towards the study of politics, to which he made a destructive contribution, Bagehot turned in his later years to wholly serious matters. *Lombard Street*, begun in 1870 and finished in 1873, is a paean in praise of money. We have the authority of Keynes for saying that, as a contribution to economics, it is of no great account. Keynes noted that it was one book which, at the time he was writing [1915], every economics student could be counted on to have read; he attributed this distinction to the desire of teachers of economics to conceal from the young student the fact that the subject was, in reality, not so amusing as Bagehot made it out to be. Bagehot did not, however, pretend that his book was a work of theory. Indeed, he went out of his way to emphasize that it was a description of concrete realities, and that is why he gave it a local instead of an abstract title. It was a study of the men who made money in the city, written by one who had a close acquaintance with many of those who dominated that scene, and who was by heredity as well as experience in the heart of the money trade.

Bagehot was writing in the great bulge of Victorian prosperity, and was conscious of these advantages, if that is what they were. His tone is that of a man showing off his plush furniture for the benefit of less fortunate people. 'Everyone is aware,' he says, 'that England is the greatest moneyed country in the world; every one admits that it has much more immediately disposable and ready cash than any other country. But very few persons are aware *how much* greater the ready balance – the floating fund which can be lent to any one or for any purpose – is in England than it is anywhere else in the world.' Money was economic power, and Bagehot never asked the critical question as to whether this unprecedented concentration was a good thing, or whether it was a proper use of the dignified parts of government, about which he had written so cynically in *The English Constitution*, to act as a screen for the *sub-rosa* activities of bankers.

199

There is an almost childish lack of moderation about Bagehot's approach to his subject. In what he blithely called 'the non-banking countries', including Germany and France, there was more cash out of the banks than there was in England. But the French people, notoriously, would not part with their money. The result, though he did not specify it, was that France remained a predominantly agricultural country – or a backward country, as Bagehot would have said – while England moved rapidly toward a state of swollen manufacture and over-population, with consequences which are still with us, for good or ill, while the rest of the world has tried with some success to catch up. The distinction of England at this time was that it had an abnormal – and, historically regarded, perhaps morbid – amount of borrowable money. The banker collected a great mass of other people's money, and the borrowers gathered round him because, as Bagehot accurately said, they 'knew or believed' he had it. With a million pounds you could think of building a railway; leave that sum in its constituent tens and hundreds and you had to be content with scattered horse or donkey-carts. These technological benefits came less from the ingenuity of engineers and craftsmen than from the seminal virtue of trusting bankers. The system had a democratic tendency, but one that did not go so far as to recognize the voices of those whom bankers did not trust. This was the *via media*, the *optimum* as far as Bagehot was concerned. He admitted that the new men created by easy credit and a wave of the banker's wand were, as a class, less honest than those who depended on a continuity of trade, and so of reputation. He admitted also that the system produced inferior goods because it relied on mere saleability, which could be achieved by relative cheapness, without regard to quality. But 'these defects and others' were 'compensated by one great excellence. No country of great hereditary trade, no European country at least, was ever so little "sleepy" . . . as England.' To prove the indubitable supremacy of that excellence Bagehot relied upon Darwin. The propensity to variation was 'the principle of progress'.

What it really amounted to was that men like Thomas Bagehot and Vincent Stuckey, placed at a point of vantage in an unsuspecting countryside, collected together the money produced by agricultural persons, who had no political thoughts, and transmitted it by way of London to Manchester and such places where entrepreneurs could then afford to pay wages which, miserable as they might be, were enough to attract people from the countryside to the mills where the new manufactures were carried on. Lombard Street was the go-between between the 'quiet saving districts of the country and the active employing districts'. Bagehot admired without reserve the prompt way in which money flew to the places where it could produce most interest for the banker. The amount of profit being made was the sole thing that interested him; the fact that what is profitable to a particular entrepreneur may, on a wider or longer view, be uneconomic or even destructive, did not detain him for an instant. He would no doubt have sneered cleverly at William Barnes's distinction between real and commercial value (see *Labour and Gold*, 1859). Barnes was a Dorchester schoolmaster, a poet and a philologist. He was also the son of a small farmer and had seen the peasantry despoiled by the saving that went on in 'the quiet districts'. Bagehot noticed the money that was made; Barnes noticed other things.

The peculiarity of the English economy, at this time, was that trade was conducted predominantly on borrowed capital. 'There never was so much borrowed money collected in the world as is now collected in London.' Nearly all of it could be asked for any day the owners pleased, and if they did, the whole structure would come tumbling down. The ratio of cash reserves to bank deposits was unprecedently low. The whole system, therefore, might be thought, by the bystander who did not trust bankers enough, to be unstable. Bagehot himself recalls the 'astounding instance of Overend, Gurney, and Co.' whose credit was almost as good as that of the Bank of England, but who none the less in a few years lost everything. 'And these losses were made in a manner so reckless and so foolish, that one would think a child who had lent money in the city of London would have lent it better.' No doubt Messrs Overend and Gurney none the less wore what appeared to be grown-up bankers' faces as they went impressively to and fro in the City. Perhaps there is some reason to doubt the efficacy of a system in which production stops or goes at the whim of money-lenders.

At the centre of this system was the Bank of England, which was conducted on much the same principle as other banks and which most people, including experts, believed to be essentially the same sort of institution. In a sense it was. Merchants kept their reserves at one of the lesser banks, which in turn kept their reserves at the Bank of England. On the board of the Bank of England they wrangled about how much money they had to keep idle, and complained that their dividend was low because they had to keep more than other people. In a manner the whole credit of the country depended on this ordinary commercial board. The wheels of trade and manufacture could stop because of the folly or misjudgment of these ordinary city characters. Everyone fortunately trusted the Bank of England but Bagehot obviously did not think that this trust was particularly well-founded. It was indeed persisted in in the face of evidence, for on various occasions the Bank had almost or quite suspended payment, or had had to he helped out in some way. What really distinguished the Bank of England from other banks was that, in the last resort, the government was behind it. That does, indeed, make a difference, not merely to the bank but to the nature of credit and, one might have thought, the standing of bankers. The whole system Bagehot describes is based on the assumption that money-lending is a private game, played by discreet men who, for reasons financial and personal rather than economic and public, could at any time interfere with the operation of the economy and regularly did so. This raises the question, which Bagehot did not pursue, as to how far such men are, for their private devices, operating in secret what should be regarded merely as part of the delegated authority of the state.

Bagehot does not pursue his enquiries in this direction merely because he has considered the matter and is so sure of his answer. 'No such plan would answer in England' – no such plan, that is, even as state management of the Bank. Bagehot's view is that the country could very well have done without the degree of intervention represented by the setting up of the Bank of England and by its special position. But for that, there would be a group of rival banks at the centre of things, as there are rival manufacturing interests, and this multiplicity would have given a greater security. But credit cannot be invented and since people trust the Bank of England it has to be left recognizably as it is. The political parallel Bagehot draws is characteristic. It would be easy, he says, to 'map out a scheme of Government in which Queen Victoria could be dispensed with... we know that the House of Commons is the real sovereign', for of course we have read *The English Constitution*, 'any other sovereign is superfluous'. But stupid people will trust the Queen. In the same way – not stupid but – shrewd men of business have confidence in things holding together round the Bank of England; better therefore, leave it as it is. The whole plan of having political nominees 'would seem to an Englishman of business palpably absurd; he would not consider it, he would not think it worth considering'.

But Bagehot saw clearly that the government of the Bank of England was in fact a national function; he would have the Board of Directors turned from semi-trustees for the nation to real trustees, with a trust deed which made their responsibilities clear. The system he recommended was, really, that the country should be run by men of business looking towards a written republican constitution, in the trust deed of the bank, while the eyes of the common people were averted in the direction of the Crown, where there was no power but, for vulgar minds, much entertainment. The theory of *The English Constitution* is really the counterpart of the theory of *Lombard Street* and it is the latter which is at the centre of Bagehot's notions of government.

The development of banking as a sort of arcane government under the cover of the publicly admitted forms was a relatively recent affair. It takes a long time to establish public confidence in a form of government, and the most stable constitutions are those which are accepted rather than explained. The growth of deposit banking, recent and still local, involved a similar growth. The essence of deposit banking was 'that a very large number of persons agree to trust a very few persons, or some one person. Banking would not be a profitable trade,' Bagehot goes on to confide, 'if bankers were not a small number, and depositors in comparison an immense number.' It was of course part of the mystique of this shadow republic, growing up within the ludicrous monarchy of Queen Victoria, that you could trust it more than you could trust the government. It was supposed to represent the private interest of the depositor, though like all government it in fact involved releasing little atoms of private power to a more remote authority. The authority in this case was not the *res publica*, confused and uncontrollable but at least in principle influenceable and subject to constitutional rules, but the mutual confidence of men in the city of London, some of the gravest of whom might on occasion behave like children, and who had no habit of responding to public criticism. The best way of encouraging the habit of deposit banking, Bagehot says, no doubt not unmindful of the affairs of the Somerset Bank and of Uncle Vincent, was 'to allow the banker to issue bank-notes of a small amount that can supersede the metal currency'. This amounted to a subsidy to each banker – from whom he does not say – to keep the banker going until people, impressed by this mysterious power which makes money out of nothing, come

204 | ENGLISH PERSPECTIVES

along bringing their deposits, real money to take the place of the
money the banker was in the first place allowed to imagine. One
can quite see the desirability of keeping this arcane privilege to
a few persons. Bagehot's account of this process is that of an
acute and interested observer. The reason for its success is that,
in the first instance, the initiative is entirely with the banker. All
he requires is a public docile enough to do nothing but take his
money and pass it from hand to hand. If people do not call his
bluff by presenting the notes for payment, all is well. In time
people begin to acquire piles of these notes. This makes them
think what a trustworthy character the banker is, so they take
along to him, and put on deposit, not merely his own notes but
good coin as well. By preserving a grave exterior the banker has
made money. One can understand the immense number of failures among early bankers, and the look of morality on the faces
of those that survived. It is this conjuror's smile that we see again
and again on the face of Walter Bagehot. He inherited it.

Bagehot recounts the history of the origin of the Bank of England, which his favourite Macaulay had told in a manner so suited
to the exuberance of the age. Here was a Whig finance company,
set up on the principle that while a Whig government was best
for the city, even with such a government it was better for city
men to trust themselves than the government. The city would
give countenance to the government rather than the government
to the city. It was a phenomenon of settled times. A large Whig
debt having been established, it became impossible to recall the
Stuarts because they might repudiate it. The money-lender's
notion of his ultimate rights over government, which coloured
so much of the city's relationship with government from that
day onwards, derives from this situation. The essence of the
Whig settlement was that the court should sue for the support
of the city rather than the other way round. Bagehot is wholly
of this tradition. 'Nothing can be truer in theory than the economical principle that banking is a trade and only a trade, and
nothing can be more surely established by a larger experience
than that a Government which interferes with any trade injures
that trade. The best thing undeniably that a Government can do
with the Money Market is to let it take care of itself.' One could
not have a more categorical demand for 'hands off' the city. Such
a demand is, in effect, a demand for the subordination of government to the men who trust one another with money. The idea
of the government keeping its own money belonged to the infancy

of the world. Happy if government had never meddled with banking at all. But in England it had done so, and a marvellous system, which would have regulated itself entirely on the self-interest of moneyed men, was now driven to rely in some measure on public opinion. The natural voice of this opinion was the Chancellor of the Exchequer, so we had better try and get one that knew his business. But Bagehot clearly conceives the Chancellor's main duty as being so to arrange his affairs that the money market is not upset, and that the game of confidence which begins with the local banker deciding whom to favour, and ends with the international market, can be played uninterruptedly in accordance with its own rules devised, of course, primarily for the benefit of the players.

It might be supposed that the Bank of England 'has some peculiar power of fixing the value of money'. Not so, however, according to Bagehot. Other people follow the Bank of England in what they charge for money, but there is no compulsion about this. They are quite free to do otherwise; it only happens that the Bank holds more money than other people and that has a certain influence on events. In effect it fixes a price, and what other people have to decide is whether they will enter into competition with this giantess, and offer money more cheaply, or whether they will charge a little more. It would seem that their freedom of action is somewhat limited. Unless anyone has an immense store of money, he will obviously get tired of offering it cheaply before the Bank bothers to bring its own rate down. As for offering money at a price above the Bank's, that is unlikely to be very alluring to customers. The caprice of the Bank is important, therefore, though Bagehot explains how, through the operation of supply and demand, it all comes right in the end, so that the Bank's power is not permanent; it is only great and sudden. A small matter, he seems to imply, though it causes some inconveniences, for 'up to a certain point money is a necessity'. It is not the necessity of buying bread that Bagehot has in mind, but the anxiety of the merchant to find money in order to make more. 'If money were all held by the owners of it, or by banks which did not pay interest for it' – if it were designed solely for such low purposes as the exchange of directly useable goods, in other words – 'the value of money might not fail so fast. Money would in the market phrase, be "well held".' But in Lombard Street money is held mainly be people who are borrowers as well as lenders. They must keep up a constant juggling of borrowing and lending, trying to make sure that the balance of the transactions is in their favour. The final secret of the market is that it must be run to the bankers' own advantage. This vital interest depending on it, one naturally wants to see a certain steadiness in the Bank of England, so that the lesser usurers are able to keep up with it.

With these important issues at stake, it is hardly surprising that 'Lombard Street is often very dull, and sometimes very excited'. It is rather on the same principle that other professions seem always to be more excited about their own jokes and vendettas than about the earthquakes and famines of the world at large. As an immense credit rests on a relatively small cash reserve, events such as a threat of invasion or the failure of a harvest bring with them the more serious trouble of a panic among bankers. A sudden apprehension that they may be short of money casts a blight on the whole community. There are 'good' times and 'bad' times; those that are good for bankers are good for everybody, those that are bad for bankers are bad for everybody. Certainly these warlocks should be propitiated! The identity of interest between capital and labour is complete, for the latter cannot hope to eat if the former is unhappy. The manufacturer, that secondary capitalist who is the banker's direct client, does not, as you might think, produce goods so that they can be *used*; he produces them 'to be exchanged' because this is the operation in which there is most scope for the money-lender. The brisker the rate of circulation, the more the scope for lending and borrowing. The harder the manufacturer can be pressed, by his debts, to get his goods moving, the better. A man who carves pieces of wood, and puts them on a shelf to grow dusty until someone happens to come along who thinks it worth while buying one, is no use at all to the banker. He wants a manufacturer whose primary concern is a return on his money, and who thinks he has completed his mission if he produces any trash which can be sold above its cost, and the more the better, so that he has always to borrow to expand and can spare a percentage for the banker in the process. A depression or a slowing down of the circulation of trade, can be caused by one of two great natural forces – a calamity to a particular industry, agriculture especially, which produces goods people want to eat even more than they want to exchange them – and a failure of credit, caused by headaches and migraines suffered by men with money who, on account of some disappointment, no longer trust one another as much as they did. The two great natural forces are not unconnected. The picture is of the soul of the banker agonizing within the crude body of industry.

A flicker of historical recollection crosses Bagehot's mind at this point in the argument. 'In our common speculations,' he says, 'we do not enough remember that interest on money is a refined idea, and not a universal one.' There are even now unenlightened countries – most of the world, indeed, Bagehot says, in his day – where people do not trust the process of letting out money at usury. The real progress in civilization came when people found they could have safe investments. There is an optimum stage of credit, attained in the year 1871 and characterized in the *Economist* as follows: 'We are now trusting as many people as we ought to trust, and as yet there is no wild excess of misplaced confidence which would make us trust those whom we ought not to trust.' These good times are times of rising prices – produced by cheap corn, which the *Economist* was founded to campaign for, and cheap money – and not very welcome to 'quiet people' of 'slightly-varying and fixed incomes', but then it is not such people that Bagehot wishes principally to consider. They are, after all, unlikely to have their minds sufficiently on the kind of money games which mark our society with its peculiar qualities. The people Bagehot admires are those who, when a long-continued period of low interest has given way, by processes he describes, to a high rate, feel a sudden excitement, 'work more than they should, and trade far above their means'. These are 'the ablest and the cleverest' – the money-makers, in short, those who have a peculiar gift for seeing beyond the vulgar surface of physical objects to the magical numbers which lie beyond.

Bagehot goes on to examine the role of the Bank of England in the panic of 1866. The Bank conceived that it had a duty to support the banking community, and so paid out its reserves till it hurt. No legitimate request for help, backed by proper securities, was refused. The *Economist* was so exuberant in its praise of these proceedings, and of what it took to be an admission by the Bank that Mr Bagehot's analysis of its function was the correct one, that Hankey, one of the directors, characterized the article as containing 'the most mischievous doctrine ever broached in the monetary or banking world in this country, *viz.* that it is the proper function of the Bank of England to keep money available at all times to supply the demands of bankers who have rendered their own assets unavailable.' And indeed one

can see that, in the round of confidence tricks desiderated by
Bagehot for the proper maintenance of credit, there might well
be some harm in the flat assertion that the Bank of England
would always pay out to the lesser bankers. No doubt he had
seen exactly where the interest of the lesser bankers lay; he was
moreover, a journalist, and his striking and simple doctrine
looked well in the *Economist*. The passage between Hankey and
the *Economist* characterizes Bagehot's position as a writer on public affairs. On the one hand he was never tired of pointing out,
to the merely intellectual world, the solid good sense of men of
affairs, himself included. On the other, he was delighted to
exhibit to men of affairs, engrossed in mere business, the
superiority of intellectuals, once more including himself. It is a
position which gave him a sort of personal invulnerability, so
long as he twisted and turned quickly enough, but one cannot
be entirely without misgivings about so slippery an Achilles,
with no heel. Bagehot's own analysis of the ineptitude of men
of affairs, in matters of theory, is admirable.

> The abstract thinking of the world is never to be expected
> from persons in high places; the administration of first-rate
> current transactions is a most engrossing business, and those
> charged with them are usually but little inclined to think on
> points of theory, even when such thinking most nearly con-
> cerns those transactions. No doubt when men's own fortunes
> are at stake, the instinct of the trader does somehow anticipate
> the conclusions of the closet. But a board has no instincts
> when it is not getting an income for its members, and when
> it is only discharging a duty of office.

Yet it is to these alarming characters, lurching as instinct directs
them towards their private profit, that Bagehot assures us that
the control of credit and the public fortunes can safely be left.
And what of the commentator? If he intrudes remarks for their
wit or general truth rather than for the appositeness to a particular
practical situation, is he more than a public entertainer who
bedevils further the problems of the men who, by virtue of their
position, have to find solutions or at any rate next moves?

Still, Bagehot is, in spite of the temptations of journalism,
something more than a mere commentator. He is a banker from
the skin inwards, and the attraction of his work on financial
matters is that it is that of a man who can actually talk, with
some facility, about the operations which his ordinary colleagues,

the ordinary sensible men of business, merely perform. *Lombard Street*, as Keynes says,

> is a piece of pamphleteering, levelled at the magnates of the City and designed to knock into their heads, for the guidance of future policy, two or three fundamental truths... Perhaps the most striking and fundamental doctrine... is, in a sense, psychological rather than economic... the doctrine of the Reserve, and that the right way to stop a crisis is to lend freely.*

Psychologically, it might be added, the appeal of the doctrine to Bagehot was that he was recommending *other people* to lend freely, in time of panic, as a way of saving Bagehot. He describes the panic of the Money Market rather as one might have described the Fire of London, and indeed it must have been rather like that. The bad news would 'spread in an instant through all the Money Market at a moment of terror; no one can say exactly who carries it, but in half an hour it will be carried on all sides, and will intensify the terror everywhere'. This was perhaps the central horror of his life, next to the madness of his mother.

Bagehot goes on to describe the government of the Bank of England, as it was in his day. The board was self-electing, and although in theory a certain number went out each year, it was always some of the younger ones who went, so that the real power lay in the hands of a collection of ripe old men. When they chose a new director they did so with scrupulous care – 'purity', is the word Bagehot uses, and it had a certain meaning for him – because if he stayed he would, twenty years later, infallibly become in turn Deputy Governor and Governor, for those offices were filled by seniority. They came to all in turn, and those who had held office – 'passed the Chair' – formed the Committee of Treasury which exercised the real power in the establishment. By custom, none of these directors was a banker, in the ordinary sense of the term; they were merchants coming from reputable city houses. No wonder they needed Stuckey's to lecture them on the principles of banking! Bagehot indeed had a revolutionary proposal. It was that, since the Bank did not have a permanent Governor, and moreover had no one but subordinates about the place who understood banking, they should

* J.M. Keynes, 'The Works of Bagehot', *The Economic Journal* (September 1915), 371-2.

employ a sort of Permanent Under Secretary, on the model of
Whitehall, to run it. Such a man as Bagehot himself would have
filled the bill entirely.

Lombard Street is, in many ways, the most personal of Bagehot's books. His heart lay not only in the money but in the game
of confidence he had inherited from his father and uncle in Somerset. He saw that banking was changing, and, correctly, expected
that private banking would come to an end. The paragraphs in
which he celebrates the life of that *milieu* – his own – come nearer
to poetry than anything he ever wrote:

> I can imagine nothing better in theory or more successful in
> practice than private banks as they were in the beginning. A
> man of known wealth, known integrity, and known ability
> is largely entrusted with the money of his neighbours. The
> confidence is strictly personal. His neighbours know him,
> and trust him because they know him. They see daily his
> manner of life, and judge from it that their confidence is
> deserved. In rural districts, and in former times, it was
> difficult for a man to ruin himself except at the place in which
> he lived; for the most part he spent his money there, and
> speculated there if he speculated at all. Those who lived there
> also would soon see if he was acting in a manner to shake
> their confidence. Even in large cities, as cities then were, it
> was possible for most persons to ascertain with fair certainty
> the real position of conspicuous persons, and to learn all that
> was material in fixing their credit. Accordingly the bankers
> who for a long series of years passed successfully this strict
> and continual investigation, became very wealthy and very
> powerful.
>
> The name "London Banker" had especially a charmed
> value. He was supposed to represent, and often did represent,
> a certain unity of pecuniary sagacity and educated refinement
> which was scarcely to be found in any other part of society.
> In a time when the trading classes were much ruder than they
> now are, many private bankers possessed a variety of know-
> ledge and delicacy of attainment which would even now be
> very rare. Such a position is indeed singularly favourable.
> The calling is hereditary; the credit of the bank descends from
> father to son: this inherited wealth soon brings inherited
> refinement. Banking is a watchful, but not a laborious trade.
> A banker, even in large business, can feel pretty sure that

all his transactions are sound, and yet have much spare mind. A certain part of his time, and a considerable part of his thoughts, he can readily devote to other pursuits. And a London banker can also have the most intellectual society in the world if he chooses it. There has probably very rarely ever been so happy a position as that of a London private banker; and never perhaps a happier.

Lombard Street was finished in 1873. 1876 was the centenary of the publication of *The Wealth of Nations*. Bagehot wrote two essays on this occasion – or perhaps one should say an essay and an article, the latter for the *Economist*, the former, closely related and in points repetitive, for the *Fortnightly*. The contribution to the *Fortnightly*, *Adam Smith as a Person*, is perhaps Bagehot's best essay. He had a subject completely to his liking, and completely within his scope.

Adam Smith was a man Bagehot felt he could patronize. A man inferior to himself, and yet who had produced such notable results in the world: What might not then Bagehot himself produce? Smith was born in Kirkcaldy in 1723, in a world far enough off in time as in place from Bagehot's English province. 'He was never engaged in any sort of trade, and would probably never have made sixpence by any if he had been.' This lack of practical experience, in a man who passed for the inventor of political economy, needed some explaining. He was an awkward, unplausible man in comparison with Bagehot. He had a scheme, typical of the more superficial side of the eighteenth century – the Whig-*encyclopédiste* side – for a vast work on the development of the human mind and of social laws, on everything, in short. He went at this with Scotch and professorial industry until the acquisition of a sinecure made all intellectual work impossible. He picked up and much elaborated the talk of Glasgow merchants, and spent three years in France as tutor to the Duke of Buccleuch and there, as Bagehot put it, observed the numerous 'errors, such as generally accompany a great Protective legislation'. The administration of France, then as now, showed a certain weakness for logical complexity. Worse still was the tendency of this legislation. Bagehot says that 'her legislators for several generations had endeavoured to counteract the aim of nature' – which was to confine her to agriculture and so make room for the English trade – 'and had tried to make her a manufacturing country and an exporter of her manufactures'. Reasoning on all these matters was Quesnay, who had a place at Court and excited himself about *'acheter, c'est vendre'* while Madame de Pompadour ran the government downstairs. The frank admiration for competition, which would infallibly produce fair prices, made an impression on Adam Smith, whose academic mind was probably also not unsympathetic to the governmental fantasies of the *économistes* who had 'the natural wish of eager speculators, to have an irresistible despotism behind them and supporting them; and with the simplicity which marks so much of the political speculation of the eighteenth century, but which now seems so child-like,' says Bagehot, 'never seemed to think how they were to get their despot, or how they were to ensure that he should be on their side'. The gruesome admiration of eighteenth-century intellectuals for such characters as Frederick the Great is no more comic than the delusions of those of the twentieth century who have imagined that a Communist government would do what they wanted. After his residence in France Adam Smith went back to Kirkcaldy and lived with his mother for six years. After this he spent three years in London, still thinking, and then *The Wealth of Nations* appeared.

There are some acute comments on Adam Smith's conception of political economy in Bagehot's *Economic Studies*. Bagehot points out that this aboriginal author 'never seems aware that he is dealing with what we should call an abstract science at all. *The Wealth of Nations* does not deal, as do our modern books, with a fictitious human being hypothetically simplified, but with the actual concrete men who live and move. It is concerned with Greeks and Romans, the nations of the middle ages, the Scotch and the English, and never diverges into the abstract world.' On the other hand, because Adam Smith's mind was rather crabbed and limited, he thought people were far more rigorous in pursuit of gain than most of them in fact are. He mentions some of the other things that people get up to, but his description is one-sided. He does not abstract more than he can help, but his mind is really of a self-limiting and so abstracting kind. People think him very practical, as compared with modern economists, because he professes to deal with the whole of man, but they are impressed by him because he deals only with part. By contrast, Bagehot says, the modern economists who make a deliberate abstraction of the economic man, while really, he implies, understanding the whole range of human nature, strike people as mere theorists. This is an argument from which we can afford to stand aside, but it may be remarked that the simplicity of mind, which led Adam Smith to the Utopia of Free Trade, is not much complicated in his nineteenth-century successors who thought that nothing could go amiss if it were established without hindrance in their native land.

One can hardly do better, if one wants an impression of the exuberance of solid men, in Bagehot's own circle, on the subject of free trade, than look at the prospectus which formed the preliminary number of the *Economist* (August, 1843). The immediate object of the new 'political, commercial, agricultural and free-trade journal' was the abolition of the Corn Laws, on which liberal opinion had fixed with the blinkered tenacity with which it has seized, since that day, on a succession of high causes which, viewed historically, are no more than successive expressions of the growing appetite of industry. The argument of free trade was from the first a financial argument. In James Wilson's eloquent prospectus the actual trades and actions of men are made to disappear before our eyes – they are explicity treated as non-existent if they do not satisfy the financial conventions of the time. 'As long as railways and canals are profitable', he says, 'they truly represent in real wealth the capital invested; but diminish the amount of traffic only so much as pays the profit – . . . and they are no longer wealth.' In these terms there was over-production, even at this early stage of mechanized industry, and 'There is no cure, there is no remedy, for all these evils but increased demand; there can be no increased demand without increased markets; and we cannot secure larger markets without an unrestricted power of exchange, and by this means add to our territory of land, as far as productive utility is concerned, the corn fields of Poland, Prussia, and above all, the rich and endless acres of the United States.' There might well be some hesitation, less than a generation after the Napoleonic wars, about a system based on the accessibility of the fields of Prussia and Poland. Even if this were not so, one might wonder how, on this basis of territorially expanding markets, 'we might go on increasing our production without limits'. The doctrine of free trade was, after all, no more than the mood which went with markets which were in fact then expanding. If it was, as for Wilson, 'this only natural state of things', it was so for people who had rejected Hobbes's state of nature in favour of a more optimistic tradition.

Bagehot had an eye for the entertaining detail of Adam Smith's work – how long it took waggons to go from Edinburgh to London, how many apprentices a master cutler could have in Sheffield, or a master weaver in Norwich. But the subject of his essay is Adam Smith himself, and there is a sort of personal curiosity about the way he treats the events of his fellow-economist's life. The parallel is never exact – indeed there is hardly a parallel at all – but Bagehot is thinking of his own involvement in practical affairs when he makes play with Adam Smith's appointment, after the publication of *The Wealth of Nations*, as a commissioner of customs. Well acquainted with the theory of taxation, 'he could have given a Minister in the capital better advice than anyone else as to what taxes he should impose'. Just like me! Bagehot no doubt thought; was he not 'the spare Chancellor'? On the other hand, Adam Smith's not very weighty duties prevented him from writing any more. A point of contrast with the banker of Langport! 'And not unnaturally, for those who have ever been used to give all their days to literary work, rarely seem able to do that work when they are even in a slight degree struck and knocked against the world.' Bagehot puts on a brave face before the loss of his predecessor's works. He says, truly enough no doubt, that what was lost was probably not very valuable. So Adam Smith lived on for fifteen years after the publication of *The Wealth of Nations*, talking sense among the lawyers and professors of Edinburgh, and saying, at the end, that he meant to have done more. His mind no doubt was still full of his great scheme, with which in the end he did not weary the world.

Bagehot himself was, towards the end of his life, occupied with a great work which R.H. Hutton appeared to think he might be finishing off in heaven. It was an economic treatise, to be in three parts, the first of general economic theory, the second a critique of some classic theorists, and the third containing portraits of great economists. The essay on Adam Smith is clearly the prototype of the work which would have made up the third part. What Bagehot had done of the first and second parts became the posthumous *Economic Studies* (1879). This work is therefore of a fragmentary nature, but perhaps we put up with the loss of the rest of it as well as Bagehot put up with the loss of the rest of the work Adam Smith did not do because he was distracted by the Customs. Bagehot is an unsystematic writer and it is unlikely that his book would have been a landmark in economic theory.

The *Economic Studies* open with an essay which appeared in the *Fortnightly* in 1876 under the title of *The Postulates of English Political Economy*. The essay starts with a reference to Adam Smith and goes on to inquire why English political economy was not popular outside England. One reason he alleges is it was 'more opposed to the action of Government in all ways than most such theories…All Governments', he says, 'like to interfere; it elevates their position to make out that they can cure the evils of mankind' – a role which, in Bagehot's view of things, is rather that of bankers who, by the stimulation of trade through money-lending, produce comfort, which is what we most desire. Another reason was simply that political economy was 'the science of business' which at that time was held to be fully developed only in this country, as nowadays it is held to be fully developed only in the United States. Although he used this phrase, Bagehot was hardly on the side of the 'scientists' in this field. He was sceptical of the excessive hope in numeracy which has now swept through the minds of experts in affairs like a blinding lunacy. He was convinced of the treachery of figures; he knew how 'the names remain, while the quality, the thing signified', changed. 'Statistical tables, even those which are most elaborate and careful, are not substitutes for an actual cognisance of the facts: they do not, as a rule convey a just idea of the movements of a trade to persons not *in* the trade.' Yet Bagehot was not on the side of mere non-statistical common sense either. He was superior to the academic student of business because he was *in* trade, and to the ordinary man of business because he was clever. He takes neither side of the argument very far and characteristically rests in a position where he feels that no-one can get at him. As a conclusive illustration he alleges that, 'extraordinary as it may seem, the regular changes in the sun have much to do with the regular recurrence of difficult times in the money market'. It is a striking assertion, which perhaps goes to the root of Bagehot's religious faith.

The essay goes on to comment on two unfruitful methods of investigation, still in principle very popular. One is what he calls the 'all-case' method, which pretends to the impossible task of collecting all the facts before proceeding to a theory. This method Bagehot traces to Bacon's early fumblings after an empirical method. The other unfruitful method is what he calls the 'single case' method, which consists in an exhaustive analysis of a particular group of facts. Bagehot quite rightly holds that no exercise in the manipulation of facts can be useful without a preliminary theory. Even so, with a sense of the fluctuation of things which almost overwhelms any belief in the existence of man as an, historically speaking, relatively unchanging species, he sees political economy – English Political Economy, as he calls it – as concerned only with a particular recent group of phenomena. 'It is the theory of commerce, as commerce tends more and more to be when capital increases and competition grows.' He proceeds to examine the conceptions of the transferability of labour and of capital in light of these limitations. He has no difficulty in showing that there are many conditions of society in which these conceptions do not hold. The revelation will cause little astonishment to any reader who stands a little apart from the Great Commerce in which Bagehot revelled, but Bagehot himself certainly did not draw the full consequences from this glimpse of the subjectivity of economic notions. His common insistence on the superiority of common sense, and of the notions of practical men, in business or politics, over those religious and political ideas which have a longer grip on the mind, is shown to be mere bravado, the valueless talk of a class of men who happen to be fashionable with themselves at a particular moment of history. Bagehot repeatedly claims that men of business, economists and bankers are concerned with 'hard' fact, as if it were a special kind of truth. It is simply the one he loves best. 'Now of course it is true that there are some things, though not many things, more important than money,' he said in his centenary article on *The Wealth of Nations* in the *Economist*, 'and a nation may well be called on to abandon the maxims which would produce most money, for others which would promote some of these better ends. The case is much like that of health in the body. There are unquestionable circumstances in which a man may be called on to endanger and to sacrifice his health at some call of duty. But for all that bodily health is a most valuable thing, and the advice of the physician as to the best way of keeping it is very much to be heeded, and in the same way, though the wealth is occasionally to be foregone, and the ordinary rules of industry abandoned, yet still national wealth is in itself and in its connections a great end, and economists who teach us to arrive at it are most useful.' The key to this passage is the equation of wealth with money, an error which Adam Smith had sought to remove, and which Bagehot understood very well, only to forget it in his passion for the refinements of credit, of which he was a powerful and hereditary practitioner.

The End of Walter Bagehot

One very suspicious circumstance about the reputation of Walter Bagehot is that almost nobody has a word to say against him. Somehow the aura of admiration which surrounded him in his domestic life has remained. There is comedy in the ingenuous praise of Mrs Russell Barrington. It is so much that of a nice lady, enthusing over the really nice man of the family. 'While Bagehot was at this time leading a stirring social and family life,' she writes of her hero at the time of the Second Reform Bill, 'and at the same time one of pressing business.' This is the buoyant character who breezes in from such important work and people, placing his hat and gloves on the hall-stand while the ladies, hearing his footstep, put aside their needle-work or their water-colours... 'while', she goes on, 'he was watching every public event at home or abroad' – like the men who talk in trains or the interminable army of commentators who broadcast perpetually about matters of which, after all, they can know nothing – 'weighing the rights and wrongs of every current question of importance and giving judgment thereon in the pages of the *Economist*' – ah! – 'interviewing and advising statesmen respecting measures to be brought before Parliament' – a television man before his time indeed – 'a subtle machinery was at work in his brain.'[*] No doubt. But the quality and importance of the products of that machine can be variously estimated. It was a former editor of *The Times* who was chosen to write 'a literary appreciation' of Bagehot for the *Economist*'s edition of his works. A Member of Parliament and publicist was chosen to edit it. It was G.M. Young, 'this generation's undisputed guide to the Victorian age', as William Haley calls him, who found that Bagehot was 'the wisest man of his generation'. A well-placed trio to carry Mrs Barrington's praises to their conclusion. There is a certain social tone about the Bagehot coterie. He comes to roost among the cocks on the middle perches, that Oxford middle

* Mrs R. Barrington, *Life of Walter Bagehot* (1914), 382.

217

class whose undue influence is only now coming to an end in the conclusions they have for several generations contrived for with varying degrees of wall-eyed percipience.

It is in this discreet class – typically of civil servants, dons, editors of the middle-brow organs of opinion – that Walter Bagehot has been plentifully re-incarnated. There have been thousands of him, and the phalanx is only now beginning to grow a little thin. G.M. Young caught a glimpse of his fellow-marchers, which is very creditable in him, for it is a peculiarity of this kind to emphasize their own individuality and differences. There 'are thousands of people thinking and even speaking Bagehot today', Haley quotes him as saying, 'who might be hard put to say when exactly he lived and what exactly he did'. No wonder. The bright, intelligent, well-informed, quietly well-off, quietly corrupt, sufficiently successful, mutually helpful, are much alike. But the succession to Bagehot is less a phalanx than a congeries of ideas, and less a congeries of ideas than a tactical attitude, the manifestations of which vary slightly with the *milieu*. Hutton noticed that Bagehot never remained long in untenable positions, and never returned to them. The secret of his attitude is that the position mattered less to him than the tenability. He was therefore a man bent on looking after himself – an economist of his person, as Smollett said of Ferdinand Count Fathom.

It cannot be denied that this is an eminent virtue in a man of affairs. In almost all professions, once a certain mediocrity of intelligence is passed, what matters is ability to live in the *milieu*. The public at large do not know a good doctor or solicitor from a bone-headed one; success goes to the one who has the *air* of being a doctor or solicitor, according to the canons of the time. Being right or wrong is rarely of any importance; the best men have their excuses even when they are most blatantly caught out. But generally they do not have the appearance of being caught out. The patient dies, or some inscrutable legal difficulty raises its head, or the knavery of somebody else springs into sudden prominence. No very searching objectivity haunts the ordinary occupations of the banker. No doubt in an extreme case his bank can fail, but normally one muddle will pay off another, and the important thing is to seem to be doing all right. These arts, we may be certain, Bagehot had in sufficient measure, in what is called practical life. All that, however, has gone the way of the bank-notes of the Somerset Bank. The question that remains is whether the tactical evasion, so useful in day-to-day business, makes a durable contribution in literature.

In a sense it may be said that it does. One cannot locate Shakespeare in a stateable position, and the many statements as to what he 'thought' serve only to emphasize that he is something more elusive. It would be the claim of Bagehot's admirers, perhaps his own claim, that it is the same sort of nakedness before reality which gives his books on government, or on the money market, their value. He does not carry theory very far, it might be said, because he sees the whole complexity of the real world, and presents that. Or it might be said that he is the 'practical' man, dealing with 'hard' facts. The dwarf is the same as the giant, and the country banker, rightly understood, operates in a way remarkably like Shakespeare's. Is there not a comparable freedom of mind? Neither cares for a principle, if it does not suit him. Neither can be nailed down. The practical man is an artist, everything he deals with is provisional. There is a difference, however. What the artist leaves is not provisional, and does not disappear with yesterday's overdraft. Shakespeare prostrated himself before reality, because he could not help it. The little man of affairs takes the bits he can use for some mean purpose he sees, and comes out on top.

Bagehot's distinction was to have carried this technique of affairs into the business of writing. He was a journalist. Nearly all his writing was done, in the first instance, for the periodical press. So was De Quincey's, but De Quincey was no mere success and all the time he was looking for a point of rest behind the confusions of the matters of the day. With Bagehot, the provisional became so far as possible a principle. You had to move smartly to keep up with him. He used his observations not to define his position, for he had none, but to defend himself. His method was not to yield to reality but to be clever about it, and to ingratiate himself sufficiently to make sure that he was not left alone. There is an affable, matey tone about his work which has made thousands of mediocrities feel at home with him. He is not only clever himself, but gives a distinct impression that he is one of a band of like-minded conspirators, to which the reader is invited to attach himself. This accounts for the destructive element in much of his work.

It is a trick which has often passed for liberalism. Bagehot's account of *The English Constitution* is based on it. Everything which has claims to be objectively important is smilingly shown to be unimportant, or important in some arcane way intelligible only to the group of conspirators, who will never submit to any truth unless it is manifestly useable to their own advantage. The plausibility of this position lies in the fact that, precisely, it is advantageous to know the truth. The real question is as to the kind of advantage it gives, and as to the order of precedence between advantage and truth. To put the advantage first, and then to accept such truths as do not interfere with it, is a political proceeding which is favoured far beyond the bounds of what are ordinarily thought of as politics. It is Bagehot's method, and accounts for the relativism which allows him to re-arrange reality incessantly to suit situations, with a foremost eye always on his own. 'Incessant changes in science, in literature, in art, and in politics – in that forms thinking minds – have made it impossible that really and in fact we should think the same things in 1874 as our ancestors in 1674 or 1774.' Of course: and it is the half truth in this that makes this emphasis acceptable to quick impenetrable minds – even, now that everyone has got used to it, to slow ones. But of course our ancestors are not so unintelligible as all that. The shape of their minds as of their bodies has a distinct resemblance to that of our own, and it is by what used to be regarded as the truth of things that the intelligibility, and the continuity, are possible, just as it is by the truth of things that people together in one place and time can come to an understanding. An absolute relativism is a form of solipsism, which is not the best of bases for the understanding of politics.

This rickety liberalism is nowhere better illustrated than in Bagehot's attack on the Church of England in his article on *The Public Worship Regulation Bill* (1874), which is one of those judgements on current questions in the pages of the *Economist* which Mrs Barrington admired so much. Needless to say the article is not an overt attack on the Church of England, any more than *The English Constitution* is an overt attack upon the monarchy. It is merely the judicious analysis of a commentator who understands the Church so much better than a convinced Anglican could do. With a sweep of false modesty, Bagehot starts by saying that if the bill 'dealt only with subjects theological or religious', he would not 'interfere in the discussion'. But of course it 'deals also with political questions' on which he did 'not think it right to be silent'. To deprive his judicious readers of his guidance would certainly be very wrong indeed! Without his help they might choose a policy which would produce just the opposite of the effect they intend – a danger against which the *Economist* is still week by week safeguarding its devoted public. There is a characteristic mock deference about this approach to the subject. 'The Church of England is one of those among our institutions which, if it is to be preserved at all' – a point which to any fair-minded man must be a matter of serious doubt – 'should be touched most anxiously'. When it was last settled, at the Restoration, Locke was still lecturing in Greek and the apple had not fallen on Newton's head. Obviously we could not have much in common with those times. All who understood the growth of banking since 1689 would recognise that religious problems could not be the same then and now. Yet Bagehot in fact ignores the actual differences between 1662 and 1874 and calls the Public Worship Regulation Bill, which was designed to enforce observance of the Prayer Book Rubrics, 'a new Act of Uniformity'. The serious purpose of the several Acts of Uniformity was to preserve the unity of Christians in the places where its writ ran. With this purpose Bagehot's argument has nothing to do; he would have said, no doubt, because he was not dabbling in theology. But in a country in which dissent of every kind – including Papist dissent – had long been allowed to flourish, the purposes of the Act of Uniformity had been abandoned and the basis for the comparison was no longer there. Bagehot is gleeful about the conspicuous way in which the recent history of the English Church had exhibited the native 'indifference to abstract truth' – only it escapes him that abstract truth is, precisely, what Christians are not primarily concerned with. Putting on the guise of a true friend – and how frequently has that been assumed by the worst enemies of the Church? – he argues that 'the real danger of the Establishment is from within, not from without'. Its comprehensiveness was 'a great evil'. Young men of intelligence and education would naturally wish to argue themselves into an extreme position. It irritated Bagehot to see the Establishment look so benignly on differences of opinion. One may say that he had not the imagination to plumb the depths of historical formularies, and his conception of the intelligent young ordinand was of one who showed a similar impatience. 'This is the sort of thought which more and more prevents intellectual young men from taking orders, and we are beginning to see the effect. The moral excellence and the practical piety of the clergy are as good as ever' – it is the Devil speaking – 'but they want individuality of thought and originality of mind.' The ironic praise of political stupidity which appears again and again in Bagehot's work is really the counterpart of an exclusive sympathy with an abstracting cleverness. 'More and more' the clergy 'belong to the most puzzling class to argue with, for more and more they "candidly confess" that they must admit your premises, but "on account of the obscurity of the subject", must decline to draw the inevitable inference.' But is not Trinitarian religion after all a somewhat obscure subject, at any rate for analytical discourse? 'Already this intellectual poorness is beginning to be felt' he goes on, 'and if it should augment, it will destroy the Establishment. She will not have in her ranks arguers who can maintain her position either against those who believe more or against those who believe less.' It is the *pons asinorum* of the rationalist. The 'more' and the 'less' are in themselves a prejudicial definition of the *via media*. The antithesis is a false one for the Anglican who understands the Establishment as merely expressing the political relation of the historic Church in the place he lives in. But Bagehot, like many publicists of enlightenment since his day, sees Romanism on one side and scepticisim on the other – either of them a possible position for a rational man – with the derisory Church of England as a refuge for those who are too stupid to adopt a logically coherent position. It should be observed that in this presentation it is not the Roman *Church* which is brought on to the stage but certain Latin habits of mind which show up as clearly in political institutions as in the regulation of ecclesiastical matters. The differences which are being pointed at are those between the Roman law countries and our own. More simply, one may say that, for a common form of imprudent liberalism, any doctrine or institution, however autocratic, which opposes itself to the Establishment, is welcome because it does so oppose itself. Communism as well as Romanism has benefitted by this indulgence. It is for the disruption they threaten in this country, not for the several orders they would like to establish if they could, that they are admired.

From one point of view Bagehot's liberalism is no more than the voice of commercial enterprise freeing itself from the tyranny of an agricultural system. Commercial enterprise was no novelty of the nineteenth century, but the pace of the industrial revolution and the expansion of credit with which Bagehot was himself concerned had by the mid-century only begun to imagine the possibility of a complete victory. Bagehot always speaks contemptuously of 'these rustics' and resented the social position of the landowning squire, but he was exhilarated by the thought that, on the national stage where bankers and the editor of the *Economist* operated, landowners and the monarchy might be thrown on the rubbish-heap, while men of business carried on the affairs of the country. No one could say that this vision of things was belied by the century that followed him. The success of his reading of events is confirmed by the smile on the faces of practically every publicist or expert who is allowed to open his mouth in any position from which his voice is likely to be heard. Government is supposed to have become the management of the economy and there is almost universal agreement that it could not be anything else. Impulses of a longer heredity some-times irrupt upon the scene, but they are the vestiges only of undeveloped minds, as Bagehot believed the monarchy to be.

Yet if there is one lesson of history which is of certain validity it is that a new age is never so new as it imagines. Another is that in this world no one knows very clearly what he is doing until he has done it and it is too late to apply the experience. It is the difficulty of prudence which affords the best argument for reckless exploitation, but in our day the exploiters usually lay claim to a monopoly of prudence as well as of other forms of good sense. There are even those who think that a study of the subordinate prudences of management is a substitute for a humane education. In this shallow world, in which benefits are represented to be as calculable as costs, Bagehot would have been a bounding and no doubt sceptical success. That certainly proves something about his foresight, but unless one holds, as Bagehot himself tended to do, that the contemporary is always right, it proves nothing as to the profundity of his views. Might not Coleridge – the 'dreamy orator', as Bagehot calls him – have been nearer to reality after all? Nothing could be more remote from *The English Constitution* and *Lombard Street* than *Church and State* and *Lay Sermons*. Coleridge's political writings cannot have had a tenth – probably not a twentieth – part of the number of readers Bagehot's have had, and they have had nothing like the same prominence in the minds of politicians, administrators, and the academics of public affairs. What Coleridge wrote, however, can still well up disruptively in the smooth, assured world of those who think like the banker, and they come from a depth and with a force which make Bagehot's little subversions of the Establishment look like a leader in the *Guardian*. It is surprising how much of the ground Bagehot covered is touched on by Coleridge, but in a manner so different that the two sets of writing are less complementary than in hostile tension. It is Bagehot's 'sufferings of the capitalist' against Coleridge's 'when the old labourer's savings, the precious robberies of self-denial from every day's comfort; when the orphan's funds; the widow's livelihood; the fond confiding sister's humble fortune; are found among the victims to the remorseless mania of dishonest speculation, or the desperate cowardice of embarrassment' (*Lay Sermons*, 3rd edn, 1852). Or against this, which might serve as an epigraph to Bagehot's work: 'I cannot persuade myself that the frequency of failures with all the disgraceful secrets of fraud and folly, of unprincipled vanity in expending and desperate speculation in retrieving, can be familiarised to the thoughts and experience of men, as matters of daily occurrence, without serious injury to the moral sense.' Where Bagehot sees the legitimate pursuits of men entitled to their complacency Coleridge sees 'the drunken stupor of a usurious selfishness'. No doubt political writings which bristle with allusions to Donne, Jeremy Taylor and Algernon Sydney are barely credible to the readers of the *Economist*, and Coleridge traces the descent of religious thinking from 'that inquisitive and bookish theology' which enabled it to touch the concerns of clever practical men on the raw. No doubt it is true, as he says, that 'formerly men were worse than their principles, but that at present the principles are worse than the men'.

A considerable part of the *Lay Sermons* is devoted to the question, which was ignored by Bagehot and has received little enough attention since, of the balance between agriculture and other pursuits. Coleridge had no idyllic view of the country. He had seen, in what Bagehot calls 'the quiet saving counties', children with their shoulders hunched about their ears, and farmers growing fatter in the very places where the cottagers starved. Nor was he hostile to trade and industry, though he was more interested in the people they produced than in the goods, and could not believe that three people at work in Manchester were necessarily better than two at work in Glencoe or the Trossachs. He was, of course, far from Bagehot's contempt for the ordinary countryman, and he had 'watched many a group of old and young, male and female, going to, or returning from, many a factory'. Although Coleridge passes for being abstracted, and Bagehot for a realist immersed in practical life, it is the latter

whose mind rests, in the end, on an abstract calculation and Coleridge who notices what is in front of his nose. In *Church and
State*, he attempts to distinguish the respective roles of agriculture
on the one hand and of commerce and industry on the other.*
He connects the permanence of the state with the land – and is
that indeed not a simple matter of fact? – but attributes progres-
sion 'in the arts and comforts of life, in the diffusion of the information and knowledge, useful or necessary for all; in short, all
advances in civilization' to the mercantile, manufacturing, dis-
tributive and professional classes – a matter of fact also. But
'agriculture requires principles essentially different from those of
trade;... a gentleman ought not to regard his estate as a merchant
his cargo, or a shop-keeper his stock'. The continuance and well-
being of those who live on the estate must be a consideration,
and 'men... ought to be weighed, not counted'. The objects of
the land-owner, with respect to his tenantry and dependants, are
precisely those of the state in relation to the country as a whole.
Both watch over the *dulcia arva* and their inhabitants. Of course
agriculture can be carried on in the spirit of trade, and this was
an aberration which had grown, with ups and downs, since the
establishment of the public debt in the reign of William III, and
had reached what it seemed must be a final pitch during the
Napoleonic Wars, then recently concluded. The love of lucre
was not less in the past, but it met with more and more powerful
checks, among which Coleridge included 'the ancient feeling of
rank and ancestry', the hold and intellectuality of religion and,
following Berkeley, the 'prevailing studies'. It was against the
vestiges of these checks that Bagehot persistently exerted himself,
and to what Coleridge called 'a *vortex* of hopes and hazards, of
blinding passions and blind practices', Bagehot gave another
name. The central object of Bagehot's writing – and it is a destructive one – was to give exclusive respectability to the pursuit of
lucre, and to remove whatever social and intellectual impedi-
ments stood in the way of it. Intellectual pursuits, and whatever
strives in the direction of permanence and *stillness*, have to give
way to the provisional and divisive excitements of gain. In the
end one is left contemplating numbers over a great void.

* S.T. Coleridge, *On the Constitution of the Church and State according to the
Idea of Each* (1839).

It is our own world. Against it, as a better compulsory reading
for the young than *Lombard Street* – which however must long
have slipped from its position as the one book that all economics
students could be counted on to have read – or *The English Constitution* – which is still prominently mentioned – might be set
The Querist. Bishop Berkeley's questions are too plain and just
to excite wide interest, but that should not tell against them.
They pose the fundamental questions of economics in relation
to government, and these questions ought to be met in a plain
form before specious refinements are attempted. *The Querist*'s
questions are set in the context of the Ireland of 1735, but they
are relevant anywhere precisely because of their appositeness to
that country then. The problems were much those that had, in
a manner which Bagehot derided, pre-occupied Swift – poverty,
luxury, the nature and use of money. He asks:

5 Whether money be not only so far useful, as it stirreth
up industry, enabling men mutually to participate the fruits
of each other's labour?
6 Whether any other means, equally conducing to excite
and circulate the industry of mankind, may not be as useful
as money?
7 Whether the real end and aim of men be not power? And
whether he who could have everything else at his wish or
will would value money?...
70 'Whether human industry can produce, from such cheap
materials, a manufacture of so great value by any other art
as by those of sculpture and paintings?

The questions pour out. They are not answered, but they point
any unprejudiced enquirer the way to look, and arm him
shrewdly to test what is emitted by the plausible expert. Berkeley
makes one assumption not shared by Bagehot – the existence of
national sovereignty, a notion which did not really interest
Bagehot because he saw the body politic, in terms which are
extremely provincial in time and place, as a rich cheese in which
men of business could wriggle in their financial contortions
undisturbed.

20 If power followeth money, whether this can be anywhere more properly and securely placed, than in the same
hands wherein the supreme power is already placed?

83   But whether a bank that utters bills, with the sole view of promoting the public weal, may not so proportion their quantity as to avoid several inconveniences which might attend private banks?

Secrecy in financial transactions, the opportunities for private profit-making at the expense of the public good or out of private trust – the rights which Bagehot held most dear – are to Berkeley so many cankers to be cut out where that is possible. What makes him so disarming is the perfect balance of his mind. The man who was dazzled by the visible universe had an equal charity like Traherne's. He is genuinely disinterested, and cares more for his country than for himself. It must pass for a strange abnormality beside the extreme normality, not to say commonplaceness, of Bagehot's busy self-preservation. Thought turns in the end on what lies at the bottom of the mind. One scarcely likes, for shame, to quote Berkeley's *Maxims concerning Patriotism*, but they are all true.

The basis of Berkeley's economics is no doubt a version of that mercantilism which was condemned by Adam Smith and which for Bagehot, in the euphoria of his enlightenment, was no longer more than a figment in an age which understood the true way of making money. But something of that kind is unkillable as long as the notion of sovereignty and of the *aris et focis* is not killed. Adam Smith on Mercantilism is like a reader of the *Daily Telegraph* on the evils of socialism, though it would greatly surprise most of those readers to learn that the exercise of a strong arm on industry and commerce was not an invention of Karl Marx. Berkeley's interventionism springs from his care for the people starving among the green acres of Ireland: '173   Whether the quantities of beef, butter, wool and leather, exported from this island, can be reckoned the superfluities of a country, where there are so many natives naked and famished?'

One might say that Berkeley recommends prudence as to the public interest, and a certain recklessness as to private interest, while Bagehot's recklessness is for the public, and his caution is for himself.

What we get from Bagehot is not so much a theory as a position, and not so much a position as a form of tactics. It is Walter Bagehot whom the successive positions are intended to protect – the Walter Bagehot who slipped down the crack between

Unitarianism and Anglicanism; who was the child of the Bank House as some are sons of the manse; whose money was better than that of the squire's but did not produce better effects on the locals; who should have been educated at Oxford but was above that sort of conformism; who conformed instead to the world of business but was cleverer than its other inhabitants; who was all the time worried about the sanity of his stock and did not have any children; who distrusted the hereditary powers and owed all his opportunities to family influence. He was a gifted man who pushed around in the world, and he liked to think that there was only pushing and shoving, though he owed more to the discretion which keeps people on the winning side. No doubt a great deal of life is like this, and more than any other writer of talent Bagehot embodies the forces of successful action. But it is successful action in a particular *milieu*, that of the rising finance and journalism of nineteenth-century England. Bagehot operated in a field of natural selection from which the more desperate assaults, and the more desperate risks, had already been eliminated. Put him beside Raleigh, and one misses the moral strength which comes of a readiness to contemplate stabbing, and of the necessity in certain circumstances of facing the block. Put him beside Swift, one misses the force of instinctive but intellectually developed loyalties. The comparisons are in a sense unfair, because Bagehot could be – and was – a man of ability without being able to hold a candle to either of the other two; but they serve to designate not only his stature but his kind. And Bagehot was not always successful, even in his world of limited practice. The election at Bridgwater shows a certain gaucherie. It suggests also that Bagehot was a man who receded from his failures rather than lived through them. Perhaps the current of petty affairs carried him too strongly. Swift the Dean of Saint Patrick's knew that he had not been as much in Harley's confidence as he had supposed, when he lived in the great world, and his real success was made out of his defeat. Raleigh drank from the bottom of the well before he had finished. Bagehot does not, in his writing, anywhere touch these profounder depths. He spins clever comment between himself and reality; he has skimmed the river not dredged it.

Yet one should not under-rate the peculiarity of Bagehot's performance. Although by definition there are common men enough, who do the ordinary business of the world and avoid doing it on any particular principle, it is rare indeed for such a man to be explicit about this performance. Even Bagehot hedges a little, but the more one reads him the more it strikes one how little it is. The references to religion are modified by a social tone; he is a man accustomed to not offending the ladies. But the irony and contempt show through. Bagehot is reluctant to abandon the ordinary direction of his vision, which is downwards, with an amused smile playing on his lips. 'Your governess is like an egg', he said to the Miss Wilsons when he first met them, and as soon as the unfortunate hireling's back was turned. The Miss Wilsons tittered. How clever Mr Bagehot was so to break in on the traditional respects. The little episode is perfectly in the tone of Bagehot's political writings. It is a tone which has for a century been sure of a certain applause, but it indicates limitations in the speaker as well as in any audience that is too readily amused by it. It excludes any sympathy which threatens the desiderated victory. It is quite different from the tone of Samuel Johnson, when he talked for victory, for Johnson cared for the truth more than for himself and the victory was mere knock-about stuff. His real purpose was to remove his opponent's pretensions till the vanquished like the victor was humbled before reality. Bagehot's anxiety is to get by, and never to admit that he has come to grief, which is, truly, the tone of affairs and the reason why they so rarely comport the seriousness of the confrontations which are habitual in the artist or other penitent.

However well Bagehot's tactics conform to the practice of everyday life, they lack the substance of a political or social theory because, with all the pretence of frankness there is an unwillingness to admit that they are viable only within a certain defence line. Bagehot's blasphemy is that of a man who feels himself to be securely protected from God. His financial confidence tricks are played out in a society which permits and encourages certain forms of depredation. He can laugh at what he pretends are the powers that be simply because the powers are in reality not there, or because he does not tax them in any way to which they would really object, however rude they might think him. A man who is really inside the spirit of his age, as Bagehot was, cannot really offend important people, because they are working within the same pre-suppositions as himself. The most he can do is to get the credit for being a little advanced. This is the very type of liberalism which grew up within the frontiers of the England who was a terror to her foes or, at the very least, could make them think twice. Liberalism does not flourish except within safe frontiers and that is, of course, one of the reasons for making the frontiers safe, so long as that is practicable. So long as there are life-and-death confrontations within a country, there are other pre-occupations than liberalism. It was not in evidence when Cranmer was burnt or when Laud was beheaded. It reached an intense florescence under the roof of King's College, Cambridge, in the twentieth century, when personal relations, without even the degree of natural realism which is imported by the phenomena of heterosexuality, were amusingly believed to hold a real primacy over the prejudices not only of religion but of patriotism. There is a classic statement in E.M. Forster's *What I Believe*, printed as a pamphlet in 1939 and reproduced in *Two Cheers* (just the number to bring an understanding smile) *for Democracy* (1951). Forster of course did not believe in belief, and that was the first irony of his pamphlet. One simply had to have a creed because all the rough chaps outside Abinger and King's insisted on having one. 'Tolerance, good temper and sympathy are no longer enough in a world which is rent by religious and racial persecution, in a world where ignorance rules, and science, who ought to have ruled, plays the subservient pimp.' By implication, it is in a world just recently invented that tolerance, good temper and sympathy are not enough – as if those qualities had ever brought home the bacon, or defined the nature of man, however desirable they might be as supervening graces. 'Science ought to have ruled'. But whatever that evocative phrase may mean – and it would certainly have been good for *three* cheers in Cambridge – the idea that there is any novelty about ignorance being on top is a new one indeed. It was just 'for the moment', according to Forster, that his favourite virtues wanted stiffening, simply as a necessary antidote to the men in jack-boots. Forster has the vulgarity to produce as his 'motto' an inversion of certain words recorded in St Mark as having been spoken to our Lord. He makes out – for in 1939 a touch of social deference was still thought prudent, as regards Jesus himself – that his opponents are simply Moses and Paul – as if that might not in itself have given him pause. But according to Mark, Jesus said: 'If thou canst believe, all things are possible to him that believeth. And straightway the father of the child cried out, and said with tears, Lord, I believe; help thou mine unbelief.' Forster's silly motto was 'Lord, I disbelieve – help thou mine unbelief.' He illustrates his folly by putting the shallow Erasmus side by side with the profoundly sceptical Montaigne.

Forster's *credo*, like Bagehot's, is an amused disowning of everything which is not himself. In place of the banker-journalist – a crude, masculine figure in comparison – is the troop of 'the sensitive, the considerate and the plucky'. Readers of the novels will know who is meant – the cosy snobs of *Howard's End*, the picnickers of *A Passage to India*, no one far away from the Abinger-Cambridge axis, for the attempts to get beyond this special *milieu*, in such a person as Leonard Bast, for example, serve only to show Forster's real incomprehension of the human animal. For in all he says it is an ambience, not the person, that counts. Indeed in Cambridge it apparently took Psychology (sic) to show 'that there is something incalculable in each of us, which may at any moment rise to the surface and destroy our normal balance'. My word! No one would have guessed that before Psychology. To Forster's special group of 'the sensitive, the considerate and the plucky' are attributed all the culture-objects Forster approves of. These people 'produce literature and art, or they do disinterested scientific research', they 'are creative in their private lives'. They even 'found religions', which you might have thought, on Forster's principles, was not a very good thing to do, but it is important that all creativity should belong to the gang. This is Forster's version of the *élite* which is authorized to be superior about the body politic, as Bagehot's is the free-masonry of *Economist* readers. Man for man, one might as well have Bagehot's lot. Bagehot is anyway more honest as to what he is about. The culture gang is perhaps naturally more aberrational. Anyhow Forster's aberration extends to claiming Dante as belonging to his set, on the ground that he placed Brutus and Cassius in the lowest circle of Hell 'because they had chosen to betray their friend Julius Caesar rather than their country Rome', though in fact they were put there because they had betrayed their *master*, the type in that circle being Judas Iscariot.

The protected world of E.M. Forster is really a pleasure-garden, for those who care for that sort of pleasure and can afford high walls to live behind. Forster's admiration for his own irradiation and that of his friends knew no bounds. With mock humility and a blasphemous allusion he says: 'And one can, at all events, show one's own little light here, one's own poor little trembling flame, with the knowledge that it is not the only light that is shining in the darkness, and not the only one which the darkness does not comprehend.' From behind the high walls where the plucky and the sensitive have taken refuge come sniggers at the

232 | ENGLISH PERSPECTIVES

ordinary affairs of men and the great historical movements. It is a mark not merely of irreligion but of lack of grasp of the concerns of mankind that Forster refers to the Christian Church as 'a worthy stunt' – like a flag-day, no doubt, or one of those petitions to which he was a never-failing subscriber. That these frolics were conditional Forster himself perfectly understood. 'While we are trying to be sensitive and advanced and affectionate and tolerant' – I am not at all sure that such *effort* is to be commended, but that is what Forster says – 'an unpleasant question pops up: does not all society rest upon force?' His theory was that 'all the great creative actions, all the decent human relations, occur during the intervals when force has not managed to come to the front'. The crucifixion, for example? It is this notion of 'the intervals that matter' which makes Forster's liberalism so fragile and artificial. He confesses to 'looking the other way' until fate strikes him, and one can admire the candour of that, if nothing else. But the corporate affairs of men are not so to be understood. The roots of trouble are always there, even in our most smiling actions. King's and Abinger are not cases of virtue, but the slight phenomena of an historical situation which for a brief space allows a few rather soft people so to amuse themselves, and to consume what others have sweated or got themselves killed for. Perhaps the esthete, like the banker, depends on 'the ruder sort of men' who 'will sacrifice all they hope for, *themselves*, for what is called an idea'.

A more important question is whether theories of liberalism, whether economic or otherwise intellectual, which can have play only because of the antecedence of less seductive institutions and doctrines, can be more than a delusive foundation for political thought. So long as they are understood to be merely a conditional arrangement, a permitted sport within a certain constitutional framework, they may have their usefulness, for they certainly embody a part of civilization. It is in their nature, however, to nibble at the framework rather than to support it. That again may have its uses, for all institutions must change and be ceaselessly in a state of adaptation. The 'hard facts' of money are not very hard, for they are the facts of a convention, and the 'values' of intellectual fashion are valuable only so far as they represent a viable existence.

The enlightenment Bagehot offered has run out. A good laugh at the monarchy, a series of little jeers at the historical Church, a jealous look at the gentry – all this comported a certain amuse-ment in its time, but it is not very funny now. The gentry has gone the way it has always gone, in England where, as Fuller said in 1648, the capacity to be gentle has not been denied to any, who so behaves himself. The 'Church is more set against the world than at any time since pagan Rome', as Eliot had it. No one can deny now that she is engaged in a life-and-death struggle, which is all she is fit for. The monarchy has gone on, not, as Bagehot suggested, because people at large have not noticed that the Cabinet really takes the decisions, but because they have begun to suspect that the Cabinet does not either. The final point in the State must rest on a certain incomprehension, and incom-prehension is the beginning of theology. Few people now would imagine that they knew what was meant by the Divine Right of Kings, but anyone might reach the point of mystification as to the coherence and persistence of national entities, which the hereditary monarchy so well expresses.

Gregory Dix reports that he met in West Africa, 'a leading Ju-Ju man' who explained his role as a magician with 'all the *aplomb* and that touch of courteous condescension which always mark the man of science explaining to the theologian' (*Jew and Greek, A Study in the Primitive Church*, 1953). The witch-doctor claimed to make spectacular things happen, and thought the priest was wasting his time. It was, of course, the former who was the typical man of the modern world. Nobody now likes to admit to being lacking in usefulness, of some kind intelligible to a vulgar utilitarianism. Yet the production of results is a less common achievement than most performers would have us believe. There is still hewing of wood and drawing of water, but such clear cases are by no means universal in an industrial society. When one gets to the men with charts and statistics – the battalions of management so characteristic of our world, whose philosophy is exclusively one of *results* – the connection between cause and effect is often so tenuous as to strain everyone's belief. The idea that a man 'makes' even money, as distinct from putting himself or perhaps merely standing in the way of it, is always to be treated with reserve. And even with the housewife, that residual handiwoman from earlier times, the role is a much larger thing than the sum of the performances. In a static, caste society, it is the role which dominates and attracts attention. The warrior occasionally fights, but is always a warrior. In our sort of society, it is conceived that the worth of a man is in the result he produces, so there is no end to this sort of exaggeration. Yet results, even when achieved, are generally very difficult to evaluate, and the idea of a whole society valuing itself on its results alone is a very difficult conception indeed. One might say indeed that it is non-sense. A simple deception has given it currency – the peculiar, not to say overwhelming, use of money in our times. A conventional numerical system establishes a common value, and it is pretended that one can calculate a Gross National Product, within which all results have their contributory number.

Bagehot was entirely a man of this world. His personal product was only words and numbers – the typical groceries of managerial man – but he was the philosopher of the consumer society, which is only the reverse of the producer obverse. The end of progress was 'the development of human comfort', then the distinguishing mark of the superiority of the Englishman. Bagehot saw this as the product of industry by the development of money-lending, and this corresponds pretty well to an obvious aspect of history in the hundred years since his death. It was a sort of liberation, involving the denigration of everything which stood in the way of it, but the liberation is hardly what we notice most about the world it has brought about.

Bagehot was reckless even on his own showing. He saw that there had to be recognized authority to hold any society together, and that the establishment of authority was a process which takes time, a lot of time. It was a sort of non-financial capital, he might have said, which could be used only when it had been collected or imagined. He was interested in the *use* – what could be done, in his case money-making – under its shadow. None the less the whole tenor of his critical effort was to assist the destruction of respect among those whom he regarded as serious and intelligent men of affairs, for what he called the dignified elements of the constitution. It was as if to ensure that no future generation should operate with such advantages. Perhaps he did not care much for the future. The old landowner planted trees for his grandchildren; the man acting in the spirit of trade wants to know only how much timber he can sell over the next five years. Coleridge's distinction goes to the root of the matter. Any political unit worth maintaining, or which is anyway to be maintained at all, must contain a principle of foresight and continuity which goes beyond the next series of trade figures, and it will be the foresight of care rather than of calculation. An unreasoning love on the part of its inhabitants is the best safeguard for any country – superior even to that love of private gain in which Adam Smith and Bagehot, like Mandeville before them, put such trust. No doubt both stimuli are necessary, the world being what it is, but it is super-stition, or worse, to suppose that the unchecked appetite for lucre can bring anything but the destruction of the commonwealth, or that it can take very long to produce that result. Art and all things made for their own sake tell in the other direction, towards permanence rather than towards change and saleability, and there is no more terrifying symptom of decay than the replacement of art, in the public attention, by the saleable products of anti-art. Those who do not believe that that is happening do not know what art is. They can never have *seen* the ordinary domestic equip-ment of the seventeenth century, or tradesmen's cards of the eighteenth century. The Devil has many disguises, and what is called liberty of expression, particularly in the great trade of sex, has more to do with the nature of the financial system than with art. In the ordinary hue and cry about the latest play or novel to poke its way to prominence, it is more instructive to ask who gets the money from it than whether the work can properly be regarded as corrupting. Indeed the financial question has more to do with serious literary criticism. It must not even be supposed that there is some special kinship between art and democracy. Indeed almost all of the great literature of the world was produced without that freedom of expression which is now generally said to be essential for such productions.

It will not quite do, in a commonwealth, to count heads as one counts money. The land is also important. It was until recently maintained that there was a labour shortage in this country. Nothing could be more absurd, in an island of this size. It was merely that people were doing the wrong things, because the wrong things were the most profitable. It is now often main-tained that if we make and sell enough of any kind of marketable rubbish, our future is assured. That also is a lie. An economics which rests entirely on financial measurement is as far from reality as any refinement of mediaeval schoolmen. It will not help if there is nothing to eat in the refrigerator, or the land is soured from Portsmouth to the Wash.

Bagehot lies under an ungainly tombstone in the churchyard of All Saints, Langport, which looks out over miles of Somerset to the Dorset hills. Standing there one may see why he was, indeed, no more than 'the wisest man of his generation'.

Epilogue on a Founding Father

There is, of course, another view of Walter Bagehot. This is that he was the innovator who pointed the way for all reasonable Anglo-Saxons in the generations which have succeeded him. It is possible to see him as pointing further than 'that, as if the give-away attitude he represents – giving away what belongs to others while holding tight to what you have yourself – were the only rational way of conducting affairs, in all times and even in those places which have not been illuminated by the light of Anglo-Saxondom. In a way it is, if by rational you mean proceeding so far as possible to a comfortable disintegration. Only you have to be sure that you have something to give you comfort as long as you need it. Not everyone has been so well placed, in that respect, as the English middle classes of the nineteenth or even the twentieth century. The case for attributing a wider relevance to this attitude is confidence in the power of technology to create, continuously, more than we manage to destroy. This confidence is inherent in all the dominant movements of our world and one can entertain the hypothesis that it may be justified.

In Bagehot's time things must have looked rather different. But the direction of movement was already marked, and the year in which Bagehot was educated by the French *coup d'état* was also the year of the Great Exhibition. It is therefore possible to hold that the adolescent who, nine years before (in 1842) had entered upon courses of study at University College, London, rather than go to Oxford, had been guided by all the lights of advancing thought. The same planets which presided over Walter Bagehot's birth had played upon the seven acres around Gower Street which were purchased in 1826 and where the foundation stone of the College was laid in the following year. Behind the founding movement were impeccable Whig minds. There was Brougham, of whom Bagehot himself said that he 'was able to rush hither and thither... and gather up the whole stock of the most recent information, the extreme decimals of the statistics, and diffuse them immediately with eager comment to a listening world.'

There was Thomas Campbell, an overblown literary man whose best work was behind him and who was busying himself with a career of public eminence. Both were Scots, educated at Scotch universities, and fell easily into the tradition of those who, since the Act of Union to which Swift had taken such exception, had contributed to the inflation of the English and Anglican world and its replacement by Great Britain or something even greater and vaguer. Other members of the founding group were Isaac Lyon Goldsmid, Joseph Hume, and 'some influential dissenters, most of them connected with the congregation of Dr Cox of Hackney'. The scheme was inspired by the same passion for freedom which motivated Thomas Bagehot – an aversion from the Thirty-Nine Articles with which Oxford and Cambridge were so degradingly entangled. The first Council of the new institution comprised representatives of nearly every religious denomination, and so demonstrated the unimportance of such differences and ultimately that of the Christian religion itself. The ideas of the reformers were much the same as those which Sir William Hamilton – another Scot – brought into play in the eighteen-thirties against the sleepy resistance of Oxford. Hamilton's aim was to lower the pride of the fellows and to raise that of the professors, as the supposed sources of learning in particular subjects. From the first it was planned that the courses of instruction in London should include languages, mathematics, physics, the mental and moral sciences, the laws of England, history and political economy. These developments must have been noted with satisfaction in the office of the bank manager at Langport, and no doubt Thomas Bagehot recoiled with horror at the reaction which led in 1831 to the opening of King's College, London. At King's a similar pattern of studies was to be followed but there was to be a connection with the national church. The sentiments of Thomas Bagehot would have been those of the contemporary cartoonist who exhibited three fat bishops huzza-ing for King's, set in a scale against Brougham, Campbell and Jeremy Bentham. The bishops bore down the scale – as if they were not fat enough already – with a weight labelled 'Money and Interest', while the reformers of University College flew up in the air, having nothing on their side but 'Sense and Science'.

There is no doubt that, in accordance with a well-known bit of social mechanics, the activities of the dissenting groups had a marked effect in stimulating, somewhat belatedly, the forces of orthodoxy. The foundation of the University of Durham from the revenues of that see may be classed as an effect of the same movement. It was to the rising forces of dissent and industry that the Bagehot family really belonged. One must not over-rate the intellectual freshness of those forces or the degree of social oppression they suffered. They followed the Whigs who, throughout most of the eighteenth century, had treated the Church with contempt while ensuring that their nominees revelled in the revenues of the bishoprics. The alliance with industry which was a characteristic of the nineteenth century was in succession to a long alliance with the forces of finance. When Matthew Arnold took up the task of civilizing dissent, from the point of view of an Oxford which by then he regarded as a home of lost causes, it was the manufacturers and their opinionated chapels he had in mind. Arnold was, rather markedly, the son of a public school headmaster – *the* public school headmaster, you might say – and himself an inspector of schools. But his class of savage mill-owners themselves begat inspectors of schools and the like in great numbers and it was finally the war of 1914–18 which split society open and made it clear that the landed aristocracy and gentry, whose dignity had offended Bagehot so much, would offend by their dignity no more. Dissent, in a wider sense than the *démodé* business of disagreement with the Thirty-Nine Articles, became the unquestionable Establishment of our society. It has been so, with an ever-widening series of topics if a certain monotony of method, ever since.

There is an intellectual succession to be taken account of in this movement away from what one might perhaps call the agricultural and religious world to the modern world of assumptions about the impugnability of technological benefits – a tradition of feeling, as Keynes has pointed out, as well as of thought. It is – to quote Keynes's essay on Malthus,

> the English tradition of humane science... that tradition of Scotch and English thought, in which there has been, I think, an extraordinary continuity of *feeling*, if I may express it, from the eighteenth century to the present time – the tradition which is suggested by the names of Locke, Hume, Adam Smith, Paley, Bentham, Darwin and Mill, a tradition marked by a love of truth and a most noble lucidity, by a prosaic sanity free from sentiment or metaphysic, and by an immense disinterestedness and public spirit. (*Essays in Biography*, 1933, 120.)

It is to this tradition, or only a little aside from it – aside on account of his personal flavour and the tinge which financial interests gave to his concern for the public good – that Bagehot belongs, as does Keynes himself, though with another, and perhaps subtler, deviation. For Keynes was, in his early years, at the centre of a little pseudo-renaissance which was a great social and, it is said, literary and intellectual success. This movement marks the passing of the non-conformist tradition into the general orthodoxy of Bloomsbury and the *New Statesman* and beyond. Keynes has given a nostalgic account of this in the short paper, entitled *My Early Beliefs*, which he wrote in September 1938, just as it became publicly indisputable that the smile of amusement which had, so to speak, passed with an immense accretion of refinement from Bagehot to himself, was not, after all, a smile at the nature of reality but the tic of a rather pampered group. Keynes was of course among the first to see this for he had, like Bagehot, a facility in withdrawing from untenable positions, though in this personal confession his subtlety in preserving his own dignity was such that, while admitting that he had been wrong, he added that it was too late to change. There had, after all, been only 'just a grain of truth' in D.H. Lawrence's assertion, in 1914, that Keynes and his Cambridge friends were 'done for', and it was only by ignoring what Keynes called 'our charm, our intelligence, our unworldliness, our affection', that the admission could be forced thus far. The centre of their doctrine, or 'religion' as Keynes appropriately called it, was an individualism which was not, like Bagehot's, that of a moneyed provincial pushing his way in a conventional society, but that of a man who felt himself safely detached from all such ugly realities.

'We entirely repudiated', Keynes says,

> a personal liability on us to obey general rules. We claimed the right to judge every individual case on its merits, and the wisdom, experience and self-control to do so successfully. This was a very important part of our faith, violently and aggressively held, and for the outer world it was our most obvious and dangerous characteristic. We repudiated entirely customary morals, conventions and traditional wisdom. We were, that is to say, in the strict sense of the term, immoralists. The consequences of being found out had, of course, to be considered for what they were worth. But we recognised no moral obligation on us, no inner sanction, to

conform or to obey. Before heaven we claimed to be our own judge in our own case. I have come to think that this is, perhaps, rather a Russian characteristic. It is certainly not an English one.

And yet it is, of course, the logical outcome of that long line of dissent which, having eluded all the authorities which it always asserted were bent on oppressing it, ends by being dissent *tout court*, or the mere pursuit of a lonely appetite. Keynes goes on:

> It resulted in a general, widespread, though partly covert, suspicion affecting ourselves, our motives and our behaviour. This suspicion still persists to a certain extent, and it always will. It has deeply coloured the course of our lives in relation to the outside world. It is, I now think, a justifiable suspicion. Yet so far as I am concerned, it is too late to change. I remain, and always will remain, an immoralist. (*Two Memoirs*, 1949, 97–8.)

Certainly Keynes has gone beyond Bagehot in the logic of his argument. He kept better logical company, and had less to fear from society than Bagehot, whose credit depended on retaining, in spite of his cleverness, a certain stodgy respectability, while Keynes was throughout his life able to cultivate a reputation as an intellectual. He was moving towards a world in which a much more rapid adaptability was required and Bagehot's gentle jeering at the Church and the landed gentry was old-fashioned stuff. Keynes's beliefs left no impediment to limitless change, and this enabled him to carry much further the sort of rationality which is needed for the uninhibited development of technology. He thought, as Bagehot did, that 'self-interest was *rational*' and that 'the egoistic and altruistic systems' would 'work out in practice to the same conclusions'. This optimistic view of human nature he claimed later to have corrected, though not, I think, so far as to take a pessimistic view of himself and his friends, whom he called, in a Forsterian phrase, 'poor, silly, well-meaning us'. Bagehot of course always made a point of the stupidity of other people, or of the mass which needed to have deceptions practised upon it so that those who could see through social and religious pretences could govern the country.

Keynes was perhaps the wisest man of *his* generation, as Bagehot was of his, and that is after all the height of worldly distinction. An hereditary member of the post-clerical university world, he was born at the right moment to rise with its fortunes as an influence on public policy. He had all the talents for a distinguished role. Eton and King's College, Cambridge, gave him a background which facilitated his access to political circles at a time when they were only just beginning to lose their aristocratic or at any rate upper class colour. He was present at the Peace negotiations in 1919. After a recession from favour said to have been due to *The Economic Consequences of the Peace*, a book which was in the rising sentiment of the inter-war years, whatever might be thought of its political acuteness, he was back at the centre of power in the Second War and afterwards, with a theory which fitted perfectly the social-democratic tendencies of the time. He was the prophet, only shortly before politicians were ready to receive the doctrine, of central controls which would establish 'an aggregate volume of output corresponding to full employment as nearly as is practicable', and consequentially of 'a large extension of the traditional functions of government'. The *direction* of output was all right; whatever was produced, was good. It was only the volume – the fact that it left people unemployed – that was wrong.

Economics used to be called Political Economy, and has lost the adjective in the search for scientific status. But political it remains, like the behavioural sciences at large, which are sciences only in a large, old-fashioned sense, whatever may be the claims of their academic exponents, scrambling for the most profitable description in order to get a full share of the money flowing into universities. Concealed under the more comprehensive propositions of these sciences, and under all their practical propositions, are assumptions about the nature of the human animal which are capable of only slight modification in the light of current observations and are mainly lore – what the human race thinks about itself. Keynes was well aware of the underlying elusiveness of his subject-matter. In propounding his *General Theory of Employment* (1936) he realized that it was uncertain 'how far it is safe to stimulate the average propensity to consume' and that only experience would show 'how far the common will, embodied in the policy of the state, ought to be directed to increasing and supplementing the inducement to invest'. The 'common will', so unobtrusively introduced, begs all the classic questions of political theory. It could only get by because of the general agreement not to question the bases of democracy. Keynes the theorist was always near enough to practice to know when to keep his mouth shut. Bagehot's conception of a managing *élite* was franker but it flattered the degree of democracy obtaining in his day. In Keynes's day the public to be flattered was larger. Enough attention has not been given to the effect of the extension of the franchise upon economic theory. Bagehot wanted to stop the tide of widening suffrage at a point convenient to him, beyond which it would have spoiled his theories and perhaps his income. Keynes did not sufficiently take account of its effects, though he clearly realized that his projects could only be executed by the intervention of the state. What sort of state? and What was it likely to do? were questions he brought his theory up against but did not, in the end, face. Both he and Bagehot assumed the sort of state they respectively needed. It is a measure of the benign good fortune of their lives, and a limitation in their usefulness to us.

Keynes concluded his *General Theory* with some words which look far beyond the subject-matter, beyond economics altogether. 'The ideas of economists and political philosophers,' he says, 'both when they are right and when they are wrong, are more powerful than is commonly understood. Indeed the world is ruled by little else. Practical men, who believe themselves to be quite exempt from any intellectual influences, are usually the slave of some defunct economist.' He might have added that economists and political philosophers, in the most enlightened epochs as in the darkness of the Victorian Age or of the Middle Ages, take their direction from religious and ethical conceptions which they are apt to think they threw out of their studies when they started their serious work. Ideas are not created by individuals; they are derived.

In our day the denial of the sources of our thinking is an indispensable preliminary to any intervention on the public stage. Debate on public affairs, and still more the actual execution of public business, has to be conducted on the basis that there are facts but no philosophies. It is a technique for securing civil peace and in view of the difficulty, historically speaking, of attaining this objective, it is not to be lightly dismissed. Whereas, however, older Machiavellian devices for achieving one's ends amidst general approval – such as, in suitable times and places, assuming a mask of religion – allow for a realistic disjunction between the thought of the governor and of the governed, this device is apt to deceive the governors as well. The modern bureaucratic machine, certainly in this country, is conducted in the full belief – tempered only by the private scepticism of individual operators

– in the objectivity of 'facts'. It needs a poet rather than a mathematician to realize vividly the shadowy and elusive connection between word and fact.

Bagehot was a founding father of the apologetics of 'fact'. Clever, sceptical men of affairs, the class whose activity consisted in deceiving the others, saw, according to him, nothing else, and what the others saw was nothing. Facts were what Bagehot could use, to clear a way for himself in society and to make money. They are likewise the weapon of the contemporary civil servant, to turn away wrath and to make a game so complicated that no one else can play it.

The function of the philosopher, the artist, or in his degree of any many worth his salt, is different. Wyndham Lewis said despairingly: 'The game of government goes on, and it is a game that no philosopher has ever been able to interrupt seriously for a moment.' Bagehot on the other hand tried to elevate to the role of a philosophy the derivative muddlings of men of affairs, to the detriment of both theory and practice.

V

NATIVE RUMINATIONS

Introduction

The conduct of government rests upon the same foundation and encounters the same difficulties as the conduct of private persons: that is, as to its object and justification, for as to its methods, or technical part, there is all the difference which separates the person from the group, the man acting on behalf of himself from the man acting on behalf of many. The technical part, in government as in private conduct, is now the only one which is publicly or at any rate generally recognized, as if by this evasion the more difficult part of the subject, which relates to ends, could be avoided. Upon 'the law of nature and the law of revelation', Blackstone said, 'depend all human laws'*. This quaint language, which would at once be derided if it were introduced now into public discussion, conceals a difficulty which is no less ours than it was our ancestors'.

It was reasonable for Blackstone, using this language, to use also language of a certain nobility in describing the functions of Members of Parliament:

> They are not thus honourably distinguished from the rest of their fellow-subjects, merely that they may privilege their persons, their estates, or their domestics; that they may list under party banners; may grant or withold supplies; may vote with or against a popular or unpopular administration; but upon considerations far more interesting and important. They are the guardians of the English constitution; the makers, repealers and interpreters of the English laws; delegated to watch, to check, and to avert every dangerous innovation, to propose, adopt, and to cherish any solid and well-weighed improvement; bound by every tie of nature, of honour, and of religion, to transmit that constitution and those laws to their posterity, amended if possible, at least without derogation.

* Sir William Blackstone, *Commentaries on the Laws of England* (1765-9), Introduction, Section I.

This is so unlike the language we should use, in relation to Members of Parliament, that it has an air of comedy. Honour and religion are – many would say, happily – subverted, and nature has become uncertain, so it is not clear what binds the Members. Are they there after all merely 'that they may privilege their persons'? They would for the most part shy away from that explanation. Many might say they were there to make innovations, as Blackstone thought they were there to avert them: and while for Blackstone 'dangerous' was the adjective which went naturally with 'innovation', for our Members other, more approving qualifications would come more readily to mind. They might well be so busy about change as not to catch sight of the fundamental problem, which remains, however. What are they there for, if not merely to 'privilege their persons'? If not tied by honour or religion, they are perhaps tied by nature, which science may study, and their innovations are in her service. It is a possibility.

A possible Anglicanism

1

The real difficulty of the Creed is the first word – I – the number and person of the *Credo*. The *ergo* of Descartes, like many others before and since, now looks like a confidence-trick.

This is a difficulty which is least in youth, when the force of desire makes a certain animism easy. Surely a spirit must dwell in that body which is the object of nascent desires? But later the reflection comes that that spirit is like one's own, which is less impressive. A more wholesome reflection, perhaps, is that one's own body is like another's. That is to say, one can explain one's own spirit in terms of another's body, and so of one's own; re-assure oneself that, however uncertain it is to be oneself, one must at least be like other bodies, which seem plausible enough. This is a pagan reflection, but it may also be a Christian one, though it is self-regarding, perhaps, in a way that the young man's animism in relation to another body may not be – but that is only perhaps, too.

Whichever way one approaches the subject, one arrives at the identification of the self and the body, whether or not the two are co-terminous. There is nothing but the body, its actions and manifestations, that has any claim to be thought of as a self. Is spirit something different? If it is, I am quite without understanding of it. Unless of course it is a hall-mark, set on the body by God, or a sort of standard pattern, the image of the Creator. But that must be an object of faith, because it cannot be perceived – believed in if at all in sheer despair at what can be perceived, and out of need for a re-assurance of one's identity, not so much with oneself as with other creatures. It therefore looks like a metaphysical projection of the common need to be like another body, and to be re-assured that the other body contains consciousness, or whatever it is that one perceives in oneself. I have always slid over these difficulties to the resurrection of the body, so little believed in, incredible certainly, but more understandable than any other apology for the life everlasting – the only understandable one, I would say. It is that or nothing.

That, as distinct from nothing, is, it seems to me, what religion is. There is nothing but God to choose. Apart from that, which we properly call Him, not on account of sex but because of an identity with ourselves, there are only the miscellaneous performances of the human body, of any sort of body – not merely that of a cat but of a stone, for if consciousness has to be inferred from external appearance stones have their performance as well as those who are more usually thought of as our neighbours. If He does not exist the miscellaneous performances of the human body are not *sui generis*, the sums you do are no more than the sums done by a calculating machine, your punch is like that of the boulder that falls on you. Indeed I am afraid we believe in Him in order to be *sui generis*, in order not to perish. And if our faith is right he chooses us – we are a mirror and there really is someone looking in.

The Christian faith is that God was made man. And what is man? Why, he is the image of God – there is no other meaning I can attach to the expression. He is the broken image which was re-made at the Incarnation, for our re-assurance. There is a circle here which may be a deceit. If we believe it is because we want to choose and be chosen. If our belief is true it is because we must so choose. Otherwise the desire to choose and be chosen is the illusory appearance of something else, a mere accompaniment of being driven on by forces which indifferently drive everything. One cannot say that that alternative is improbable.

There is a trick in the abstraction of language which could deceive us either way. Because there is nothing of us but our bodies and their manifestations, the language which reminds us least of them seems most promising of a truth beyond them. But in fact what we say is said in words which have their start in the operations of the body. Words are not ours but the words of a myriad, having point only because of their history, ultimately of their prehistory. The man who speaks, if there is Man, is the same who (I think it was Frobenius who put me on to this) at some stage of pre-history – and it may be in some of contemporary consciousness – could have sexual intercourse without being aware of it, as I might scratch my head without knowing it. We speak as historical persons – well, to say persons is to beg the question, but we do not speak as ourselves. If we are selves, it is by virtue of other selves that we are so. And our speaking is that of a race, of a tribe, of a time. There is no speech which is not of a here and now and it is nothing except in terms of other times and elsewhere. That is why the historical church is so apt to our needs and meaning. It is a congregation of meaning and there is no meaning without congregation.

There is no meaning except in terms of a time and a place. If one could understand it would be at one altar, in a stone building, in such a place, at perhaps eight o'clock on a Sunday morning. If there were no sacraments there would be nothing. If there were not England there would be no church, for me who happen to have been born here. I am an Anglican.

2

If the *ecclesia anglicana* is the vehicle of meaning for me, it is the centre of England, however little it seems to be regarded. That is to say, it is so so far as England enters my consciousness – to which word I prefer *conscience*, and consider the French are more fortunate (and more exact) than we in having only one word for the two (English) conceptions. The *ecclesia anglicana* is the centre of the political England no less than of the others, and the political conceptions which omit it are not merely incomplete; they are without middle. It is no less true, however, that any consideration of the Church which ignores the vulgar exterior of doing and intriguing – the ordinary behaviour of men – is an abstraction of an individual mind, the invention of a non-imagination – a partial, protestant mind like Kant's, trying to elevate our thinking above the world of sense. The truth is that churches have their politics, in the most vulgar sense, no more deserving of pity than other politics. There is no reason to adopt a soppy, Christianish way of talking about these things, as if everything to do with the church demanded the manners of the Ladies' Working Party. This soppiness is of course a new thing, the product not of sweeter and more gracious ways of thinking but of the progressive realization that the church is socially unimportant and can (nearly) be ignored. It was not very nice that people should burn one another for their faith, or that Archbishops should be executed for their political devotion to their sovereign, but these things were done because, at the time when they were done, there was not the present facility in extracting from theological conceptions all trace of practical meaning.

The progress of democracy – for which Locke's *Letter on Toleration* is an early apologia – has been a process of laicisation. It has succeeded in driving religion into the recesses of a thing called the individual conscience, which has to be less than the *consciousness* people have of their physical environment, including themselves, so that it bothers nobody. Then, it is said, we can ignore people's beliefs, indeed the proprieties of our politics demand that we should do so. We will debate in parliament about the things we can really agree about – what we all want, food, keeping the enemy away, never mind who we are or what form we give to the food we eat. The end of this is a material world which there is no-one to observe. There is the food secured for us by our governors, the fuel that warms our bodies, the machines which carry us around or replace our labours. All this system is to be promoted and no questions asked, for *conscience* has nothing to do with it. It is the Neanderthal man, with his mind closing upon him as he reaches the end of his path. Of course the conception is muddled. If politics are planned as a system of doing things to people (which, so far as it ignores consciousness is the same thing as doing things to things) it assumes a supreme political group who do the doing, who are not merely some *thing* but some *bodies*, not merely some bodies but bodies with consciousness. There could be a new serfdom which would make this possible, but it is an oppression which would so much impoverish the human race, the conception of what man is, that even for the governors it would in the end be of little interest.

Under this negative debate of our public affairs, once excused under the name of liberty and now, more often, under the name of economics or production, the conscious, including the ecclesiastical, groups still stir. Not only stir, but exhibit all those political symptoms which are admitted to exist only in relation to groups concerned with the matters the consciousness of the commonwealth admits. Just as, in westernized Africa, black habits are likely to break out and disrupt the internationally admitted plans for a century ahead, the suppressed political forces of ecclesiastical politics are likely to irrupt one day, amidst profound misunderstanding, on the surface of our political life which denies them. The forces are, in the last analysis, only those of the *ecclesia anglicana*, with its tail of protestant sects fading imperceptibly into the great mass of what might be called the *prejudice of disbelief*, and the Popish non-conformity which has its political centre elsewhere. Meanwhile, so far as a residual theory of establishment is still admitted, the *ecclesia anglicana* is inhibited by (its own and others') belief that it occupies a seat of political influence, while the Roman conspirators, unhampered, plan the destruction of the whole edifice, political and social. Coleridge, so far as I know, was the last man of first-rate intellect who took this possibility seriously.

3

Does it matter an awful lot? one might ask. I will not here enter upon the doctrine of papal infallibility, which is an absolute bar to liberty of conscience, as it used to be called, or to the free admission of all that comes to our consciousness, as one might more lucidly put it now: except to say that it is also an invention, in its final form, of the democratic eighteen seventies, the earliest ·moment at which it became politically possible for the Curia to get the explicit endorsement of its long-nurtured, but hitherto always partially thwarted, ambitions. The essential thing is whether we want, in this country, a Roman *imperium in imperio*; as to which I agree with Coleridge that we do not. Rome has since the Middle Ages understood the necessity of government, and she has progressively insisted on the superiority of her own. But her government is like other people's, as was well enough understood in the old Catholic monarchies and given rational form in the Reformation conception of the Sovereign as Governor of the church in his own dominions – a conception of greater antiquity, it could be claimed, than the notion of papal infallibility; it is, indeed, much the conception of Constantine. It has often puzzled people, in recent times, that in the sixteenth century men should have attached so much importance to the subject following the religion of his prince. What we may think of as mere tergiversations, however, conceal a profound sense of the identity of the church and the commonwealth, as aspects of the same body, so that a failure to follow the prince in his religion partakes of the nature of schism. And as for the theology of it, given that the Church is one, but is torn, is our Catholicity more injured by being out of communion with the Bishop of Rome than by being out of communion with our prince and those among whom we live? Note the *non-conformist* quality of the papists among us.

Of course the identity of church and commonwealth was never

more shadowy than it is now – or never since, say, the days of Constantine. But one cannot be complete without the other, and the notion of the solitary catholic is ridiculous. We are a broken-down lot, whichever way you look at it. If you look at it from the point of view of the ordinary non-Christian subject – he is not now even legally called that, he is a citizen, if you please – is there any point in monarchy at all? There is because the truth is not a matter of his or of anyone else's opinion. He cannot help being human, poor devil, if that is what we are. Therefore he exists as we (the obscure Christians) do, in virtue of the existence of others. And if Man exists only by God, the fact is not altered by Mr Jones thinking otherwise. And if he does not think – a better and happier condition than being all the time in exacerbated error – he may still feel that a King or Queen can stand for us as policies and the ministers who promote them can not. Already in the Cabinet, with its score of ministers, whose policies are the subject of analytical discourse, the human mind – which is the same as the human body – has begun to disintegrate; but it is one in the crown, which is as mysterious and unknowable as we are ourselves. It is by virtue of that that we are one. The need for this identification is not likely to become less, in the future, whether the future lies in an abstracted world of international organizations or in a physical devastation which sends us back to our primitive concerns. It is probably only for the local group that this can have any meaning. Others should not be discouraged from shedding the burden of loyalty. It may well be that the Crown will end, as it began, as the Crown of England.

An Essay on Identity

1

It is, indeed, very hard to understand what makes up 'I'. And the mere existence of the pronoun should not at once persuade us of the existence of the thing.

There is, of course, a sense in which 'I' is self-evident. But it is a pretty silly sense, a sort of tautology. 'I' is the fact of the assertion being made. It does not get one out of the prison of solipsism, but when we say 'I' exists, what we are really hoping is that there are other 'I's. If we do not mean that we do not mean anything, indeed there would hardly be such a thing as meaning.

We are therefore talking about the existence of 'Man', and this is a very difficult conception indeed. Moreover, it is a conception rich in history; it is history. It is also biology. To discuss 'Man', in fact, one can only proceed by taking some traditional universe of discourse, and defining him in terms of it. There is nothing else.

The answer to 'what am I?' can only be that I am one of those two-legged creatures of which we see so much. Biology and history tell us something about them – their relations with other species of animal, their relations with one another. 'I' become at once a term for a variant, though it could also mean one of two identical twins, identically brought up, if that were possible. In any case what makes 'man' is not the fact of 'I', the individual, but the fact of the species. Unless one can say 'I am a man', i.e. one of a kind, 'I' does not say anything. Yet what is meant by 'I', the individual, is something more overweening than that. The something is historical and conceptual. It has been invented by man, I suppose as a comfort. It is a reason why you should not kill me – which is something living creatures seem to be constitutionally against, though few take it as hard as man.

Taking it hard, however, is merely a function of consciousness. And consciousness – as is not perhaps widely understood – is purely traditional. Adam did not know what he was doing. That was his innocence. There was a point at which consciousness emerged, presumably out of the frustration of wishes. It has grown and been handed down. What it amounts to is determined by the traditions of particular societies. A 'culture' is partly a style of consciousness. It can however be more easily studied as a style of behaviour. Behaviour and consciousness are two related aspects of 'Man'. They are not identical; there is plenty of behaviour without consciousness. But the style of one affects the style of the other.

The individual 'is', or may certainly be identified as, a sub-style of consciousness and behaviour. The variant is not important, except in terms of a tradition which says that it is. Tradition, once developed beyond a certain point, has to say something about 'Man'. The subject is so difficult that it usually starts by saying something about gods. These are projections, which is not to say that God might not be there all the time, watching all this. But mythology is about man, the first sketch of a difficult subject.

The individual is nowhere in this. And what did God become, in Christian history? He became Man, one for all. The meaning of the first Adam was Man, and so with the second. His incarnation was like the descent of a Platonic form into physical shape. It was a re-affirmation of the kind. Every bit of the kind was important. In the end the bits thought they were important as 'individuals'. The claim is ill-founded.

2

The incarnation is a tall story. But of course if you believe in God you can believe it. If you do not believe it, you can still believe that the kind is important, though without giving a reason for it. Is the difference between the importance attributed to kind by the Incarnationist and that attributed to it by the rest of the world of any significance in relation to the 'individual'?

The matter is not free from difficulty. Is every 'individual' included in the Christian salvation? It has generally been supposed not. The saints are a subkind. Those who believe in Christ shall not perish, but have ever-lasting life. The rest shall perish in some sort. Cowper thought himself one of these: ACTUM EST DE TE, PERIISTI. The saints are, as it were, a wealthy class, those to whom, having already, more shall be given. The Christian looks for a more precise identification by hoping to approximate to this class, he is a kind of snob. His 'I' is not merely the two-legged animal; it is an 'I' with paraphernalia, more or less realized. The rest of the world no doubt has its own snobbisms, their 'I's are variants of sub-kinds, more sharply defined on that account. Is there any possibility of an 'I' which is not, as it were, re-defined by a snobbism?

It is in fact impossible to conceive it. Is an Idiot a man? Yes. A monster? Yes. A man in a long coma preceding death? Yes. I give the answers of fashion. At other times it might have been said that the idiot was possessed, and so out of kind. And so on. But in fashionable terms where does the man begin? At the mouth of the womb? How premature must a foetus be to be disqualified? Are the ovum and sperm constituent parts of a man? You must choose your snobbism rather arbitrarily. And when you have chosen it, you say to those outside it: Periisti. Identity implies the election of a sub-kind, and henceforth a course of conduct which may be described as the management of the sub-kind. The object of this management is to collect the sub-kind into some ark or paradise. For the Christian it is theologically prescribed. For the self-justifying abortionist – as distinct from the abortionist who is willing to murder for money, who belongs, of course, to a species with wider terms of reference – it is the group of healthy people, as contemporaneously conceived. The two-legged may be handled without scruple in relation to those out-side the group. This health is something which can be ascertained in relation to other people. Medicine and surgery at large are the treatment of other people. They are the technics of humanist management. Its objects are the preservation of a kind. It ought not to be too scrupulous about incidental 'individuals'. The Christian should not be too careful with the damned; the kindness so often exhibited is a symptom of weakened faith.

Is there a Christian management of the sub-kind? Since God became Man, would it not be reasonable to seek an objective salvation for the holy, to attempt a kind of eugenics for God's people? 'Not one of these little ones should perish', to be sure, but what about these and these? The ones not yet born? The ones whose parent orgasm is being mounted at this moment? Those who will tear one another's eyes out, in a hundred year's time, for the last food in Asia? Is every bit of mankind important? What does number mean in relation to holiness? Would it not be a kindness for old men to kill themselves?

3

What makes up the 'I'? If the separate parts of our kind are 'individuals' there would have to be identifiable minds in the separate bodies. But are there? 'Creation's matter flows through us like a river.' It flows, but the question is whether there is an 'us' that it flows through. And so with consciousness. It flows, but its contents are historical rather than individual. It is a matter of 'culture' what we are conscious of. The 'thought' is a common thought; only so could it be understood. A stream loaded with old bottles, the vegetation of several countries, rags of clothing perhaps, flows around the world. It makes no sense to talk of the individual mind. The individual body, perhaps. That is made of matter that flows in this changing form, comes from and goes to other things. But for its limited history of growth and decay it is defined by its skin, it is one in the clear sense of being separable from other things. The individual, if anything, is this, without regard to consciousness. It begins with the egg and the sperm; it ends, not with certified death but with the disintegration which follows. In the end it is not there, as an identifiable thing. There is no 'personality' apart from it. If that were ever collected again, it could only be at the resurrection of the body.

'Call no man happy until he is dead'

1

Conduct is supposed to be of the individual. And so, it is supposed to be directed from the inside, for that is how the individual is conceived of as being directed. That is what used to be called being a 'rational creature'. There are no such creatures nowadays, but the conception of being directed from the inside persists. Indeed it was never so popular. The preferred theory is now that not only the direction, but the rules of conduct themselves, come from inside.

There is something in this. Man, like other machines, moves according to the laws of his construction. There may be question as to how absolute those laws are, but nobody doubts that there are limits within which he must operate, whether or not those limits are held to be fully known. The limits are the range of human conduct, and it is generally held that the individual has to choose points within that range, and that this is his freedom.

It may be so. But, whether or not freedom is an illusion, there is at any rate an apparent question of how I should act. And so of where to look for the rules. Or what motives to admit, which is the same thing. Those in search of the individual usually prefer the motives of non-conformity, or said to be so. If the differentiation goes far enough, whom may they not find? Them 'selves', no doubt, as the unattainable end; meanwhile in observable particulars their conduct resembles that of other people. At best they contribute to the fissiparousness of groups; more generally merely share in the popular fickleness, which heaves to and fro between accepted opinions.

It is better, perhaps, to accept the external direction of one's conduct. There is then no nonsense about one's 'self', no attention to the pathology of the moment. The mind can be used to reflect the outside world, as is the case with the best animals. There is a duty of discrimination, which cannot be avoided, but one makes as little as may be of internal doubts and hesitations – the flaws in the mirror, the ripples on the surface of the reflecting water, or the unidentified objects lying below the surface.

One should be glad to find social conceptions one can conform to. They represent possibilities of one's nature, and the most one can hope to do is to embody certain of those possibilities.

2

The person who takes this orientation finds a kind of renewal. The 'individual' sinks from sight and is extinguished; in exchange, one has all the benefits of history, not as an emporium to choose from, but as they bear down upon one at a particular point of time, like a column of air. The famous 'conflict between the individual and society' – that Byronic conception – is resolved, because one term is lost. One enters, as a negligible quantity, on a vast playing field and has all the possibilities of the game being played there. One chooses roles and tries to perfect them – not one role, but as many as one can discern. Instead of the 'problem of conduct' there is the matter of discernment. The attention is shifted from the subject to the object. Indeed one does not bother about the subject; perhaps it is not there.

'Call no man happy until he is dead' is a paradigm of this conception of things. The happiness is not an affective condition, it is a state of prosperity, judged as such by others rather than by the subject. Or if the subject judges of himself, he judges as he would of another man, because it is of a man that he is judging, not of a 'self'. Health, wives, children, cattle or other riches according to the custom of the time, the marks of honour accorded by other men – these are the constituents of this happiness. In all this there is room for a large discrimination. One need not keep many cattle to be sure of one's milk, in a society in which it comes to door in bottles. One may not get an honour one cares for by owning a bigger car than one's neighbours. Diogenes is an early example of sophistication in this kind. He sought an objective condition, as much as any patriarch in the Old Testament, but he was on the brink of the terrible discovery of him'self' which would ruin everything.

3

The roles one chooses – the husband, the father, the soldier, the man of affairs – one plays them more or less well according to the richness of one's inherited conceptions. There is no way of acquiring such conceptions except by inheritance, but of course whereas any fool can inherit money the ability to inherit conceptions depends a little – though less than is usually thought – on the capacity of the heir. This capacity of the heir is, however, a small thing compared with the capacity of the society he lives in to remember and to transmit, in short to embody. You cannot be Plato in Bechuanaland or George Herbert in Connecticut. You cannot be in the Italy of the twentieth century a man of the first century A.D. So in fact you are largely directed from the outside, however little you like to think so, and it is not so much a recommendation I am giving you as a short view of the nature of things.

To seek to discriminate among your inherited possessions, to understand more profoundly the roles it is your chance to be called upon to play, is more than enough to occupy anybody. Of course there are wilful persons who imagine that they stand outside society and change it, but it is merely that they have struck a not very rich vein of tradition. Their ideas of changing come from where other people's ideas come from; they cannot be got from anywhere else. And if those who talk most of changing society also talk most of individual liberty, it is merely that they are confused. To make a change is to make other people bend. If one can do that at all it is only by putting them in the way of a current. And what is the meaning of acquiescence, to the reed the stream catches?

4

Acquiescence is perhaps a joke. At any rate it is clear that, for the most part of our lives, there is no more in it than is involved in going quietly. What opinions do you hold about being born, growing, declining, and dying? You will do these things even if you are against them. And how? You will do them as they are done in these parts, at this time. How much less acquiescence is involved in being compelled by someone who says he understands your role better than you do yourself? Is there really much difference between persuasion and compulsion? The mythologies of the moment say that there is, and they have to be obeyed. In the very act of obedience to them the man who understands his role will see that there is no freedom of choice, that a compulsion underlies all our persuasions. But if it does, should we deny it?

The word 'democracy' is now so full of air that it is about to burst. Its bursting will not be the end of everything but the recognition, in passing, of a truth. There is reason to believe that it may mitigate the boredom of our society. If hunger does not drive us, do we not need more than ever those who will put us in a corner and make us fight? The ease of technology will, in any case, in the end produce a race of diminishing consciousness, for whom the only persuasion is by force. The triumph of technology would be to leave people with so little consciousness that they did not notice the change.

On the Eros of Poetry

Ernst Robert Curtius says, in *Europäische Literatur und lateinisches Mittelalter* (1948), that most of the themes employed by modern lyrical poets, 'out of their own experience', are to be found in late classical antiquity, where they appear as the themes of rhetorical exercises. It is uncertain how much is swept away by this observation. Certainly most of what has been thought about poetry in the last two hundred years, at any rate in the form in which it has been thought. The poet was after all not expressing *himself*. The very existence of the conception of *self* may be in doubt, from other causes, and what Curtius says comes to demolish the notion of expression.

Certain literary curiosities fall into their place. It would generally be said that Shakespeare, in his sonnets, was expressing himself in some more personal sense than in his plays. But this is an absurdity, from several points of view. In the first place, it is ludicrous to suppose that the author of the plays was the helpless victim of his own biography, when it came to inventing material for the sonnets. And secondly, if the notion of self-expression is fundamental to the notion of poetry, how does it come that Shakespeare is expressing himself more radically in the sonnets, because of their supposed biographical reference, than in *Lear* or the other great plays of his maturity?

It would usually be thought that Spenser and the other Petrarchans wrote lyrics of a more 'artificial' character than, say, Donne, because they are more evidently the coherent members of a group – those who succumbed to the 'Petrarchan tradition'. They might well not be expressing 'their feelings', because their sources are known to be literary. Because Donne is outside this tradition, he is often thought to be not only 'more original' but writing more directly from his own experience. It is the very notion of experience which Curtius is, by implication, questioning. The difference between Donne and the Petrarchans is perhaps not the closeness of the relationship between the subjects of their verse and what actually happened to them, but the degree and nature of the psychological insight which these authors respectively brought to their themes which, like 'experience' itself, are merely traditional.

It is too readily supposed that there is a 'personal experience' which can be conveyed in words. In fact, the consciousness we have is a product of history, and we think we feel as we do as much as feel that way. We can only feel as we do, because only so will our forms of words and thoughts allow us to feel. There may be some uniformity between the feelings of men who have their legs cut off, whether in the forests of hundreds of thousands of years ago or in London now, but certainly even in so patent a matter there will be differences. But when it comes to the feelings of a woman abandoned by her lover, the whole force of a civilization is in play. There is no original feeling of such a situation, and no overlay of tradition. The whole is an invention of thousands of years, places, times, religions, cultures. The individual variant which could be 'expressed' – if we admit the conception – must be negligible by comparison.

3

The fact that our thoughts are not our own does not mean that there is no distinction to be made between the thoughts of one and another. There are degrees of relevance of thoughts to situations; there is variety in the capacity of different people for assimilating and applying what they have assimilated. The first symptom of a wide intelligence is its receptivity. The colour-blind who cannot distinguish red and green are the type of imperfect awarenesses – imperfect that is within the possibilities of a particular culture. The depth, coherence and relevance of what one person has to say will immeasurably exceed those qualities in what another says, and the poet has his place in this scheme of things. In a sense he will be less concerned than other people to be original, because he will be seeking among forms of thought long current for the formulation which will apply most exactly to the new situation.

4

The prominence of the erotic in the thought of the twentieth century is not the mark of any increase in the activity of the erotic organs, or even of the reverse. It is a result of the desuetude of other thought-forms which are recognized as being of general interest.

The problem – which was perhaps one of the problems of Catullus – is how much weight the contemporary Eros can bear. It will clearly not bear very much unless it is re-inforced by streams coming from more profound sources. There are only two – the stream of classical mythology and that of the Christian faith. Both are erotic, though they have proceeded side by side through the centuries, burbling at one another like quarrelsome water-gods.

The poet who can still draw on these sources will not merely illustrate the contemporary Eros. He may revivify the popular apprehension of the Christian and pagan worlds, so that, for example, in fifty years' time, people might sing hymns of which the imagery did not seem grotesque. But it would need more than a few bedraggled poems to have such an effect.

A Note on Morality

To say purpose would be to beg the question, but the effect of moral rules is to produce coherence – and from one point of view, perhaps an important one, it does not matter what the rules are so long as the coherence is there. Of course coherence is also a word that begs some questions. There are modes certainly, but the essential thing is that everybody should think the same, or same enough. When that happens you have a culture in which, typically, all the vases are the same shape. The importance of the sameness, from the individual's point of view, is that it provides expectations. It is immoral to disappoint this expectation, roughly speaking. The sameness also produces conventions about the meaning of actions, which again is reassuring. For it is above all meaning that actions are in need of, if we are to be human. This means attaching actions to traditional patterns of thought, preferably the general view, at any rate a view which enough of us hold to make it respectable. In an evolved society it seems that everything has been thought about, and everything has a meaning. In a disrupted one the meanings are inadequate.

Are there any morals apart from those of particular societies? 'Thou shalt not steal', 'Thou shalt not commit adultery', are already notions with a particular sort of society in mind. This 'thou shalt not' is not absolute; it relates to an existing idea of what is the done thing. It is dependent on the form of property and the form of marriage established. If there were Christian morals would they go beyond the needs of particular societies, and what would their relationship be with the laws of a particular society, formerly seen as the law of God? The first Christians solved this question, in relation to Jewry. Having burst into the Gentile world, they then found another question. Was there a Christian social form (sc. morality) to be imposed? The answer was yes, but it has never been an entirely satisfactory one. It is least satisfactory in the less stable societies. In the Middle Ages, and long after, Christian morality had taken the place of the Law, and the finer breath of Christianity blew over it, as it had over

266

the Law. In an unstable world, Christian morals have to justify themselves, a task for which they are not altogether equipped because, like all morals, they prefer to be taken for granted.

Take the famous morality of marriage. It could not be said that the gospels do more than bless the morality of a society in which, by that time, monogamy had become general. Certain dicta may even be held to equate adultery with the ordinary thoughts of man. If there is a pattern of behaviour as well as the dicta, it is not of monogamy but of abstinence. The only family exemplified is strictly inimitable.

Is it then the duty of Christians to establish a certain relationship with the morality of the day, whatever that may be? This is not antinomianism but it may be held to come too near to it. The alternative is to wage a war of Christian morality against whatever else is current, as if an agrarian or even a sheep-rearing society could replace a society of contraceptives and euthanasia.

On poetic Architecture

1

There is no reason to suppose that the state of mind of the poet, when he writes a poem, is reproduced in the mind of the reader. It has sometimes been said that the poem represents an 'organisation of impulses' which is transmitted – it is generally supposed with beneficial effects – to the reader, who in this way manages to live for a moment with the sages. If you believe that you can believe anything about the relationships existing between members of the human race.

In the first place, one should try to be clear – or as clear as one can – about 'the state of mind of the poet, when he writes a poem'. What sort of correspondence has it with the poem produced? The poem is, of course, some of what is passing through his mind. It is certainly not all, even though he is likely to be more nearly absorbed by this activity than by many others that he engages in. And 'passing through his mind' is not an easy conception either. The only proof, really, is that the words get written. What accompanies the act of writing may be various. The poet may be exalted or he may be merely numb. He is just as likely to feel the emotion he is (as they say) 'conveying', *after* he has written as at the time of writing. He may be frozen as it comes to consciousness. In any case he is using words which are not his own (words are not a man's own), though his organization of them owes something to his own physiology and, of course, history. He speaks with the voice of a civilization and if anyone understands him it will be people who 'understand' what he 'understands', whatever that may mean. But what does it mean?

2

Does it make sense to talk of 'understanding' a person as distinct from 'understanding' a thing? There probably is no distinction, except so far as affinity between the subject and object (the same sort of animal, the same civilization) give a peculiar quality to one's relationship with things like oneself. That people share states of mind is obviously true in the sense that consciousness is historical and within a particular civilization there will be commonly accepted explanations of various classes of events. But the only proof of your understanding of a person is your ability to adjust yourself to him or her, or her or him to yourself, just as the only proof of your understanding of a motor-car is your ability to handle it in various ways and to do what it wants to do (if it is to go at all). The more complex the machines the wider the range of mutual adjustments, but one is usually more stupid than another, as a car is more stupid than a man, and will normally come sooner to the point of exercising its will, i.e. refusing to adjust itself any further.

3

'The poem' is words on a piece of paper, or spoken, just as 'the building' is erected before you and you must make of it what you can. Nobody supposes that you feel what the builder or architect 'felt', as he sweated through his work, even in cases where there is one man to whom a 'feeling' or an original creative act could with any plausibility be attributed. Of course buildings are in styles as well as being in materials, and many people have a hand in them. And so have poems although one man will, these days, put his name on the title page. Take no more than a due amount of notice of it; it is to get the money, or the reputation, or in hopes of the same.

Le Roi Soleil

1

Does consciousness of one's own body differ from consciousness of other things? 'One's own body': an expression already heavy with metaphysic. At first it seems obvious that it must. 'One's own body': the one that is always there; the least interesting of bodies. If consciousness is the centre, or perhaps the maggot, then that body is the nut and the surrounding world the shell. Most of what goes on in our own bodies we are unconscious of; it is the microcosmos. The macrocosmos is hardly more mysterious, or unknown; its size alone is impressive.

What we see, what we touch, we do with our own eyes, our hands, parts of our bodies. But it is also our eyes which see what we see of ourselves, our fingers which touch our skin or our tongue which touches our teeth. What of our consciousness of what goes on inside our bodies? The bellyache, the sudden lesion? These pains are not external to our bodies, but they are as external to our consciousness as events we perceive in Mars. Is not consciousness a convention, more or less, a matter of history? Could not an animal have a belly-ache without being aware of it? It would not be an ache, no doubt, but there would be the visceral disturbances, the vomiting would follow, and then quiescence. How much we perceive of the convulsions of the macrocosmos is a matter of the tradition we have inherited. But so it is, surely, with the belly-ache. If two states of consciousness could be compared (as they cannot, with any accuracy, because only one is known) the neolithic pain would differ from our own, for there is no pain, certainly no located pain, without meaning.

2

But if the relationship of the consciousness to the microcosmos and the macrocosmos is the same, what becomes of the notion of personality? It is more extensive. Instead of trying to conceive of a consciousness which corresponds to a physical person, as if

270

such a person could float out of space and time, one takes the consciousness *de facto*, with all there is in it, which is something of the world as well as of a single body. A person becomes, not what he thinks he is, but what he is, or at any rate what is. The 'what is', like the person in other conceptions, can be seen from inside or outside; the more or less of correspondence there is between these two views is a commonplace of morality.

Who was Louis XIV? He was what he was seen to be, or if he was not, it was because there was more to be seen and not because a 'reality' was hiding in Versailles behind an appearance. Subjectively, he was what of his world he was aware of, and in building Versailles he was to some extent building himself. A whole skein of connections met in his hand, and it matters more whether a king dies than whether a beggar does. What profound sense has it that not a sparrow falls without the knowledge of your father which is in heaven? It is supernatural.

By Way of Explanation

About a month before George Herbert's death (according to Walton), a conversation took place between him and a Mr Duncon, who had been sent by Nicholas Farrar:

> 'I desire you to pray with me.'
> 'What prayers?'
> 'O, sir! the prayers of my mother, the Church of England: no other prayers are equal to them!'

The point needs no illustration, but when he prayed, daily, 'Lighten our darkness, we beseech thee, O Lord' it was 'Illumina, quaesumus Domine Deus, tenebras nostras.' The prayer is in the breviaries of Sarum and York, in the sacramentaries of Gregory and Gelasius. The *mother* of George Herbert was the Church, looking on him with her English countenance. It was 1633, the year in which the King first greeted Laud, then Bishop of London, as 'my Lord's Grace of Canterbury', adding, 'you are very welcome.' It was only eleven years before the Archbishop, on Tower Hill, said: 'Cupio dissolvi et esse cum Christo' and passed through 'a mere shadow of death, a little darkness upon nature,' as he said in his prayer.

2

A less austere character, Robert Herrick, who welcomed the king into the west when he published his *Hesperides* in 1648, looked towards death through the ordinary sensualities, and hardly distinguished the sacred from the profane:

> Holy waters hither bring
> For the sacred sprinkling:
> Baptize me and thee, and so
> Let us to the Altar go.
> And (ere we our rites commence)

272

Wash our hands in innocence.
Then I'le be the *Rex Sacrorum*,
Thou the Queen of *Peace* and *Quorum*.

Herrick had been deprived of his living before his book came out; and he is not heard of again till he goes back to Dean Prior in 1662, aged seventy-one. In this year was issued the edition of the Prayer-Book we now have, the use of the Elizabethan book, as it more or less was, having been illegal from the Ordinance of Parliament, Die Veneris, 3 Januarii, 1644, for the taking away of the Book of Common Prayer, and for the establishing and putting in execution of the Directory, until the Restoration.

3

Roger Clark, rector of Ashmore in Dorsetshire,

When the Rebellion broke out... adhered Immovably to his Majesty's cause, and betook himself to the army under my Lord Hopton; for which he was Plunder'd of all that he had, the Soldiers Tearing a broad the very beds, and Scattering the Feathers out of the Ticking:... they took the Two Young Sons, being Twins, the Elder named Roger, and the Other, Richard, and laid them stark-naked in a Dripping-Pan before the Fire, with a design to Roast them; but a certain woman, whose name was Pope, came and snatched them away in her Apron. (Walker, *Sufferings of the Clergy*, 1714)

It happens that the minute-books of the Parliamentary Standing Committee, which sat in Dorset during the Rebellion and inter-regnum, have been preserved: perhaps the only ones of their kind; there was good reason for destroying such books: 'Whereas we are informed that Leonard Snooke of Stower pvost, one Combe of Fifehead and Thomas Dowden of Kingston have been in armes against the Pariament, it is therefore ordered that you seize, inventory and secure their estates...' It is a matter of taste, or perhaps something more, whether you sympathize with these men or with John Hampden, that model of the bourgeois who makes a virtue out of not paying his taxes. Somebody gained by the losses of such men as Leonard Snooke, one Combes and Thomas Dowden: 'shall hold and enjoie the farmes called Grange and Waddam, beeinge part of the sequestred estate of Robt.

Lawrence, Esqr, for delinquencie...' And instead of ecclesiastical discipline – 'It is hereby ordered that noe minister whatsoever shall psume to preach in the pish church of Blandford in this Country without leave first obtained from Mr. Trottell, minister of Spettsbury.'

4

At the Restoration, Jeremy Taylor was consecrated Bishop – to an Irish see – and some other reparations were made to tired men.

Thomas Ken, whose sister Anne was married to Isaac Walton, was ordained in 1661 or 2. He became Bishop of Bath and Wells in 1684. In 1688, with six other bishops including Sancroft, Archbishop of Canterbury, he submitted To the King's Most Excellent Majesty (James II) the petition which humbly sheweth

> That the great averseness they find in themselves to the distributing and publishing in all their churches your Majesty's late declaration for liberty of conscience proceedeth neither from any want of duty and obedience to your Majesty, our holy mother the Church of England being, both in her principles and constant practice, unquestionably loyal.... nor yet from any want of due tenderness to dissenters, in relation to whom they are willing to come to such a temper as shall be thought fit, when that matter shall be considered and settled in parliament and convocation; but yet among many other considerations, from this especially because that declaration is founded upon such a dispensing power as hath often been declared illegal in parliament, and particularly in the years 1662 and 1672, and in the beginning of your Majesty's reign....

The seven bishops were taken to the Tower 'for contriving, making and publishing a seditious libel'. But Ken would not take the oath to William; nor would Sancroft and seven other bishops. Ken went to Wells and from his chair asserted his canonical right. The rest of his life he spent at Longleat, where he wrote two thousand pages of verse, as a form of laudanum, he said, which shows how dangerous it is for a man to have time on his hands.

5

One does not often think of Swift as a cleric, because his imagination was unbridled, and because he was Irish and the merits of a later (rebellious) nationalism are supposed to have washed away the stains of his loyalty. But Swift said: 'Might not those who enter upon any office in her Majesty's family, be obliged to take an oath parallel to that against simony, which is administered to the clergy?' And in *A Letter concerning the Sacramental Test*:

> As to the argument used for repealing the Test, that it will unite all the Protestants against the Common Enemy; I wonder by what figure these gentlemen speak, who are pleased to advance it.... 'Tis an odd way of uniteing parties, to deprive a Majority of Part of their antient Right, by conferring it on a Faction, who never had any Right at all, and therefore cannot be said to suffer any loss or injury, if it be refused them. Neither is it very clear, how far some people may stretch the term of Common Enemy. How many are there of those that call themselves Protestants, who look upon our Worship to be idolatrous as well as that of Papists, and with great Charity put Prelacy and Popery together as terms convertible?

6

Queen Anne died in 1714 and the country has been more or less given over to Whiggery ever since. In 1717 Convocation was suppressed so that it should not condemn the invisible bishop of Bangor, Dr Hoadley, to whom William Law wrote (in the *Defence of Church Principles*)

> But, my Lord, as human nature, if left to itself, would neither answer the ends of a spiritual or civil society; so a constant visible government in both is equally necessary; and I believe, it appears to all unprejudiced eyes that, in this argument at least, your Lordship has declared both equally unlawful.

7

George Hicks, the non-juror who in 1694 was consecrated titular

Bishop of Thetford, used the First (and more Catholic) Prayer Book of Edward VI, and in 1717 the Nonjurors published their own office, which was closely allied to it. Those who followed the latter book were called the *Usagers*, from the mixing water with the wine, saying the prayer for the dead and other usages prescribed in it.

> What can be more heinously wicked [wrote Law, himself a Nonjuror], than heartily to wish the success of a person on account of his right, and at the same time, in the most solemn manner, in the presence of God, and as you hope for mercy, to swear that he has no right at all.

From Johnson it is enough to quote the *Dictionary*:

> TORY. One who adheres to the ancient constitution of the state, and the apostolic hierarchy of the church of England.
> WHIG. The name of a faction.

Not wholly irrelevant are certain curious verses of Charles Wesley about Methodist preachers:

> Rather than suffer them to dare
> Usurp the priestly character,
> Save them from arrogant offence,
> And snatch them uncorrupted hence.

Omitted in the second edition. John did not like them.

8

The Tories of the nineteenth century are Samuel Taylor Coleridge and the Duke of Wellington, and the latter was already intent upon ruinous calculations: 'What I looked on as the great advantage of the measure (for Roman emancipation) was that it would unite all men of property and character together in one interest against the agitators.' Coleridge upon fanciful conditions:

> a declaration, to which every possible character of solemnity should be given, that at no time and under no circumstances has it ever been, nor can it ever be, compatible with the safety of the British Constitution to recognise in the Roman Catholic priesthood, as now constituted, a component Estate of the realm, or persons capable, individually or collectively,

of becoming the trustees and usufructuary proprietors of that elective and circulative property, originally reserved for the permanent maintenance of the National Church.

But, on any terms, the emancipation of the Papists was the end of even the possibility of that system which Coleridge himself defined:

> the Constitution, in its widest sense as the constitution of the realm, arose out of, and in fact consisted in, the co-existence of the constitutional State.... with the King as its head, and of the Church, that is, the National Church, with the King likewise as its head; and lastly of the King, as the head and Majesty of the whole nation.

The political device of the latter part of the seventeenth century was not the Restoration but the Revolution which is sometimes called glorious, and indeed you might call it that by comparison with the one which took place in France in 1789. From the time Charles raised his standard at Nottingham, Toryism as defined by Johnson has almost always been a doctrine of opposition, and so it will remain.

Sources

I *Orientations 1937-1940*
Published in the *New English Weekly*: 'Charles Maurras and the
Idea of a Patriot King', 22 July 1937; 'Remarks on a Letter of
Junius', 16 December 1937; 'Prejudice as an Aid to Govern-
ment', 7 April 1938; 'English Liberalism', 9 March 1939; 'A
Study in Public Opinion', 5 October 1939; 'The Argument
for Federal Union', 7 March 1940; 'Reflections on a Bureau-
crat's War', 24 October 1940.
Published in *Purpose* XI:4: 'Order and Anarchy', October-
December 1939 (in shortened form).

II *Post-war Reflections*
Published in the *New English Weekly*: 'Charles Péguy', 14
November 1946; 'Epitaph on Nuremburg', 15 May 1947; 'T.S.
Eliot on Culture', 2 December 1948; 'Lord Beveridge Explains
Himself', 20 January 1949; 'The Crisis in the University', 16
June 1949.
Published in *The Catacomb*, New Series, 1:3: 'Charles Maurras',
Winter 1950-51.
Published in *Poetry Nation Review*, IV:1: 'Looking Back on Maur-
ras', 1976.
'Philip Mairet': introduction to *Philip Mairet, autobiographical and
other papers*, ed. C.H. Sisson (Carcanet), 1981.

III *The Practice of Government*
Published in *The Cambridge Journal* VI:7: 'The Nature of Public
Administration', April 1953.
From *The Spirit of British Administration and some European com-
parisons* (Faber and Faber, 1959): 'Administrator and Law in
France', 'The Judge and the Administrator', 'The Adminis-
trator as Governor', 'The Politician as Intruder', 'The Mind
of the Administrator'.
Published in *Church Quarterly Review* CLIV:313: 'A Note on the
Monarchy', October-December 1953.

IV *A Touch of Whiggery*
This section from *The Case of Walter Bagehot* (Faber and Faber), 1972.

V *Native Ruminations*
Essays, privately printed (Knole Park Press, Sevenoaks), 1967.

Index of Names

Adler 100-101
Alvarez-Gendin 137, 138
Amouretti 73
Anne, Queen 187, 275
Arnold 22, 32, 238
Auden 44, 45, 90

Bagehot 11, 108, 167, 168, 171, 179-243
Bainville 75
Barfield 96, 106
Barnes 201
Barrès 79, 88
Barrington 217, 220
Beaudouin 52
Beer 164
Belgion 11, 55-6
Benoit 105
Bentham 237
Berkeley 157, 226-7
Beveridge 63-7
Bismarck 82
Blackstone 79, 247
Blum 52, 89
Bolingbroke 15, 16
Bridges 111-14, 166
Browne 60
Brougham 236
Burnham 162-3

Calvin 107
Campbell 237
Cato 130
Catherine 155-6
Catullus 265

Chambord 72
Chapman 146
Charles I 22, 77, 86, 132, 172, 173, 277
Chateaubriand 74
Churchill 92, 159
Clarendon 168, 169, 170, 223-5, 234, 276-7
Clark 273
Claudel 81
Cohen 112, 114
Coke 129
Coleridge 223-5, 234, 276-7
Coomeraswamy 99, 100
Cowper 256
Cox 237
Cranmer 230
Cross 129
Curtius 263-4

Dante 73, 94
Darwin 196, 200
Daudet 91
Debré 121
Demant 102
De Quincey 219
Dix 233
Donne 263
Douglas 97
Dreyfus 74, 88, 89, 94
Duncon 272

Eliot 10, 57-62, 68, 69, 87, 99, 102-7, 233
Eschenburg 149-51

Farrer 272
Ferry 74
Filmer 187
Ford 157
Forster 94, 230-2
Fox 181
Franco 83, 91
Frazer 176
Frontinus 113

Gambetta 162
Geddes 103
Gide 53, 104
Goering 153
Goethe 104
Goldsmid 237
Gowers 155, 156

Haecker 161
Haley 217
Hamilton 197, 237
Hamlyn 122
Hamson 122-7
Hankey 207-8
Henry I 22
Herbert 262, 272
Heron 99, 100
Herrick 272
Hewart 130-3
Hicks 275-6
Hitler 20, 21, 84, 91, 92, 149
Hoadley 275
Hollis 174
Hulme 15, 89, 90
Hume 237
Hutton 214
Huxley 196

James II 170
Jaurès 52, 53, 81
Jennings 168, 170, 171
Johnson 229, 276-7

Joinville 71
Julian 78
Justinian 126, 127

Keir 169, 172
Ken 274
Keynes 97, 199, 209, 238-42

La Fontaine 71, 89
La Rochefoucauld 40
Laski 116
Laud 230, 272
Laval 95
Law 275
Lawrence 239
Lewis 25, 243
Locke 221, 252
Louis XIV 271
Louis Napoleon 181, 185
Ludovici 22-3

Macaulay 204
Machiavelli 160, 173
Maclise 104
Mairet 10, 62, 96-108
Maitland 132
Malherbe 94
Malthus 238
Marismas 123
Martin 176
Marx 162
Massis 93
Maudsley 196
Maurras 15-16, 23, 58, 71-95
Michelet 74
Mitrinović 99-101
Moberly 68-70
Monk 84
Montesquieu 19, 36, 79, 132
Montherlant 55, 114
Montgomery 101-7
Munro 112, 114

Murry 108
Mussolini 91, 92

Napoleon 121, 125-6
Naudy 52
Newton 271

Oakeshott 10
Orage 10, 97, 103

Pascal 40, 157
Pater 93, 190
Patmore 194
Péguy 10, 51-4
Pepys 112-13
Pétain 84, 86, 89
Pilate 160
Plantey 120, 121, 125
Plato 261
Pompadour 212
Pound 133-5
Pujo 75

Quesnay 212

Racine 71, 89, 155
Radcliffe 129
Raleigh 228
Read 44
Reckitt 192
Rivarol 161
Robson 132, 133
Rolland 119

Sainte-Beuve 17, 74
Saklatvala 90
Sancroft 274
Sandulli 137

Shakespeare 155, 219
Shelley 166
Smith 211-16, 227, 235
Smollett 218
Sorel 90
Spender 90
Spengler 93
Spenser 263
Stalin 83, 84, 173
Stuckey 182, 193, 200
Suarès 53
Sunderland 159
Swift 228, 275
Symons 102

Taylor 70, 274
Tocqueville 144

Vaugeois 75
Victoria, Queen 189, 203
Vidler 103
Voltaire 71, 87, 89

Waline 122-3
Walker 273
Walpole 181
Walton 274
Weber 162
Wellington 276
Wesley 276
Wilson 82, 193, 213
Wright 108

Yeats, J.B. 114-15
Yeats, W.B. 87
Young 217-18

Zola 157